Foreword by Henry T. Bl

RICHARD
BLACKABY

THE WAYS OF GOD

How God Reveals Himself
Before a Watching World

Printed in the United States of America

978-1-0877-5701-8

Published by B&H Publishing Group
Brentwood, Tennessee

Dewey Decimal Classification: 231
Subject Heading: CHRISTIAN DEVOTION

Cover design by Cover design by B&H Publishing Group.
Illustration by Joshua Noom/Closer & Closer LLC.
Author photo by Renee Carolla Photography.

1 2 3 4 5 6 7 • 27 26 25 24 23

CONTENTS

FOREWORD

I believe the church would be radically altered for the better if its people ever came to understand and practice the ways of God. God has made it clear: his ways are not our ways (Isa. 55:8–9). He has told us, but we don't believe him. The church continues to develop its own goals and plans and then asks God to bless its efforts. Pastors lead their congregations the same way a CEO would guide a secular company. Worship leaders conduct themselves as if they were the star of a Broadway musical. Church members behave as if they belonged to a political organization. Then we wonder why God is not working powerfully in our life and church. It is imperative that we return to the ways of God!

In 2000, I wrote a book with Roy Edgemon called, *The Ways of God*.[1] In it, we outlined the ways God works in our world. I am so pleased that my oldest son, Richard, has returned to this important matter to provide a fresh look at this important subject. Richard has a keen eye for biblical truth as well as a knack for drawing practical applications from profound theological doctrines. I know you will be challenged, encouraged, and inspired by what he has written.

We live in an age where people assume that the end justifies the means. But with God, this is never the case. It matters to God how things are done. That's because the way we do something reflects on him. It is possible to do the right thing, the wrong way. I have known well-meaning Christians who sought to defend Christian orthodoxy, but they did it in a prideful, condescending, vindictive manner. I have known sincere pastors who diligently served the Lord, but they did so in a way that alienated them from their family. I have known churches that attracted large crowds, but they failed to build a church. When you serve God the wrong way, you present God in the wrong light. And God cares very much how you represent him to a watching world.

Thankfully, God has revealed to us, through his word, the way he acts. It is all there in the pages of Scripture. You will find that when you do God's work, God's way, power, and resources are released to you. The world does not need you to give them your best. It desperately needs what only God can give. There is an enormous difference between your ways and God's. Now is the time to reflect on how you have been leading, serving, and living. Don't assume that if something makes sense to you, it is from God! I have often said, if something makes perfect sense to you, it probably is not from God!

Read this book carefully, thoughtfully, and prayerfully. There is too much at stake for you to continue living as you have been. Ask God to reveal areas in your life in which you have been doing things your way instead of God's. Then quickly repent of your presumption and adjust your life back to God. The world desperately needs what only God can give. They will receive it, in abundance, when God's people, serve God, God's way.

Henry T. Blackaby
President Emeritus, Blackaby Ministries International
Author of *Experiencing God*

PREFACE

There are many people today who are urgently praying for revival to sweep across their land. Our world desperately needs to experience God's life-transforming power. Nations need healing. Families require restoration. Sinners yearn for forgiveness. The broken long for mending. This only happens when the Holy Spirit moves powerfully among his people as he has done repeatedly throughout the ages. Looking at the current spiritual condition around the world, it appears that darkness is prevailing, and God's kingdom is in retreat in many places. Yet revival is closer than it might seem.

Since Christ's resurrection, he has assigned the church the Great Commission. That is, to make disciples, by the enabling power of the Holy Spirit, of all nations (Matt. 28:18–20). After 2,000 years, there is still much work to be done. The church is struggling in much of the western world. Attendance in most of today's churches is plateaued or declining. Thousands of congregations close their doors each year. A growing percentage of Americans no longer attend church or claim to believe in God. The nation's moral condition is plummeting. Behavior traditionally considered to be immoral is now publicly celebrated. Politicians, rather than addressing the nation's ills, only seem to make them worse.

Obviously, the church cannot keep doing things the way it has been. Something must change. The church, as it functions now, is not the salt and light the world desperately needs. God made it clear that our ways are not his ways (Isa. 55:8–9).

Tragically, the church has become enamored with secular thinking. It is foolish to assume we can conduct God's work, the world's way. Historically, such thinking has always led to catastrophic consequences for the church and the people it serves.

The problem is that we are so immersed in the world's ways, we don't recognize when we have departed from God and his ways. We are working hard and praying for God's kingdom to come, but we are not seeing the results we should expect from almighty God. This ought to alarm us. We ought to grieve at the absence of power and advance in today's church. We must take a spiritual audit of our ways to discern where we have jettisoned God's ways for worldly methods. We must study God's ways, so we know what they are. Then we must fervently embrace them.

In 2000, my father, Henry Blackaby, and his good friend, Roy Edgemon, wrote, *The Ways of God: How God Reveals Himself Before a Watching World*.[2] In that insightful book, they clearly outlined the difference between the world's ways and God's ways. If you have never read that book, I encourage you to do so. Dad and Roy asked if I might produce a new version of this important book. God's people still need this message! The book you are reading is the result.

The more I studied and wrote on this topic, the more convinced I became that the church desperately needs this message. We simply cannot keep doing "business as usual" in God's kingdom. We ought to be wholly dissatisfied with the meager results we have been achieving. In light of our nation's current spiritual condition, we ought to long for the mighty power of God to be expressed in our life and ministry. We must radically adjust our ways back to God's.

Can you imagine what would happen across our land if God's people started to act the same way God does? What if we began serving God in holiness? What if we truly denied ourselves, took up our cross, and followed Christ wherever he led? What if our speech was seasoned with grace? What if we were quick to forgive? What if we began to love people, even our enemies, with the love of Christ? How long do you think it would take before the world felt the impact?

As you read the following pages, ask the Holy Spirit to alert you to any of God's ways you are not currently practicing in your life and church. When God shows you, quickly make whatever adjustment is necessary and begin to enthusiastically think, serve, and live God's way. The world around you will be forever grateful that you did.

ACKNOWLEDGMENTS

I believe this is one of the most important books I have written. Several people deserve special thanks for the invaluable contribution they made so this would be possible.

First, thanks to my father, Henry Blackaby, for the way you taught, and modeled, that God's ways are not our ways. You have always lived contrary to the way many ministers and Christians lived, and you have repeatedly demonstrated that God's way is best.

Thanks also to Roy Edgemon, who wrote the original version of *The Ways of God* with my father. You were the first person to encourage me to work on this project. I so appreciate your heart for God and for the church.

A special thanks goes to my wife Lisa. As of this writing, we have been married thirty-nine years. Thank you for "coming out of retirement" to edit this book! You are still the best editor with whom I have ever worked! Thank you for your unfailing love and support over all these years.

Thank you to my two sons, Mike and Daniel, who both offered important contributions to this material. Thanks Daniel, for helping me think through chapter 13 on "Beauty," and letting me draw ideas from your PhD dissertation!

Thank you also to special friends, Rick Fisher, Bob Royall, Scott McLellan, Lou Leventhal, and my sister, Carrie, for taking time to read over the manuscript and offer me rich insights that made this work incalculably better.

This has been a challenging project. At one moment I felt like I had a handle on what I was trying to say, and the next moment I realized I was barely scratching the surface of some amazing truths that God's people desperately needed to hear. I could have taken years to ponder over and think through this material. Hopefully it will spark many thoughts and insights for you as you read.

INTRODUCTION

WHY STUDY THE WAYS OF GOD? AREN'T THEY OBVIOUS?

"He revealed his ways to Moses, his deeds to the people of Israel."
(Ps. 103:7)

Your Money or My Life

On January 4, 1987, evangelist Oral Roberts announced that God had told him, "I'm going to call you home . . ." if he did not raise eight million dollars for his university and medical center by March. This was certainly not the first time a television evangelist had made a dramatic appeal for funds, but it struck many people as odd that God would kill one of his servants if he did not take in a certain amount of money by a particular deadline. No one could cite a Scripture passage that provided biblical precedent for such a homecoming. In the end, sufficient money was garnered by concerned supporters, so Roberts was spared, until he died twelve years later at the age of ninety-one from complications of pneumonia.

In 2018, evangelist Jesse Duplantis announced that God had told him to obtain his fourth private jet, a Dassault Falcon 7X, at the cost of 54 million dollars. Duplantis explained, "If Jesus was physically on earth today, he wouldn't be riding a donkey." He proclaimed that God had instructed him to preach the Gospel to every creature on earth and that would be an impossible task if he travelled by car or train. But he could accomplish that goal with a state-of-the-art airplane. Duplantis also revealed that God occasionally asked him for advice.

Assertions like these understandably raise the eyebrows of many Christians. Though these claims are passionate and accompanied by ample tears and biblical proof-texts, they appear contrary to the clear teaching of Scripture. These preachers zealously proclaim that their teaching aligns with what God has done throughout the Bible. Others suggest God is doing a new work in the modern day.

The question is: How can you know if a statement is "from God" or not? How can you identify false claims about God? Are there means by which you can evaluate what you sense God wants you to do? To help us grapple with these questions, we must ask, does God act consistently, and if so, how does he act? What are God's ways?

Biggest, Boldest, Best Ever

God's ways dramatically captured my attention several years ago. The head of a large Christian organization asked me to dinner. I was a young minister in the early stages of my ministry. The veteran Christian leader invited me to undertake a role at a massive conference he was developing. His vision was awe-inspiring. It would be unprecedented in scope and magnitude. It seemed like the chance of a lifetime, especially for an unknown speaker such as me.

As he waxed eloquent about his vision for the conference, I couldn't help but be impressed. It would be the largest event of its kind. It would be headlined by some of the biggest names in contemporary Christian music. The venue would be amazing. The crowd, immense. The technology, cutting edge. I'd be a fool to decline his invitation and I was no fool. But something seemed odd. I had difficulty putting my finger on it at first.

Here was a man who sincerely wanted to strike a mighty blow for God's kingdom. Shouldn't I jump at the chance to join such an undertaking? Eventually, it dawned on me what was "off." Everything he was saying about the Christian event sounded like an advertisement for an impending Hollywood blockbuster, or the release of the next iPhone. He spoke effusively about the size of the budget and venue, but little about God's leading. He boasted of headliners and concerts, but never mentioned prayer. In essence, he was speaking the same way the world talks about its major events. And that seemed wrong.

Over the years I have had many Christian leaders explain that God deserves the very best. They conclude that if businesses are going to spend millions of dollars advertising their products, then Christians ought to be even more zealous about promoting God. If places of business are constructed with impressive architecture, then places of worship certainly ought to surpass commercial outlets in beauty and grandeur. Such people will argue that if people in the marketplace will develop sophisticated programs and systems to increase sales and profits for their business, then surely God's people ought to produce cutting edge programs that will accelerate the advance of God's kingdom as well.

On the surface, such arguments appear to make sense. After all, doesn't God deserve the best? Shouldn't we use our best thinking and most advanced resources to promote his causes? Why should secular endeavors enjoy our best efforts while

Christian enterprises are relegated to leftovers? Why shouldn't the church learn from the dizzying success of popular music stars, professional athletes, and politicians, so it, too, can garner a larger, younger, and more enthusiastic following?

As I listened to the Christian leader effuse about his plans to take the best the world had to offer and baptize it for the cause of Christ, I couldn't escape the nagging feeling that everything I was hearing was ringing hollow. If God really does need the best, why was his Son born in a stable? If God's work requires sophisticated systems, why did Jesus build his leadership team predominantly using unlettered fishermen? If God's work requires the best marketing campaigns, why is Jesus's "brand" symbolized by a cross, a gruesome symbol of torture and death? Yes, almighty God does deserve the best, but at least on the earth, he generally chooses to forgo it. And, perhaps more importantly, who says that our best is the same as God's? I think it was at that dinner when I first realized that God doesn't accomplish his work the same way people do. His values do not match those of Wall Street, Washington D.C., or Hollywood. What gets us excited doesn't necessarily impress him. In short: God's ways are not our ways (Isa. 55:8–9).

Nevertheless, I agreed to participate in this grand undertaking for God. After all, what if it was a great kingdom building, soul-winning, God-glorifying success, and I passed on it? But alas, it was not to be. The result was, to put it mildly, an unmitigated disaster. Sadly, it was another case of God's people trying to do God's work, the world's way. The results were, as should have been predicted, a catastrophe.

Understanding God's Ways

Jesus was different from every other rabbi of his day, or any day. He stood out. He went against the cultural norms of his generation. Notorious sinners generally liked him. He was invited to parties. He would attract enormous crowds and then make statements that turned away followers. Jesus was so unconventional that even his own disciples were bewildered by him even after having lived and worked with him for more than three years. He acted so differently, in fact, that society's gatekeepers ultimately killed him.

This book is about the ways of God. There are some great books on the attributes of God. There are heavy tomes on the doctrines of God. There are also books on the names, commands, and promises of God. But here, we will specifically focus on the ways of God. Some clarification will be helpful as we begin:

1. God's Ways Are Not His Acts

It is important to understand that, while God's acts reflect his ways, the two terms are not interchangeable. This has caused God's people no end of confusion over the years. The psalmist observed: "He revealed his ways to Moses, his deeds to the people of Israel" (Ps. 103:7). The Israelites witnessed the mighty miracles God performed when he freed them from slavery in Egypt. They observed the ten devastating plagues that humbled Pharaoh. They walked through the Red Sea on dry land and then watched the Egyptian army drown in it. They saw a cloud leading them through the desert by day and a pillar of fire guiding them by night. They collected manna every morning that God miraculously provided.

Have you ever wondered how the Israelites could watch God annihilate the seemingly invincible Egyptian army by manipulating a sea, but then worry and fret that God would not provide them enough to drink when they were in the desert? Does it seem strange that they could witness so many amazing miracles and then be filled with anxiety over something as mundane as drinking water? The reason is simple. They never made the connection between God's acts and his ways.

The acts, or deeds, of God were obvious for all to see. It was impossible to miss devastating plagues descending on Egypt, or a Red Sea parting. But the ways of God were something entirely different. Only Moses, and a handful of others, including Caleb, Miriam, and Joshua, recognized those. The *Oxford English Dictionary* defines *ways* as "a method, style or manner of doing something. One's characteristic or habitual manner of behavior or expression." To understand a person's ways, you must connect the dots between their character and their actions. People's ways derive from their character. God may accomplish his goals through various deeds, but he will never act contrary to his unchanging character and ways.

For example, every day for forty years, the Israelites needed food while they wandered in the wilderness. So, God sent manna every morning. The people received nourishment every day for forty years. Each morning when they emerged from their tents, there was manna scattered over the ground. However, one day they needed water (Num. 20:1–13). Panic ensued! What were they going to do? They were certain they would all die. Sure, God had provided manna for them like clockwork, but this was different. Now they needed water!

What did Moses see? He saw that God's way was to keep his covenant. As promised, he hadn't let them miss a solitary meal. And, if God was faithful in providing food, he'd be just as reliable in providing water, protection, or whatever else they needed. God's character is trustworthy, so his *ways* are always faithful. This faithfulness would be expressed in a wide variety of specific actions. When you don't recognize the ways of God, then dozens of previous miracles will not be sufficient to prevent you from panicking the next time you need one. But when you learn the ways of God, you'll understand that God always acts in a manner consistent with his character. You can take that to the bank.

Unfortunately, many Christians today still operate at the same level as the Israelites. They have been blessed over the years by God's practical involvement in their life, yet they have never moved beyond the specific acts of God to understand his overarching ways. As a result, every new need or problem they face provokes within them the same worries and fear as the previous ones. They fail to learn from their encounters with God.

$400 or $40? When I was in university, I walked a financial tightrope every year. Each summer I worked hard to save enough money to pay for another year of school. One winter I asked a teenage friend to move my car for me. I erroneously assumed he knew how to drive. He drove it right into the back of a parked vehicle. He had no money or insurance, so I ended up owing $400. At that time, $400 might as well have been four million dollars. My only hope was to land a temporary job during spring break. Considering the fact that minimum wage at that time was $3.25/hour, earning $400 in a week was a long shot. All my friends were praying for me, but no job materialized. I grew discouraged. As spring break commenced, some college friends invited me to accompany them as they went home for the week. It seemed irresponsible to quit trying to find work and go away for a week. However, in my distress, I decided that if I hadn't found a job by then, perhaps what I needed was a vacation!

When we arrived, I learned that one of my friend's father was going into the bush country to check on his logging operation, and I was welcome to tag along. I ended up spending the next four days helping to clear brush. At the end of the week, my friend's dad took me aside and asked what I felt I deserved to be paid for the work I had done. I said, considering how much I had eaten, if he would simply not bill me for the food I had consumed, we could call it even. He insisted on paying. I adamantly refused to give him an amount. He finally handed me a $400 check.

After that marvelous provision, I should have been forever convinced that God was absolutely trustworthy. After all, this was Friday and the $400 was due on Monday. God had proven himself faithful and timely once again. We headed back home early Sunday morning. We planned to arrive in time to attend our church's evening service. On the ten-hour drive, I was struck by a troubling thought. My parents had taught me to tithe on everything I earned. That would be $40. But the entire $400 was due on Monday. Surely God would understand if I gave him an IOU until the upcoming summer when I had a job once more. I was torn. It seemed foolhardy, to say nothing of legalistic, to tithe on money God had just given me to pay a bill. But I could get no peace. So, I wrote out a check for $40 and then fervently prayed we would experience car trouble on our way home, so we missed the church service that evening.

Everyone who had been praying for my financial need asked how I was doing. Rather than celebrating God's $400 provision, I was sullen about the $40 shortfall I was about to incur when the offering plate was passed.

Imagine! God had proven he could provide for a $400 need, but now I fretted about $40. But that is what happens when you see the acts of God but fail to learn the ways of God. God could graciously perform 1,000 acts on our behalf, but unless we translate those into an understanding of his ways, we will worry when we face our next need.

I reluctantly gave my tithe. I was not a cheerful giver. After the service, Erin, a sweet girl from my college group, hugged me and told me she had been praying for my financial need. I mumbled a thank you and hurriedly excused myself. When I got home, I discovered an envelope in my jacket pocket. It was from Erin. She must have put it there when she hugged me. Inside was a note telling me she had prayed for my financial need throughout spring break. She said she wanted to do what she could to help. Enclosed were four ten dollar bills. I fell to my knees, overwhelmed. I realized in that moment that my God was not a God who gives $400 or $40. He is a God who provides for his children's needs. Period. Whatever they might be. That evening I began to understand one of the ways of God.

Many people who have attended church all their lives, who read their Bibles regularly, and pray daily, still don't know God very well. They may realize that God periodically intervenes in people's lives, but they have never come to know his ways.

2. Troubling Bible Passages

God's ways sometimes confuse us. They can appear troubling, or even offensive from our modern perspective. Common examples include when God commanded the Israelites to obliterate every person in Jericho, or to stone adulterers to death. Some people claim they cannot believe in a God who is so harsh and merciless. Other actions, such as calling for the sacrifice of untold thousands of animals in Old Testament worship, or kosher laws where God's people are forbidden from eating prohibited foods (such as bacon), seem unduly harsh.

There are some who view the Old Testament God as far more wrathful than the New Testament Jesus, as if the Bible portrays two different Gods. There are many modern Christians who are happy to dispense with the Old Testament altogether as outdated and no longer applicable, thus excising many of the most troublesome biblical portrayals of God. Other Christians resort to picking and choosing which of God's behaviors are to be jettisoned from modern Bibles so God's ways do not offend the sensitive souls reading it today.

An important issue we'll address is, where do we learn what the ways of God are? Should we even look in the Old Testament for them? Are those revelations of God outdated? Do we restrict our search for God's ways to the life of Jesus? Even there, though, Jesus overturns tables (Mark 11:15–17), curses a fig tree (Mark 11:12–14, 20–21), and casts a legion of demons into 2,000 swine, causing them to rush headlong into the sea and drown (Mark 5:1–20). Jesus also said that if someone rudely slaps you in the face, you should turn your other cheek toward them so they can slap it too (Matt. 5:39). Did Jesus really expect people to live that way in the modern world? Or was that just the way he lived his life? After all, living that way got Jesus killed.

As we study this subject, we'll see that we can't be selective about God's ways. They are revealed in the Bible. They come as a package. And they don't change. God's ways are the same today as they were in the biblical era.

3. Confused Christians

A final problem related to God's ways concerns those who claim to be following his ways, yet their behavior, and its consequences, appear incongruent with clear biblical teaching. Many of the worst abuses in Christendom have been perpetrated by people asserting they were following God's scriptural teaching. The infamous Crusades of the Middle Ages were based on stories of Joshua and the Israelites conquering the land of Canaan. European Christians grimly marched off to conquer it once more to the glory of Christ. The Prosperity Gospel is based largely on certain passages (typically in the Old Testament) that appear to teach that God intends for his people to grow wealthy and to enjoy old age. Television preachers will point out an isolated Bible verse and zealously proclaim it summarily represents how God works in people's lives today.

There are also sincere people who assume they understand God's ways, but when they attempt to live out what they believe, they experience painful failure. Devout pastors may assume that if they preach God's Word faithfully and keep their heart pure, God will protect them from their enemies and grow their flock. Then they are cruelly fired by an oligarchy of deacons or elders and left bewildered as to why a loving God would allow such a cruel injustice. Or a Christian businessperson decides to be salt and light in her workplace, assuming God will honor her courageous efforts. Then she is summarily fired by a hostile boss. Or a Christian entrepreneur starts a new company that is to be run on Christian principles, for God's glory. But a large chain store opens an outlet nearby and the smaller business is forced into bankruptcy. A young man believes the Bible teaches that if he delights himself in the Lord, God will give him the desires of his heart. He immerses himself in Scripture and prayer, volunteers at his church, and tithes on his income. Yet the woman of his dreams turns him down flat.

And what about sincere young people like William Borden, who gave away an enormous fortune, investing it in missions. Then he travelled to the Middle East where he intended to be a missionary. He fully devoted his life to the cause of Christ, only to die of meningitis before ever beginning his missionary service. Why does God allow the lives of some of his finest saints to be cut short while he allows brutal dictators to live long, diabolical lives? Let's face it. On the surface, at least, God's ways can be confusing.

Have you known people who grew disillusioned and disheartened by God's ways? They thought they understood biblical principles, but when they attempted to live according to this understanding, they experienced grievous disappointment. Perhaps this describes you. Hopefully this book will help you understand the ways of God. God wants you to know his ways, and to live your life accordingly (Isa. 30:1–2). Those who grasp and follow God's ways can change the world. But we must know what they are.

Some people insist on doing things their own way, or in ways that make sense to them. Frank Sinatra famously crooned, "I did it my way!" History is filled with the carnage of people, churches, and nations that chose their own way rather than God's. It is enormously costly to ignore God's ways and choose to live according to our best thinking. The prophet Isaiah noted,

> "Who gave Jacob to the robber and Israel to the plunderers? Was it not the Lord? Have we not sinned against him? They were not willing to walk in his ways, and they would not listen to his instruction. So he poured out his furious anger and the power of war on Jacob. It surrounded him with fire, but he did not know it; it burned him, but he didn't take it to heart." (Isa. 42:24–25)

What may be more tragic than brazenly refusing to follow God's ways, however, is to mistakenly assume you are following God's ways when, in fact, you don't know what they are. Many people who have attended church for most of their lives assume they know what God's ways are. Yet they do not know God's Word beyond a surface level, and they are unaware of how the world's thinking has saturated and influenced their own. As a result, there are powerless, defeated Christians today who erroneously assume they are living the life God intended. The truth is, only by understanding and following God's ways will you be able to experience genuine Christianity.

Questions for Reflection/Discussion

1. What are some examples of churches and Christian leaders using the world's methodology rather than following God's ways?

2. Consider your own Christian life. Do you have habits that reflect the world's way of operating, but not necessarily God's way?

3. In focusing on God's acts, how have you sometimes missed his ways?

4. What are some Scriptural examples that trouble you? What are some that encourage you?

5. When was a time you misunderstood God's will and made a bad decision? What did you learn from that experience?

CHAPTER 1

GOD'S WAYS ARE NOT OUR WAYS

"For my thoughts are not your thoughts, and your ways are not my ways." This is the Lord*'s declaration. "For as heaven is higher than earth, so my ways are higher than your ways, and my thoughts than your thoughts."*
(Isa. 55:8–9)

Make your ways known to me,
Lord*; teach me your paths.*
(Ps. 25:4)

God's Ways

Take a moment to consider God. Infinite. Spirit. Dwelling in an unimaginable celestial world. Governing trillions of galaxies and stars. Creating a universe so vast it takes more than thirteen billion light-years for the glimmer of distant stars to reach Earth. Not only does God know the furthest extent of the vast universe, but he is cognizant of the minutest details of every human being, animal, and plant on Earth. God knows the future, including every event still to come. God will bring time to a climactic close at the precise moment he has sovereignly destined. He comprehends every mystery in the universe. He is fully aware of every creature lurking in the depths of the sea, every cosmic activity in the far reaches of the universe, and every interaction of each cell on Earth. Consider also that God knows every sin that every person in history has committed, and he fully intends to execute perfect justice upon every wrongdoer.

Now imagine the audacity of assuming, or demanding, that God act in ways that make perfect sense to us or in a manner that we, ourselves, would behave. Ponder the hubris required to insist that we will not believe anything God says unless we understand it completely. We can't grasp what it is like for God to act today while he already knows what will happen tomorrow. We can't imagine how God can be fully aware of what billions of people are doing and thinking simultaneously. We are exceedingly ignorant of much of what exists in our physical world, yet we assume God, who inhabits a heavenly, spirit domain, should act in ways we understand. We are but creatures of dust. How could we assume the source of life would conduct affairs in ways that are logical to us?

Misunderstanding God's Ways

A god who makes perfect sense to us is no God at all. This is, of course, the absurdity of idol worship. Frail humanity cannot begin to fathom the vastness of God. That is the insanity of carving an idol out of wood and assuming you have captured the likeness of the almighty. A. W. Tozer said, "Among the sins to which the human heart is prone, hardly any other is more hateful to God than idolatry, for idolatry is at bottom a libel on his character. The idolatrous heart assumes that God is other than he is—in itself a monstrous sin—and substitutes for the true God one made after its own likeness. Always this God will conform to the image of the one who created it and will be base or pure, cruel or kind, according to the moral state of the mind from which it emerges."[3] Idols are humanity's misguided attempt to downsize God to a level they can understand and control.

Frail humanity cannot begin to fathom the vastness of God.

The prophet Isaiah described the foolishness of worshipping a god that is microscopically less than is the true God:

> All who make idols are nothing,
> and what they treasure benefits no one.
> Their witnesses do not see or know anything,
> so they will be put to shame.
> Who makes a god or casts a metal image
> that benefits no one?
> Look, all its worshipers will be put to shame,
> and the craftsmen are humans.
> They all will assemble and stand;
> they all will be startled and put to shame.
>
> The ironworker labors over the coals,
> shapes the idol with hammers,
> and works it with his strong arm.
> Also he grows hungry and his strength fails;
> he doesn't drink water and is faint.
> The woodworker stretches out a measuring line,
> he outlines it with a stylus;
> he shapes it with chisels
> and outlines it with a compass.

He makes it according to a human form,
like a beautiful person,
to dwell in a temple.
He cuts down cedars for his use,
or he takes a cypress or an oak.
He lets it grow strong among the trees of the
forest.
He plants a laurel, and the rain makes it grow.
A person can use it for fuel.
He takes some of it and warms himself;
also he kindles a fire and bakes bread;
he even makes it into a god and worships it;
he makes an idol from it and bows down to it.
He burns half of it in a fire,
and he roasts meat on that half.
He eats the roast and is satisfied.
He warms himself and says, "Ah!
I am warm, I see the blaze."
He makes a god or his idol with the rest of it.
He bows down to it and worships;
he prays to it, "Save me, for you are my god."
Such people do not comprehend
and cannot understand,
for he has shut their eyes so they cannot see,
and their minds so they cannot understand.
No one comes to his senses;
no one has the perception or insight to say,
"I burned half of it in the fire,
I also baked bread on its coals,
I roasted meat and ate.
Should I make something detestable with the
rest of it?
Should I bow down to a block of wood?"

> He feeds on ashes.
> His deceived mind has led him astray,
> and he cannot rescue himself,
> or say, "Isn't there a lie in my right hand?" (Isa. 44:9–20)

The admonishment is clear: if people attempted to create their own version of God, it would be infinitely inferior to the reality of who he is. People cannot comprehend God's nature. He is exceedingly greater than we can possibly imagine. He inhabits a world we have never seen. He has power we cannot fathom. He functions with wisdom that dwarfs ours. No wonder the first of the Ten Commandments is, "Do not have other gods besides me" and the second is, "Do not make an idol for yourself" (Exod. 20:3–4).

The reason for the first commandment is obvious. God tolerates no rivals for his people's affections. But why would he care if his people crafted images and idols that represented him, the true God? Many religions construct elaborate idols to symbolize their god. The worshippers understand that the idol is not the actual god. However, it makes their god tangible and hence easier to worship. If you went to a temple of Zeus, you would find an idol of Zeus inside. The same is true for Apollo, Athena, and Buddha. But God will have none of that. Inside the holy of holies in the temple was the ark of the covenant but no image of God. History records that when the Roman general Pompey conquered Jerusalem, he brazenly forced his way behind the veil into the holy of holies to examine the Jews' most sacred place. To his surprise, there was nothing there. He couldn't understand how people could revere an invisible god. How could they worship a being when they had no idea what he looked like? Why was God so insistent that his people refrain from portraying him with an idol or image?

God undoubtedly had many reasons, but the most obvious is that any image, no matter how grandiose, and regardless of how much gold and precious metals were used, would merely be a pathetic attempt to duplicate something that was far beyond human comprehension. It would be like handing a two-year-old child a paintbrush and asking her to paint a replica of the *Mona Lisa*. I have visited Buddhist temples in Bangkok. They house large statues of Buddha. You can purchase gold leaf to apply to the statue as an expression of your devotion. Over time the metal statue becomes clothed with a thin layer of gold, pressed upon it by thousands of worshippers. God refused to be subjected to such a demeaning exercise, for it was infinitely beneath him and it misled worshippers into believing he was far less of a God than he really is.

The problem with fashioning idols, beyond grievously insulting God's majesty, is that we don't know what we don't know. We have no idea what God looks like. He is spirit, inhabiting a spirit world. He rules the universe and is fully aware of what every person, star, planet, asteroid, and black hole are doing. How do you portray that? You don't. So whatever image you envision for God falls vastly short of reality.

We become like that which we worship.

The psalmist declared, "Those who make them [idols] are just like them, as are all who trust in them" (Ps. 135:18; see also Ps. 115:8). We become like that which we worship. If we make wrong assumptions about what God is like, we will also develop erroneous beliefs about how God acts. And, if we misunderstand the ways of God, our Christian life will inevitably experience disappointment, frustration, and failure. A. W. Tozer advised:

> Our real idea of God may lie buried under the rubbish of conventional religious notions and may require an intelligent and vigorous search before it is finally unearthed and exposed for what it is. Only after an ordeal of painful self-probing are we likely to discover what we actually believe about God. . . . I believe there is scarcely an error in doctrine or a failure in applying Christian ethics that cannot be traced finally to imperfect and ignoble thoughts about God. . . . The man who comes to a right belief about God is relieved of ten thousand temporal problems.[4]

Common Misconceptions about God

Because people tend to envision God in terms that match their personal preferences, they view the ways of God through a variety of lenses. Although not himself a Christian, Jonathan Haidt, in his book *The Happiness Hypothesis,* argues insightfully that people generally choose their beliefs based on their feelings.[5] Then they use their reason to justify what their emotions have already decided. He gives the analogy of a monkey riding an elephant. If the monkey represents our reason, the elephant symbolizes our emotions. Haidt suggests that though the monkey is in the driver's seat, the elephant will go wherever it chooses. We like to assume we are rational beings, driven by reasonable decisions. Haidt suggests we base our religious beliefs far more on our feelings than we care to admit.

Haidt points out in his book *The Righteous Mind* that when it comes to political or religious beliefs, people tend to have six primary values that influence their decisions about such things as politics and religion.[6] He found, not surprisingly, that Democrats and Republicans have different hierarchies of what they value most. Likewise, various religious denominations prioritize different values, so their members often develop their view of God and his ways based more on their feelings and values than on how God has revealed himself in his Word. We can be drawn to Bible verses that support our view of God and ignore other verses that challenge our theology. There are, of course, many faulty views of God. The following are some of the most common:

Greek God Model

The Greeks developed a religion in which their gods were essentially larger-than-life versions of themselves. Greek gods were lustful, adulterous, jealous, spiteful, vengeful, and prideful. They were no more moral than were ordinary people, and often their behavior descended to levels of depravity that would have shocked the average Greek. The difference was that the gods were immortal, and they were more powerful than mortals. Rather than setting a high ethical standard for people to follow, the gods behaved shamefully, pursuing their lusts and nursing their pride. Because the gods supposedly hungered for sacrifices that were offered to them in worship, the Greeks hoped to influence them through generous sacrifices and homage. At the same time, these mythological gods could be capricious and turn against you on a whim.

Stories of Zeus, Poseidon, Athena, and Hades have entertained people for centuries. It is man-made religion at its most creative. The gods were nothing more than sinful people writ large. Yet this same approach to religion has permeated Christianity, as is demonstrated in numerous ways. When someone claims they prayed and God granted them permission to divorce their spouse and to marry their lover, they treat God like a Greek deity who is equally as lustful and deceitful as the adulterer. When Christians justify their greed, cruelty, pride, or dishonesty by claiming they are doing God's will, or that the ends justify the means, they are acting as if God is nothing more than a Greek deity who shares their vices.

This attitude is evident when people say things like, "I just can't believe God would not want me to be happy" or "Why would God give me this desire if he didn't want me to satisfy it?" Be careful! If your religion perfectly matches your preferences and desires, you may in fact be the author of your faith. Whenever you act as if God always agrees with your desires, never chastises your indiscretions, or upgrades your lapses in character, then your god probably belongs on Mount Olympus.

Whenever you act as if God always agrees with your desires, never chastises your indiscretions, or upgrades your lapses in character, then your god probably belongs on Mount Olympus.

God in a Bottle

A similar faulty view of God's ways is the Aladdin model, owing to the popular ancient tale of the young man who discovers a magical lamp occupied by a powerful genie who grants him his wishes. In the story Aladdin encounters problems in part because he does not always know the best things to ask for. Nevertheless, the genie never questions his wishes but grants them immediately.

Many people treat God like a genie in a bottle. This is most infamously seen in the "health and wealth," or "prosperity" gospel pervasively promulgated through the media. Proponents boldly proclaim that God is there to grant you whatever will make your life more prosperous, happy, and comfortable. Want a new Cadillac? Rub the lamp. Want to be rid of that chronic back pain? Summon the genie. Want a bigger house? Well, you get the picture. In this misguided theology, God serves us. He exists to fulfill our every desire. When he does not provide what we ask, the fault must be that we lacked the requisite faith. Faith is the equivalent to rubbing Aladdin's lamp. Our faith opens the door to God's power in our life, so God will grant our every wish. Though this view of God can be found on the Internet, you will look for it in vain in the Bible.

Laissez-Faire God

Another theology holds that, while there is a God, he is either preoccupied or disinterested in peoples' day-to-day affairs. Famous Americans, such as Benjamin Franklin and Thomas Jefferson, were deists. They believed God was like a cosmic clockmaker who created the universe and then left it to run according to laws he established. People were to use the reason God bestowed on them to solve their own problems. Such thinking led Franklin to famously declare, "God helps those who help themselves." God is viewed as uninterested in humanity's daily endeavors, so people must do their utmost to create the best possible life.

A second variant, promoted by many Christians, insists that God granted Christians the Bible, and thus we have in its pages every command and principle needed to live a God-honoring life. It is true that "all Scripture is inspired by God and is profitable for teaching, for rebuking, for correcting, for training in righteousness, so that the man of God may be complete, equipped for every good work" (2 Tim. 3:16–17). However, we must not minimize God's active involvement in our daily living (Heb. 4:12). This view has no practical role for the Holy Spirit in the life of believers (John 14–16). But the Holy Spirit does not indwell believers at conversion and then mutely take a back seat and hope we make wise choices. There are those who squirm at the thought of God directly communicating with people (despite his doing so regularly throughout Scripture). Rather than God guiding us specifically, some hold that if we need direction, we simply follow biblical principles. Absolutely, the Bible *is* indeed the best guide for Christian living. But biblical principles can only take us so far. For example, when choosing a spouse, the Bible admonishes us to marry a fellow believer and someone of Christlike character, but there is little more direction than that. Likewise, in choosing which job to take, or where to live, how to respond to a prodigal child, or many other crucial decisions, principles are a good place to start, but they still leave much of our decision-making to our own best thinking.

Many Christians have been taught that God does not give specific guidance to people. He gave us a brain, and he intends for us to use it. Of course, that's what Abraham was doing when he slept with Hagar to have a son, or Moses when he murdered an oppressive Egyptian. Likewise, deists lived their lives by God-given principles, but they had no personal relationship with Christ. Yet the consistent testimony of the Bible is that God wants to be intimately involved in our life. He promises to give specific guidance if we seek his will (Jer. 33:3). Whether it was giving Adam and Eve clear guidelines on living in the garden or the risen Christ delivering a vividly detailed message to the apostle John on the Isle of Patmos, the Bible is filled with examples of God's being practically involved in the lives of his people. If you assume that, when you become a Christian, God provides you a Bible and says, "Take it from here," then you will believe God's ways are impersonal and general. When facing a decision, you may search the Bible for pertinent commands or injunctions. You might make a list of pros and cons. You could ask friends for advice. But you won't go to God himself for guidance (Isa. 30:1). In this you behave just like an eighteenth-century deist.

Totalitarian God

Antithetical to the laissez-faire approach is one that suggests God is a universal micromanager. He enforces his will on everyone and leaves no room for individual choice or free will. This type of thinking, known as determinism, is based on certain assumptions. It holds that God has predetermined every detail of your life, and therefore your free will is an illusion. Though God tells you to believe and obey, the reality is that every one of your actions has been predetermined and you have no choice but to do what God has decreed. Events unfold exactly according to his preset and detailed agenda. If you lose your job or come down with the flu, God must have wanted that to happen. This approach contains inherent problems.

It is crucial to understand that God can retain his sovereignty while still allowing people free will. We will discuss this subject in greater depth in chapter 6. For now, A. W. Tozer offers this counsel: "God sovereignly decreed that man should be free to exercise moral choice, and man from the beginning has fulfilled that decree by making his choice between good and evil. When he chooses to do evil, he does not thereby countervail the sovereign will of God but fulfills it, inasmuch as the eternal decree decided not which choice the man should make but that he should be free to make it. . . . Man's will is free because God is sovereign."[7]

Tozer provides this helpful analogy. He notes that God's sovereignty and people's free will are analogous to an ocean liner sailing from New York to Liverpool. The destination has been determined, and the ship moves steadily on its course. But aboard the ship, passengers exercise their autonomy in various ways. They choose which meal to eat. They decide what recreation to engage in or whether to enjoy a nap in their cabin. While passengers are living out their lives aboard the ship, the captain continues with his plan to steer the vessel to its desired end. Of course, passengers have limitations. They may decide they would rather swim to Liverpool, so they leap into the water, but they will drown. They are not able to change the destination to the Bahamas. There are certain aspects of the journey that they have no freedom to alter. However, for those freedoms granted to them, they can exercise a wide variety of choices, though it will not in any way affect the captain's overall plan. If a passenger determines to spend the entire trip in the cafeteria, gorging himself at the buffet, he will reach the destination far worse for the wear, but he will arrive, nonetheless. If the passenger frequents the ship's exercise room instead, he will arrive in a much different condition. Granting people freedom to choose does not in any way hinder or thwart God's grand design for human history.

While holding a high view of God's sovereignty is rightly a biblical perspective, there is a danger in equating sovereignty with determinism (the belief that your life has been predetermined to the smallest detail). We must not assume that for God to grant people free will, he must necessarily yield a portion of his sovereignty. God has established his rules and the consequences for breaking them. Within those divinely set parameters, we are free to choose.

Just as laissez-faire theology leaves too much for us to handle on our own, the micromanager approach leaves us too little. In it, we are merely spectators of our life, helplessly watching it unfold before our eyes. It is impossible to read the Bible and not see that God demands much more responsibility from us than that. God is fully in charge of history and world events. His power is even more impressive because it is not in any way infringed upon by people's choices. God is still sovereign, and he will achieve his purposes, regardless of what people choose to do.

Political God

This is a misguided mindset that assumes God accomplishes his work the same way people do, by using power, money, and influence. Clearly this is not the case. For example, God's way of reviving a nation is to first revive his own people and then release his Holy Spirit to work powerfully across the nation to initiate spiritual awakening. The Holy Spirit works through the preached Word of God, which leads people to repent of their sins.

The human, worldly approach plays out differently because it does not depend on the Holy Spirit's working to accomplish its work. Instead of trusting the Holy Spirit to convict and transform, supporters are enlisted to boycott those with opposing beliefs. The focus is on getting the "right" people in influential positions so power can be leveraged to pass laws that curtail sin. Celebrities and politicians are enlisted to support "Christian" causes. One danger of this approach is eagerly embracing people who are unbelievers, or who have questionable morals, because they are willing to support our goals. At times these efforts, though ostensibly for good causes, can look more like a political campaign than an endeavor to advance God's kingdom.

There is an alluring temptation for believers to place our trust in people rather than in Christ. The focus is on whom we know rather than Whom we know. When we have a need, we immediately begin reaching out to our contacts rather than calling out to Christ in prayer. Those who trust well-placed people rather than God are constantly expanding their network and sizing up others based on who can help promote their causes or meet their needs. Such people focus on persuading or manipulating people in order to achieve their desired ends. The key for them is having the right people on their side.

Oftentimes this is how churches conduct their business. If church leaders want to build a new auditorium, they may approach the task in a similar way to getting a bill passed through Congress. They enlist the support of influential members. They cast the vision for their plan and then campaign for people's votes. They seek to win popular support; they develop a slick promotional campaign; they make promises and say what people want to hear. This is a classic example of trying to do God's work the world's way.

The mindset of trusting people instead of God is perhaps most evident in the way many Christians view politics. Christians certainly ought to be active and informed citizens who work to elect the best candidates possible for the office. We have been commanded to pray for our government leaders (1 Tim. 2:1–2). But we must be cautious about placing our hopes for national revival or moral renewal on getting our preferred politicians elected to office. We often assume that if our candidate is elected, God is blessing, and if our candidate loses, all hope is lost. Some go so far as to believe even God cannot save their nation if the "wrong" people hold office. When we begin to act as if God's work is best accomplished through politicians, our view of God's ways is far too small! We must always remember that God's kingdom is conducted in ways that are vastly different from today's politics. For that we should be exceedingly grateful.

Businesslike God

God is masterful in his management of people's lives, churches, and his kingdom (Isa. 40:6–31). He knows how to earn a hundredfold return on his investments. He owns "the cattle on a thousand hills" (Ps. 50:10). Yet, again, he does not operate the way we do. His plans always succeed because of the power of his Spirit and because he is omniscient; he alone knows the future. When Zerubbabel was concerned about how to lead his people, the Lord told him, "Not by might, nor by power, but by my Spirit, says the LORD of hosts" (Zech. 4:6 ESV).

We can mistakenly assume that God's will can be accomplished through business and leadership principles, apart from the working of the Holy Spirit. Many best-selling business/leadership books, podcasts, and blogs circulating today herald guaranteed methods for success. Christians often look at these and conclude that what works well in the marketplace will be equally effective in God's kingdom.

Just as many business books highlight a successful company so others can copy their methods, so pastors of megachurches write books and hold conferences teaching other pastors how they, too, can experience "success" (which usually equates to a large and financially prosperous congregation). The faulty assumptions are: (1) numerical growth equals spiritual success; (2) growth is the result of leadership decisions rather than God's guidance and blessing.

Some church leaders believe God intends for his people to always live within their means and to never take financial "risks." It is true that God's property and money should be carefully stewarded. Yet biblically, God often told people to take actions that *appeared* risky if not hazardous. Jesus stated that if you tried to save your life, you would lose it (Matt. 16:25). Of course, apart from the working of the Holy Spirit, this can seem foolhardy. If you give yourself away, how can you prosper at the same time? But for a Christian, the key is not your business savvy but the power of the Holy Spirit working in your life. God's power comes by faith. The writer of Hebrews claimed that "without faith it is *impossible* to please God" (Heb. 11:6). Yet many Christians believe God would never ask them to do anything that required them to exercise faith. Walking by faith might have been encouraged by Paul, but it will alarm your accountant!

Congregations, using the business approach to God's ways, might assume success depends on how businesslike they conduct themselves. Churches can act as if accomplishing their mission depends on their location, attractive and accessible facility, well-run programs, high-tech equipment, and professional quality worship band. While none of these is inherently bad, the danger is trusting in strategies and marketing over the working of the Holy Spirit. Efficiency can be cherished more than evangelism. If churches don't function any differently than popular retailers, they are grossly limiting their capacity to experience the Holy Spirit at work.

There has been a spate of high-profile leaders who grew massive ministries using creative marketing, high-tech worship performances, *New York Times* best-selling books, and large doses of charisma. Tragically, many of these popular figures have been exposed for adultery, staff abuse, dishonesty, or addiction. It becomes painfully clear that their numerical success is primarily due to their adept use of business principles, not the power of the Holy Spirit working through their sanctified life.

This businesslike view of God's ways can motivate Christians to take their cue from Wall Street rather than from the Holy Spirit. For example, if you assume God relates to you in a businesslike manner, you may be surprised by what God tells you to do. He may lead you to pass on a promotion that would require extensive overtime hours, so you have time for your volunteer work. Or he may want you to quit a lucrative job and assume a modest position at a nonprofit. Or he may ask you to give generously to Christian and charitable causes rather than investing more into your retirement portfolio. These directives may not line up with astute career moves, but they align with God's ways of strengthening families and building his kingdom.

Military Model

There are some similarities between how the military operates and God's ways. Yet again it is hazardous to assume God's ways follow common military strategies. How does the military operate? It follows a clear hierarchy from the top commanding officer down to the lowest level recruit. Officers design strategy and expect their ranks to obey their orders. Some churches assume God works much like the modern general, so they should too. As a result, senior pastors or religious leaders may lead their followers much like General Patton led the Third Army. Questioning authority is considered treasonous. This view places different values on people, based on their position. It makes celebrities of those on the highest rungs of the organizational chart.

Viewing God with a military mindset sees him waging continual warfare against his enemies and enlisting people to engage in his battles. The apostle Paul noted that Christians do not wrestle against flesh and blood, but against "the rulers, against the authorities, against the cosmic powers of this darkness, against evil, spiritual forces in the heavens" (Eph. 6:12).

The danger of using a military lens to view God's ways is that we can begin to regard people as our enemy. Paul said we *don't* wrestle against flesh and blood. God does not call us to be constantly embroiled in conflict with others. We may like the lofty idea that we are waging "holy war" against God's opponents (or at least, our opponents). It is a point of pride for some Christians that they have so many enemies. They proclaim, "I must be doing something right. After all, look at all the people who are angry at me!"

Such people tend to view others as either allies or enemies. Them or us. Much of their Christian life is invested in developing tactics that will defeat their perceived opponents. When you view people as your enemy, it is easy to justify all manner of unChristlike behavior to defeat them. Gossip campaigns, deception, manipulation, or whatever it takes to oust someone viewed as an enemy to God's cause. After all, "All's fair in love and war!" This mindset has led to countless family estrangements, broken relationships, church splits, and pastoral firings as zealous Christians levelled their guns at those they consider threatening.

Social media has become a war zone. If you view someone as an enemy of the faith, you can ambush them on social media. Lies and misinformation are launched like an aerial bombardment. Character assassination and vicious trolling are fair game. Everyone is classified as friend or foe. Some people love a "good fight," and thus they are often attracted to this understanding of God's ways. Such people often celebrate more joyously when an enemy is felled than when a sinner is saved. They might not be overly inspired to attend a prayer meeting, but they come running the moment a new crusade against the heathen is launched. Mention "grace," and they will sigh and cite the time in the Bible when Jesus cleansed the temple. Such people long for God's judgment to fall. They just don't expect it will land on them.

Summary

Humankind has not fundamentally changed since the Greeks fashioned gods to reflect their worldview and values. People continue to hold beliefs about God that coincide with their feelings and desires. Therefore, it is critical to base our view of God and his ways on what is revealed in Scripture. Picking and choosing our preferred verses will quickly lead us to a god that is nowhere to be found in the Bible. In the following chapters, we'll take a closer look at what the Bible reveals about the ways of God.

Questions for Reflection/Discussion

1. What is a misconception you have had about the ways of God?

2. How have you inadvertently assumed God was like you and did things in ways that made sense to you?

3. To which of the incorrect views of God have you been most susceptible? Why?

4. Why is it so important that you have a sound, biblical view of who God is?

5. What might you need to do so you have a more accurate view of God and his ways?

6. Why is measuring success by worldly metrics dangerous for Christians, churches, and ministries?

CHAPTER 2

GOD'S WAYS ARE BIBLICAL

For forty years I was disgusted with that generation; I said, "They are a people whose hearts go astray; they do not know my ways." So I swore in my anger, "They will not enter my rest."
(Ps. 95:10–11)

Let whoever is wise understand these things, and whoever is insightful recognize them. For the ways of the LORD *are right, and the righteous walk in them, but the rebellious stumble in them.*
(Hosea 14:9)

People often become confused trying to understand God's ways as they are presented in the Bible. They read of God destroying humanity with a cataclysmic flood or raining down fire and brimstone upon Sodom and Gomorrah and hasten to claim that they prefer Jesus to the "God of the Old Testament." There is a common misconception that God's character, or at least his ways, drastically changed between the testaments. Those with a dispensational view of the Bible emphasize that in the Old Testament, God was relating to the nation of Israel, while in the New Testament, God is relating to individual Christians and the church. The implication is that the ways of God change, depending on the time in history and those to whom he is interacting. Yet this is not so.

As we saw in the previous chapter, God's *character* does not change. He remains the same throughout the ages. His *ways* are based on his unchanging character. For example, because his character is holy, the ways God expresses himself are always holy as well. His *methods* can change over time, based on the circumstances. Still, his methods, or acts, are always consistent with his ways. In holiness, God, by his Holy Spirit, can convict people of their sin, or he can rain fire and brimstone down upon Sodom. In both situations, God's ways are holy, yet one method is far more severe than the other.

It is important to take our view of God's ways from Scripture. A proper view of God's ways in the Bible reveals he is entirely consistent from Genesis to Revelation. God's methods may change over time, but through the ages, his ways remain true to who he is. The God of the Old Testament was no less loving than Jesus in the Gospels. Likewise, our sin is no less grievous now than it was in the time of Noah.

God's Ways Are Found Exclusively in the Bible

To know what God is like, there is only one authoritative place to look: the Bible. We live in an age where opinions are prized, and feelings are supreme. But our reasoning and emotions do not dictate what God is like. God is God. There are not billions of gods, each corresponding to the preferences of everyone. God has provided everything we need to know about him and his ways in one repository: the Bible. So, to know the ways of God, we must search the Scriptures. If God's biblical revelation about himself does not align with our view of him, it is not Scripture that needs adjusting!

The Bible tells us everything we need to know to properly relate to God. It tells us that God never changes: "Furthermore, the Eternal One of Israel does not lie or change his mind, for he is not man who changes his mind" (1 Sam. 15:29). "Because I, the LORD, have not changed, you descendants of Jacob have not been destroyed" (Mal. 3:6). The way God related to people as revealed in the Bible is the same way he will relate to you.

A fundamental characteristic of God is love (1 John 4:16). Because God's nature is love, he will not act any other way but lovingly toward people. It would contradict his character to do so. God is not loving and gracious in the New Testament but holy and wrathful in the Old Testament. God's love and wrath are two sides of the same coin. He is equally loving (and holy) on every page of the Bible.

In one of the most intimate and glorious personal revelations of God in Scripture, he disclosed that his nature is compassionate and gracious, abounding in faithful love. Exodus 33:18 tells us that Moses asked to see God's glory. God told Moses he could not look upon his glory and live. Nevertheless, God agreed to pass by in physical form while he protected Moses in the cleft of a rock. God declared his name (the Lord) which was a revelation of his character (Exod. 34:5). Then God revealed what his character was like: "The LORD is a compassionate and gracious God, slow to anger and abounding in faithful love and truth, maintaining faithful love to a thousand generations, forgiving iniquity, rebellion, and sin" (Exod. 34:6–7). Here God's loving-kindness is expressed, not in the New Testament but in the heart of the Old Testament books of the Law.

Deuteronomy reveals the most sacred command in the Old Testament. It is this: "Love the LORD your God with all your heart, with all your soul, and with all your strength" (Deut. 6:5). When Jesus was asked what the greatest commandment in Scripture was, he cited this verse (Matt. 22:37). Through the prophet Jeremiah, God declared to his people, "I have loved you with an everlasting love; therefore, I have continued to extend faithful love to you" (Jer. 31:3). This is just a small sampling of the numerous verses in the Old Testament describing God's loving ways.

Some argue that in the Old Testament, God loved his chosen people, such as Abraham, Moses, David, and the Israelites, but expressed wrath toward others, such as the Canaanites, Assyrians, and Babylonians. God expects all people to worship and obey him, and he expresses wrath on those who reject him. Nevertheless, Scripture provides numerous examples where God demonstrated his love toward those who were not his followers.

God did indeed destroy Sodom and Gomorrah, which were legendarily wicked, yet he agreed to spare them if even ten righteous people could be found among them (Gen. 18:32). When Sarah, mother of Isaac, mistreated her Egyptian slave Hagar, God rescued Hagar from peril in the wilderness and promised to bless her and her descendants, even though they would ultimately become enemies of God's people (Gen. 16:1–16). When God knew that Egypt would suffer a horrific drought that could cause widespread starvation, he warned Pharaoh in a dream so he could prepare for the impending disaster (Gen. 41). The Assyrians were infamously cruel to their captives. Nevertheless, God sent Jonah to warn them of imminent judgment so they could repent and be spared God's wrath (Jonah 1–4). Naaman led the people of Aram to fight against the Israelites, yet God healed him of his leprosy (2 Kings 5). Through the prophets, God proclaimed his intention for every nation to worship him, not just the Israelites (Isa. 66:18–23).

In New Testament times, God continued to express his love for all people. One of Scripture's most famous passages tells us: "For God loved the world in this way: He gave his one and only Son, so that everyone who believes in him will not perish but have eternal life" (John 3:16). Throughout the New Testament, God's love is continually highlighted. Paul asked, "Who can separate us from the love of Christ?" and he concluded: "For I am persuaded that neither death nor life, nor angels nor rulers, nor things present nor things to come, nor powers, nor height nor depth, nor any other created thing will be able to separate us from the love of God that is in Christ Jesus our Lord" (Rom. 8:35, 38–39). The apostle John succinctly concluded: "God is love" (1 John 4:16).

We will talk more about God's love in a later chapter. For now it serves as an example to demonstrate that the Bible reveals God as loving both in the Old and New Testaments. Now you might ask, "But if God is loving, why does he command Joshua to kill Achan and his family, or why does God smite Ananias and Saphira?" Good question. The simple answer for now is that God is not one-dimensional. He does not merely act in love. He also acts in holiness. But his holiness does not diminish the fact that he always acts in love.

We must carefully differentiate between those traits of God that are consistently manifested throughout the Bible and those actions that appear to be rare or unique. If you only find God doing something once in the Bible, be careful not to generalize it. For example, the Scriptures only tells of one time when God struck down a couple for lying in church (Acts 5:1–11). God was being perfectly consistent in his *ways* at that point. God's ways are always holy. However, this method was an isolated incident applied to make a dramatic and unforgettable example. We must be careful not to draw the wrong conclusions based on that one incident.

Dallas Willard offers this wise counsel: "It is the *principles,* not the incidentals, of Scripture that count here. Study of the Scriptures makes clear that certain things are fundamental, absolute, without exception. If the Bible says something once, notice it but don't count it as a fundamental principle. If it says it twice, think about it twice. If it is repeated many times, then dwell on it and seek to understand it."[8] Certainly we are to take *everything* in the Bible seriously and consider it to be true. But we should exercise caution in what we conclude about God based on one incident.

Scripture records only one person who put out a fleece to be certain of God's will (Judg. 6:33–46). Yet many Christians today speak about "putting out their fleece." It is wrong to take this one example and assume God is pleased for us to regularly test what he says by asking for a sign. Furthermore, Gideon's example is never praised or lauded as a commendable precedent. In fact, when Thomas asked for a sign, Jesus said those who do not see and yet believe are more blessed than those who insist on proof (John 20:29). What the story of Gideon and the fleece represents is the consistent way in which God relates to people—with patience and grace. You can see God's long-suffering throughout Scripture. You see a fleece only once.

The ways of God are consistently evident throughout the Bible, and that is our only source for discerning them. Moreover, we must study and read the Scriptures carefully and prayerfully because the temptation is to overlay our own thoughts and feelings over Scripture and not keep in mind God's unchanging character, as expressed through his actions.

God's Ways Are Different from His Methods

God's ways don't change because they are driven by his character. However, the methods he employs can vary dramatically. For example, God's character is always holy. God will never act in an unholy way. To do so would violate a fundamental aspect of his character. Because of his holiness, he will never overlook sin, and he will discipline sinful people using various methods.

The tools God uses to discipline people for their sin are many and diverse.

One of the most troubling Bible accounts for many people is when God commanded Joshua and his army to kill every man, woman, child, and animal in the city of Jericho (Josh. 6:17–21). Such judgment, even on wicked people, seems excessively harsh and certainly uncharacteristic of Jesus, as portrayed in the Gospels. So we must go back to God's character and examine his ways to shed light on his actions in this case.

The land of Canaan was filled with (unsurprisingly) Canaanites, comprised of various peoples such as the Hivites, Girgashites, Amorites, and Jebusites (Josh. 3:10). Their religion was idolatry. Their primary gods were Baal and his consort, Asherah. These were fertility gods, which meant that farmers sought to placate them so they would grant rain and abundant harvests. When gods are primarily responsible for your farm animals procreating and seeds germinating, you can imagine the depravity that could develop in religions designed by people. A popular feature of such religions was having male and female prostitutes available to engage in sex with worshippers at the temple as an expression of worship. Worse yet, the god Molech ostensibly called for people to demonstrate their devotion to him by sacrificing their children on his altar. Even some of the Judean kings, such as Ahaz and Manasseh, participated in this horrific evil by causing their children to "pass through the fire" (2 Kings 16:3; 21:6 HCSB).

Imagine God's righteous indignation as he watched the Canaanites rejecting their Creator and practicing their depraved, man-made religion. Consider God's thoughts as men had their wives wait outside the temple with the children while they went inside to "worship" with a prostitute. Ponder God's heart when he saw farmers, greedy for a bumper crop, handing their babies to a priest to be burned on an altar. This was not merely a different world religion from Judaism. It was a debauched, sexualized, violent, and materialistic religion that destroyed people for selfish gain. How offensive to a righteous God!

The Bible is silent on how God had thus far sought to turn the Canaanites from their horrific, sinful ways. However, when God led Abraham to journey into Canaan, God told him that one day his descendants would occupy their land. But not yet, God said, "for the iniquity of the Amorites has not yet reached its full measure" (Gen. 15:16). The Amorites had already descended into abominable depths in their culture and religion, yet God said he was not yet prepared to judge them. God would wait while Abraham had a son Isaac and reared him into adulthood. Then he would wait while Isaac had a son Jacob. Then God would wait while Jacob raised his twelve sons and ultimately moved with them to Egypt. Then God would delay four hundred more years while the Israelites toiled in bondage. Then God would tarry forty more years while the Israelites wandered in the wilderness because they doubted God's Word. Finally, God told Joshua that the time had come to judge the Canaanites for their evil. For over five hundred years, God continued to allow the people of Canaan to practice their wicked religion. God's actions on cities such as Jericho can only be understood in light of the patience God showed them over the centuries.

Throughout Old Testament times God used a variety of means to discipline his people. Deuteronomy 28:15–68 itemizes an extensive list of the methods God would employ, if necessary. This could include defeat at an enemy's hands, an infestation of locusts, or a host of natural disasters. God continued to correct his people in New Testament days. Jesus warned that Jerusalem would be destroyed and the temple torn down as a result of God's judgment (Luke 19:41–44). Jesus instructed the church to treat a sinful brother like a tax collector, ostracizing him, if he did not repent (Matt. 18:17). In the early church, God struck

Ananias and Sapphira dead when they lied to the Holy Spirit (Acts 5:1–10). The book of Revelation lists numerous means by which God will unleash his judgment on Earth (Rev. 6; 8–9; 16). The Bible closes by giving a glimpse of the great white throne of judgment, and of those whose names are not written in the Book of Life being thrown into the lake of fire (Rev. 20:11–15).

This indicates that the ways of God are always holy and righteous, but how he expresses his righteousness varies depending on the situation and the severity of the sin. Whether God is judging an entire city like Sodom or an individual such as King Herod (Acts 12:20–23), God always behaves in a holy manner. It is, therefore, crucial to distinguish between the ways of God and the methods of God. God's ways remain the same, century by century. The actions God takes to express his ways, however, are adjusted to times, cultures, and circumstances.

God's Ways Are Not Subject to Changes in Culture or Popular Psychology

Our world has experienced enormous shifts in how people view themselves and society. The Bible declares that humanity's foremost problem is sin (Rom. 3:23). Modern culture often disdains the concept of sin and prefers to focus on inequality, intolerance, and other social ills. While these certainly are legitimate issues, they are at their root the outgrowth of sin. God claims the primary response to sin is repentance. During the 1960s in America, many of God's standards were turned on their head and explained away in new, psychological and sociological terms. God says, "Do not steal" (Exod. 20:15). But modern society may justify stealing if it is from a company that is considered exploitive or if the thief is homeless or a hungry drug addict or a victim of generational poverty or a lack of education. God said, "Do not commit adultery" (Exod. 20:14). Yet modern society excuses such behavior if you have fallen out of love with your spouse or you do not feel your needs are being met.

A problem inevitably occurs when people feel the need to adjust God's ways so they line up better with current societal trends. In today's culture it is considered boorish and insensitive to call on someone who is addicted to drugs or pornography to repent of their sin. If a person has been victimized, society feels they should be excused for whatever evil they commit in response. Many assume, therefore, that God must update the ways he relates to people so he is better aligned with modern ways of thinking.

One problem, of course, is that sciences such as psychology and sociology are fluid and constantly changing. Social sciences are far better at observing symptoms in people's behavior than diagnosing root causes for people's problems. Furthermore, much of modern theory is not based on truth and certainly not on God's Word. Today, scientists and medical professionals are being pressured to conform their views to popular societal thought and feelings. God's Word, on the other hand, has remained consistent through the centuries. A god who is continually updated and conformed to shifting trends will be a god who has no power or authority to tell people how to live.

Consider just one example. Scripture teaches that parents who love their children will discipline them (Prov. 13:24). Furthermore, God provides the model of a loving Father who disciplines his children (Heb. 12:3–11). But in the 1960s, a growing trend claimed it was barbaric to chastise children and preventing them from doing as they pleased would stifle their growth, causing emotional harm. Time typically sheds light on the wisdom and efficacy of new parenting styles. That is not to say that each generation can't improve on our child-rearing skills, but it is precarious to allow modern psychology or sociology to alter the way we view God's ways or how we understand divine directives found in his Word.

A god who is continually updated and conformed to shifting trends will be a god who has no power or authority to tell people how to live.

Likewise, many churches and denominations have attempted to modernize their approach to what God has always labeled as sin. Again, there is a need for compassion and kindness—both being godly traits, but by seeking to appear more enlightened, compassionate, or inclusive, these churches have ended up compromising the clear Word of God. As a result, they have generally become more powerless and irrelevant. The truth is, the ways of God don't change, regardless of how gauche they may appear in light of popular opinion.

God's Ways Don't Adjust to Your Personal Experience

Scripture tells us that God is a loving heavenly Father. "Father" was Jesus's favorite term to use when he prayed (Matt. 6:9). Yet many people associate negative connotations with that term. Their father was absent, abusive, or impossible to please. As a result, they struggle with God acting as a father because to them fathers are evil and hurtful. This is why we must gain our view of God's ways from how God reveals himself in Scripture and not from our personal experiences.

My father and I were once leading a conference for Christian leaders from across Europe. My dad stated in one of his presentations that God's people had lost the fear of God. Afterward, a young man approached us and vehemently argued that Christians should not fear God because he is a God of love. My dad pointed to numerous examples in Scripture that exhorted people to fear God (Ps. 119:20; 147:11; Prov. 1:7; 9:10). Nevertheless, the young man would have none of it. He grew increasingly agitated that a Christian speaker would promote the fear of God. Finally, I asked him a few questions about his past. His countenance completely changed. His father had been a tyrant. For him to acknowledge that he should fear God came dangerously close to conceding that God was like his father. That was something he could not do. It mattered not what Scripture said; this man's personal experience demanded that he view God differently from the way the Bible revealed him to be.

Whenever people say, "I know what the Bible says, but I just can't believe God would do that today," it could be they are imposing their personal biases on God's revelation. Rather than interpreting God's ways to match our experience, we must understand our experience in light of God's revelation.

Worship Affects Our View of God

Worshipping the Lord can lead to life-changing encounters. God cares greatly about how we worship him. We know this because his Word lays out, clearly and frequently, what he desires. For instance, God forbade images being made of him. Moreover, he was concerned that his name, or character, not be treated inaccurately or lightly (Exod. 20:4–7). Numerous other passages address the prescribed manner and attitude of our worship. Scripture warns that we become like what we worship (Ps. 115:8; 135:18). Therefore, it is imperative that we worship God based on an accurate understanding of who he is. But we must worship him as he reveals himself in Scripture and not how we imagine, wish, or feel him to be. The irony is that oftentimes our misguided worship leads to false conclusions about God's character and ways.

Scripture provides two primary focuses for how we worship God. First, we are to praise him for who he is. Isaiah witnessed this when he heard the mighty seraphim proclaiming, "Holy, holy, holy, is the Lord of Armies" (Isa. 6:3). The book of Revelation provides breathtaking glimpses into the celestial throne room. There heavenly beings worship God for being holy (Rev. 4:1–11), while the Lamb is praised for being worthy (Rev. 5:11–14). When creatures in heaven see God as he is, their instantaneous response is to worship him. Scripture records that when people encountered almighty God, their typical response was to fall to the ground, overwhelmed (Isa. 6:5; Acts 9:4; Rev. 1:17).

Second, we are to praise God for his deeds. Worship is, or should be, a natural response when God provides for us or answers our prayers. After God rescued the Israelites from the Egyptians at the Red Sea, the people exuberantly praised him (Exod. 15:1–21). When God heard Hannah's pleading and granted her a child after years of praying, she responded with worshipful prayer (1 Sam. 2:1–10). During the reign of King Jehoshaphat, the Ammonites and Moabites invaded the land with a large army (2 Chron. 20:1–30). God assured Jehoshaphat that he would deliver his people without their lifting a weapon in their own defense. Sure enough, the Israelites went out praising God even as God was destroying their enemies.

Martin Luther once claimed that if he were allowed to write the hymns of the church, he could shape people's theology. He was undoubtedly correct. His famous hymn, "A Mighty Fortress Is Our God," is filled with exalted descriptions of God and his ways. Many hymns, such as "Holy, Holy, Holy," "Amazing Grace," and "How Great Thou Art" have done much to educate people on the person and work of God.

However, numerous other popular Christian hymns, choruses, and carols contain unbiblical statements about God. The songs we sing affect our theology. A casual survey could well reveal that people's views of the incarnation come predominantly from Christmas carols rather than from Bible study. We are certain there were three kings who came to bring gifts to newborn Jesus (who, incidentally never cried), because we sing about that every Christmas season. At times Christmas carols and other songs merely speculate about what the Bible is silent about and are relatively harmless. However, dangers abound when we incorporate into our worship statements about God that are entirely untrue.

Today's church is inundated with a steady stream of new worship songs. They vary widely in quality and theological depth. Some songs, though popular, have lyrics that completely misrepresent the person and ways of God. Church music is particularly vulnerable to this danger. For one, church musicians often have not attended seminary to receive biblical and theological training. Even when they earn a degree in church music, they are more likely to have taken classes that enhanced their singing and musical abilities rather than sharpening their biblical and theological acumen. At times songwriters face the need to make their words rhyme, so they choose words that match but are not theologically accurate. Or, they are seeking to evoke a specific emotional response, so they fashion their lyrics accordingly. Some songwriters are attempting to write a popular chorus, so they write music with a strong emotional appeal.

Church leaders should be sensitive to certain criteria. First, the words, not the melody and rhythm, should drive the song choice. A song with an upbeat tempo can get a congregation swaying in their seats and dancing in the aisles, but it might have shallow or even unbiblical lyrics. People are naturally wired to respond physically to music, and there is nothing wrong with an upbeat tempo, but we should beware of songs that substitute a heavy beat for the moving of the Spirit. There is a profound difference between worshippers being moved by the Holy Spirit and people inspired to rush on to a dance floor. A song may have a beautiful, emotionally uplifting melody but contain poorly written lyrics. We can be deeply affected by the melody yet fail to evaluate the words we are singing. It was said of the great evangelist D. L. Moody that he was so musically untrained that if he asked for "Rock of Ages" and his daughter-in-law played "Yankee Doodle" slowly with soulful chords, he would wipe tears from his eyes.[9]

Worship is ultimately driven by truth, not feelings. Worship music should present God as the Bible does. At times songwriters mistakenly present God more like a frail person than a divine and powerful being. He is portrayed as a friend who may suffer from limitations or weaknesses just as we do. In our effort to "humanize" God, we can inadvertently misrepresent his divinity. Any song that portrays God as less than all-powerful, all-knowing, or perfect should not be used in worship. We are made in God's image, but God is not "just like us."

Some popular Christian songs elevate people too highly. These songs speak as if we humans are the center of God's universe. That everything God does is performed with us at the forefront of his thoughts. Some songs imply that Jesus endured the horrific crucifixion just so he could enjoy the pleasure of our company in heaven. While this can be an extremely moving thought, especially when accompanied by a powerful melody, it is not biblical. In truth, Jesus's crucifixion was not primarily about us. It was about God the Father. Ever since Adam and Eve's fall in the garden, God had been steadily working to redeem his fallen creatures. The cross was the Father's plan. Jesus went to the cross because his Father sent him. As Jesus hung on the cross, his thoughts were not focused on me and my salvation; they were fixated on pleasing his Father (Matt. 26:39, 42; 27:46; Luke 23:34, 46; John 19:30).

Why does this matter? Because some worship songs are extremely self-centered. They essentially praise self rather than God, as if God exists to love us rather than the reverse. The truth is, God does love us with an infinite love, but to assume his redemptive plan centered on me is supremely egotistical. My story is interwoven for a few brief years with God's eternal plan that spans the ages. God does love me. But he is not a doting grandfather figure, nor is he a "buddy." He is almighty God!

If I continually sing about how special I am and how God would do anything for me, I can gain an improper view of God, and I can begin to have unrealistic expectations for the way God will act toward me. If I assume God will protect me from all pain or harm since he loves me so much, what happens when I lose a loved one or contract a grave illness? I will be bewildered. How could a loving God who thinks I am so special allow me to suffer?

A final caution concerning worship music. Some songs rely on a catchy tune and a few pithy phrases repeated over and over. Psychologists, marketers, and politicians all understand that oft-repeated words or catchphrases exercise a powerful influence on our minds. One example of this is what psychologists refer to as the "priming effect." This occurs when people are exposed to certain words that *prime* them to respond in a particular way. In one famous experiment, John Bargh enlisted students from New York University.[10] The students, most aged between eighteen and twenty-two, were given five words and asked to compose a sentence. One group of students was given the words, "Florida, forgetful, bald, gray, wrinkle." All the words are obviously associated with the concept of being old. Afterward, students were asked to proceed down a hallway for the next experiment. Students were timed as they walked down the hallway. The students who had been primed to think of old age walked measurably slower than those who had not. Merely being exposed to terms associated with being elderly affected the behavior of college students.

There are also psychological studies to demonstrate that hearing the same thing repeatedly makes it easier to believe. Daniel Kahneman, author of *Thinking: Fast and Slow,* notes: "A reliable way to make people believe in falsehoods is frequent repetition, because familiarity is not easily distinguished from truth."[11] When worship songs repeat the same phrases repeatedly, they can imbed thoughts and beliefs into our mind, regardless of whether they are biblical. In Martin Luther's day, each verse of a hymn was often infused with deep theological truth. Today, songs may repeat the same few phrases over and over again. There is, of course, no harm in this if the phrases are theologically sound. But beware of songs that rely on repetition for effect rather than biblical truth.

Music is, of course, not the only avenue to misguided worship. At times preachers can be careless in their sermon preparation and make false or misleading statements about God. Examples abound. I recall as a college student being struck by a speaker who dramatically declared that Jesus was ugly. He based this on Isaiah 53:2: "He didn't have an impressive form or majesty that we should look at him." Of course, this doesn't mean he was ugly. It simply means that people weren't attracted to him because of his appearance. I was so concerned that the preacher called Jesus ugly that I later asked my theology professor about it. He noted that Isaiah 53 focuses on Jesus on the cross and that nothing about a man being crucified is attractive.

Over the years, many preachers have declared that we must, at times, wrestle with God, just as Jacob did (Gen. 32:24–32). Of course, there is nothing honorable about wrestling with God, and the outcome is never in doubt. Some preachers will pronounce that the eleven apostles sinned in choosing Matthias since "God intended Paul to take Judas' place" (see Acts 1:15–26). This, despite the fact the Bible never indicates that was God's intention, nor does God ever chastise the apostles for their choice. Other preachers boast about being a "doubting Thomas" as if that disciple's example were to be emulated (John 20:24–29). Such sloppy exegesis misrepresents God and the way he relates to us.

Public prayers can be another source of confusion for worshippers. People will often pray things that, though they might elicit an "amen," are misleading, nonetheless. One of the most common requests people pray in churches is, "Lord, would you be with us today?" In some services the worship leader will "welcome" God to join their service. People often exclaim, "God really showed up today!" Of course, all of this ignores the fact that Jesus promised he would be with us always and that he would never leave us (Matt. 28:20; Heb. 13:5). We are, in fact, the ones who "show up." What effect does this type of messaging in worship services have on people? When congregants constantly hear church leaders publicly asking God to be with them, they get the impression God is arbitrary about when he decides to join in his people's worship.

The way people pray can also misrepresent God. When people pray flippantly, without thinking about what they are saying, or they speak to God without the respect due him, they give the wrong impression of who God is. Some are critical when a person writes out a prayer ahead of time. They feel prayer should be spontaneous. However, the key is for prayer to be thoughtful. Understandably, many laypeople are nervous about praying in public. It behooves pastors to teach their people how to pray (especially in public). A brief, simple, but biblical prayer is far better than a lengthy, flowery stream of heresy. Many worship teams will use public prayer as a time to enter or exit the stage while people's eyes are closed, as if it were a magic show or a stage play.

These are the worship leaders, and they are busily taking care of business while God is being addressed during the congregational prayer.

Even the overall "tone" of a worship service can deter us from the fact that God is holy and worthy of our reverence. Worship should be joyful, but it ought to feel different from attending a rock concert. Worship is the lifeblood of a Christian. It is based on our understanding of God. It also shapes that understanding. If we are continually exposed to statements about God that are false or misleading, we will gradually develop incorrect views of God. Our misguided worship will lead us to idolatry as we fashion false gods in our minds based on what we erroneously assume God is like. These observations may seem overly critical or even nitpicky, but knowing the true character of God is crucial. Why? Because we cannot live in sync with God's activity if we do not understand his ways. How tragic to spend a lifetime attending church, singing Christian songs, listening to sermons, hearing prayers, and yet never truly knowing God.

Conclusion

God's ways are not our ways. He does not adjust his ways over time. He does not accommodate them to our feelings or preferences. But he is willing to reveal them to us. They are found in Scripture, and they haven't changed. If we fail to learn his ways, God's actions will continually confuse and disappoint us. If we don't know God's ways, we won't recognize his activity, even when he is working all around us. But when we learn God's ways, we will discover that he is indeed at work, and we will be swept up into his eternal purposes. Never be satisfied merely seeing the *acts* of God. Strive to move from seeing God's actions to being intimately familiar with his ways.

Questions for Reflection/Discussion

1. What are some of the ways of God you have appreciated most that are revealed in the Bible?

2. Have you struggled with some of the ways God worked in Old Testament times? If you have, what has troubled you?

3. What is an example of the difference between God's ways and his methods?

4. What are some worship songs you feel represent God and his ways well? What are some that may have questionable lyrics?

5. How have you been tempted to shape your view of God's ways so it matches your personal experience or beliefs?

6. What are some ways of God that modern society might view as being out of date or contrary to popular opinion?

CHAPTER 3

GOD'S WAYS ARE HOLY

God, your way is holy.
(Ps. 77:13)

For you alone are holy.
(Rev. 15:4)

God Is Holy

People act according to their nature. What people are is what people do. God's holiness is fundamental to all his attributes. Without understanding God's holiness, you will struggle to comprehend many of his actions. A. W. Tozer claimed: "He may fear God's power and admire his wisdom, but his holiness he cannot even imagine."[12]

Celestial beings are overwhelmed by God's holiness. The mighty seraphim continually cry out, "Holy, holy, holy is the Lord of Armies; his glory fills the whole earth" (Isa. 6:3). When the apostle John received a glimpse into heaven's throne room, he saw four heavenly creatures proclaiming, "Holy, holy, holy, Lord God, the Almighty, who was, who is, and who is to come" (Rev. 4:8). God's character is multifaceted, but the quality that infuses every other aspect of his being is holiness. His ways are all expressions of his holy character.

God's Word exhorts us to strive for holiness, but God alone is perfectly holy. He is distinct from his creation. No other being is remotely like him. After Moses witnessed the parting of the Red Sea, he declared: "LORD, who is like you among the gods? Who is like you, glorious in holiness, revered with praises, performing wonders?" (Exod. 15:11). When God granted Hannah a child, after her years of barrenness, she proclaimed: "There is no one holy like the LORD. There is no one besides you!" (1 Sam. 2:2). In the last days angels will declare: "Lord, who will not fear and glorify your name? For you alone are holy" (Rev. 15:4). People commonly assume that because we can express love, forgiveness, or faithfulness we share God's character. Yes, we are made in God's image, but God's attributes are perfect and so vastly superior to our own that we cannot begin to comprehend the enormous gap between God's attributes and our own.

For God to be holy means he is entirely pure, without blemish, unspotted, and perfectly consistent. While we might be loving most of the time, or to a certain degree, God is entirely loving in every moment. Keeping God's pure and perfect nature at the forefront of our thinking helps us understand certain Bible passages that can otherwise appear confusing. For example, Scripture notes that God is jealous (Exod. 20:5; Deut. 4:24) and that he becomes angry (Exod. 32:10; Judg. 2:14; Ps. 2:12). At first glance, it seems unbecoming for almighty God to be jealous for the love of creatures of dust. Jealousy is generally considered unattractive in a Christian. Yet we must understand that God's jealousy is holy. It is not spiteful or petty. It is expressed in perfect righteousness. He is jealous for our love because his holy love is all-consuming. God's anger, likewise, is not evil. It never leads to sin, as ours often does (Eph. 4:26). God's anger demonstrates his holy passion for justice and righteousness. God is slow to anger

(Exod. 34:6). When he does express his wrath, it leads to good, not evil. God's holiness ensures that *all* his ways are perfect and righteous.

God's Ways Are Holy

The psalmist Asaph wrote: "God, your way is holy" (Ps. 77:13). Scripture is filled with references to God's holiness. Everything he does bears the mark of his holy character. We see this truth manifested in several specific ways.

God's Actions Are Holy

The psalmist David declared: "The Lord is righteous in all his ways and faithful in all his acts" (Ps. 145:17). Modern-day believers may miss the magnitude of such a claim. "Righteous" and "faithful" certainly did not describe the pagan gods during the biblical era. The mythical Greek gods on Mount Olympus were a lustful and egotistical lot. Zeus, the chief god, ruled over the other deities as well as over mortals, dispensing justice. However, Zeus had multiple affairs with goddesses other than his wife Hera and produced numerous illegitimate offspring. Zeus had children with his wife Hera, including Ares and Hephaestus. He also went to great lengths to seduce other women, including transforming himself into an animal to gain sexual conquests. As a result, Zeus had many illegitimate children from his numerous escapades. Zeus fathered Apollo and Artemis with Leto. He sired Hermes with Maia. Persephone was the daughter of Zeus and Demeter. Dionysus was the son of Zeus and Semele. Zeus procreated three daughters with Eurynome. Athena was the daughter of Zeus and Metis. Zeus transformed himself to look like Alcmene's husband so he could sleep with her. Their son Hercules was the result. These were some of the better known of the numerous offspring he fathered with various goddesses and mortals. While Zeus may have been passionate about justice, he certainly could never serve as a model for holy living. In fact, few mortals could descend to the level of prolificacy in which Zeus indulged.

The Canaanite religion was a depraved, man-made system that appealed to base passions but provided few moral guidelines for living or answers to life's ultimate questions. It was rife with human depravity in the guise of worship. The Canaanite gods were believed to encourage human debauchery, such as encouraging farmers to have sex with religious prostitutes so their land produced bumper crops. The ancient gods were largely unconcerned with immorality (otherwise they would be hypocrites). They merely required sacrifices, and in return they would bestow favor. Tom Holland, an expert in Greek mythology, notes, "'Are there no guidelines set by heaven for mortal men, no path to follow that will please the gods?' This question, which the sick, the bereaved or the oppressed could hardly help ask, had no ready answer. The gods, inscrutable and whimsical as they were, rarely deigned to explain themselves. They certainly never thought to regulate mortals. The oracle at Delphi might offer advice, but not ethical instruction."[13]

Israel's God differed vastly from the false deities of other nations. Most ancient religions had a male and a female god. This led to sexual liaisons between the deities as well as between gods and their followers. But the true God is spirit. There is no male and female version of God. There is one God, and his conduct in all things is above reproach. The Greek world was unfamiliar with such a holy God. Because God is holy, he can demand holy living from his followers (Lev. 19:2).

God will never act in an evil way in your life. He would have to contradict his fundamental nature to behave in an unrighteous manner. God will never diminish his standards or use questionable means to accomplish his purposes. No matter the crisis or the stakes involved, God never compromises or bends his own rules. In every imaginable condition or situation, God acts with supreme holiness.

This truth has caused people great consternation over the years. When a devout Christian dies prematurely of a terminal disease, or a missionary is killed in a car accident, or a child contracts leukemia, people often accuse God of being cruel or unjust. When people suffer as the result of a natural disaster, crime, or warfare, many charge God with being capricious. In truth, far less disastrous events have led many to conclude that God is uncaring or powerless.

Job famously wrestled with the question of how a just God could allow him to suffer so grievously since he was a righteous man. He assumed, as did his friends, that God was the author of his calamities. Convinced there must be a mistake, since he believed he was innocent of sin, Job pleaded for an opportunity to present his case (Job 27:2; 31:35).

Ultimately, God spoke to Job out of a whirlwind (Job 38:1). We can learn several important lessons from this profound book of Scripture. First, though God may permit evil, he does not cause it. It was Satan who assaulted Job, not God, though the devil needed permission to do so. Second, God values free will. This leads inevitably to people committing evil as they exercise this prerogative. Human choices have resulted in enormous wickedness and suffering throughout history. Nevertheless, Job discovered that he could not indict God for poor management of the universe because God was infinitely wiser and superior to humanity. Job's every breath was an undeserved gift from his Creator (Job 12:10). In the end, Job could not point to one incident where God had acted wickedly, broken a promise, or been deceitful. Job learned that evil occurs in the world and yet God continues to maintain his holiness in every instance.

God Speaks in Holiness

God communicates differently from people. Holiness permeates God's every word. We mortals contaminate our words with lies, half-truths, exaggerations, and innuendoes. People today are so accustomed to the manipulations of advertisers and the spin of politicians that words are received skeptically at best. The definition of a word can change to have a completely new meaning. No wonder people are confused.

What does it entail for God's words to be holy? It means every word he speaks is pure with no ulterior or hidden meaning (Ps. 18:30; Prov. 30:5). God's words are not too difficult to understand (Deut. 30:11–14). They are entirely true with no mixture of error (John 17:17; 2 Tim. 2:15). His words stand the test of time (Isa. 40:8). His words never lose their relevance. God's words always accomplish their intended effect (Isa. 55:10–11; Matt. 24:35). Every word of God is inspired and profitable (2 Tim. 3:16). God's words may well seem politically incorrect over time, but they always lead to life (John 1:1–4). Peoples' words require frequent amending, explaining, or retracting, but God's words demand faith and obedience.

Because God's words are holy, we require the Holy Spirit's aid to fully understand them. To an unregenerate person, God's wisdom appears foolish (1 Cor. 1:18). When the risen Christ was delivering a message to the seven churches in Asia, he kept announcing, "Let anyone who has ears to hear listen to what the Spirit says to the churches" (Rev. 2:7, 11, 17, 29; 3:6, 13, 22). Only those with spiritual discernment can recognize spiritual truths.

Though God might speak the same word to many people, their responses can vary greatly (Matt. 13:1–23). Those with a pure heart see God (Matt. 5:8). Those with an evil heart think God's Word is ridiculous (1 Cor. 1:18). The key is not to adapt the word to the listener. The words God speaks are always true, and they unfailingly bring life to those who believe. The problem is that people hear God's Word when their own life is unholy, and an unsanctified person cannot comprehend holy words.

Jesus's parable of the sower addresses this issue (Matt. 13:1–23). He said the word of God comes to a wide variety of people. Yet the condition of people's hearts determines how they process his message. Some people's hearts are so hardened, busy, or cluttered with worldly concerns they cannot respond properly to God's Word. However, a holy life is pure and uncontaminated by worldly traffic and sin. Hearts that are free of sin, distractions, and competitors can immediately respond to God's Word and bear much fruit. Preachers and Bible teachers regularly witness this phenomenon. As they present God's Word to an audience, the response to the message varies widely. One person will be in tears, deeply moved by what was said. Another person, sitting right next to the one weeping, is indifferent. A third is angry and offended by what was said. A fourth is bored and anxious for the meeting to end so he can go home and watch sports. God's Word is pure, undiluted truth. It is best understood and received by hearts that are clean and undistracted (Matt. 5:8).

God Relates to Us in Holiness

God never acts wickedly. He is long-suffering, but ultimately, he will not tolerate sinful behavior. The psalmist declared: "For you are not a God who delights in wickedness; evil cannot dwell with you" (Ps. 5:4). God expects people to be holy just as he is holy (1 Pet. 1:15–16). Therefore, he will never instruct us to sin, though some have claimed as much. They say God granted them permission to commit adultery and abandon their spouse to marry someone else. They are mistaken. God would never lead us to break one of his commandments (Exod. 20:14). Some act as though they have a special dispensation to be unforgiving since their hurt runs deep. The Bible says otherwise (Matt. 18:21–22). Those who justify taking things from their workplace, since they are underpaid, are misguided. We grossly dishonor God when we blame him for our wicked behavior. He would not be holy if he condoned our sin in any form.

The prophet Habakkuk declared: "Your eyes are too pure to look on evil, and you cannot tolerate wrongdoing" (Hab. 1:13). How does a holy God relate to sinful creatures? The third chapter in the Bible makes clear that sin exerts a dreadful effect on our relationship with God. Adam and Eve were accustomed to walking with God in unencumbered fellowship (Gen. 3:8–9). After they sinned once, they were expelled from the garden, and a cherub with a flaming sword was stationed at the eastern entrance to Eden to prevent them from ever entering again (Gen. 3:24).

In a powerful message to God's people, the prophet Isaiah declared: "Indeed, the Lord's arm is not too weak to save, and his ear not too deaf to hear. But your iniquities are separating you from your God, and your sins have hidden his face from you so that he does not listen. For your hands are defiled with blood and your fingers with iniquity; your lips have spoken lies, and your tongues mutter injustice" (Isa. 59:1–3). Our sin dramatically harms our fellowship with God. God will not allow us to willfully sin and rebel against him and yet continue to bestow upon us the rewards of obedience.

Holy God abhors sin. He alone knows the full magnitude of suffering, pain, and death that sin unleashes. He understands the enormous loss people experience when they forfeit what God intends in exchange for evil's vaporous promises. The moment you sin, the Holy Spirit begins to convict you so you can quickly repent and return to God. If you resist the Spirit's efforts, he will steadily increase your discomfort (John 16:8). He is determined to make you holy as he is holy, no matter what it takes.

David aptly confessed, "How joyful is a person whom the Lord does not charge with iniquity and in whose spirit is no deceit! When I kept silent, my bones became brittle from my groaning all day long. For day and night your hand was heavy on me; my strength was drained as in the summer's heat. Then I acknowledged my sin to you and did not conceal my iniquity. I said, 'I will confess my transgressions to the Lord,' and you forgave the guilt of my sin" (Ps. 32:2–5). David committed adultery with Bathsheba. Then he murdered Bathsheba's husband, Uriah, so he could marry her. Yet despite David's perfidy, he initially refused to acknowledge his sin. David described the devastating conviction the Holy Spirit brought to bear upon him. Finally, in one of the classic prophetic moments in history, God spoke through Nathan and confronted David directly, declaring, "You are the man!" (2 Sam. 12:7). God's unrelenting work in David's life ultimately brought about genuine repentance and restoration.

Because David resisted God's convicting work for perhaps a year, he experienced the intense discomfort and pain of guilt. The most miserable people on Earth are those who resist the Holy Spirit as he convicts them of sin. But incredible joy and freedom come when we confess our sin and finally turn from our wicked ways.

David was a man after God's own heart (1 Sam. 13:14). He was a giant killer with a huge faith in God. He was Israel's mightiest king. He wrote many of the psalms, praising God. He conquered Jerusalem and made it his capital city. He made extensive preparations for the construction of the temple. From his descendants would come the Messiah. Yet God made no allowance and accepted no excuse for his sin. David was held fully accountable and was expected to confess his transgressions and to repent, just like every other sinner.

Make no mistake. God despises sin. Sin cost the life of God's only Son. It offends his holiness. It blocks our divine communion. It brings death. The Lord will not tolerate or excuse it. He has only one remedy for it.

Responding to God's Holy Ways

We readily acknowledge that God is holy, but we can soon begin making excuses as we realize God intends for us to be holy too (Lev. 19:2). It would not be difficult to be as holy as Zeus or Poseidon or Baal, but to live according to God's standards is an entirely different matter. It is impossible to maintain a proper relationship with God while excusing unholy behavior. The Old Testament is the account of God continuously instructing, correcting, convicting, and forgiving people, with the goal of having close fellowship with his people. It is the story of an eternal, holy God teaching a perpetually sinful humanity how to properly relate to their Creator.

When God first called the shepherd Moses, he told him to remove his sandals because God's presence made the ground he stood upon holy (Exod. 3:5). The Israelites mistakenly assumed they could serve God any way they chose. God set that misconception straight. When they gathered at the foot of Mount Sinai, "All the people witnessed the thunder and lightning, the sound of the ram's horn, and the mountain surrounded by smoke. When the people saw it they trembled and stood at a distance. 'You speak to us, and we will listen,' they said to Moses, 'but don't let God speak to us, or we will die'" (Exod. 20:18–19). God's awesomeness was on display, and the children of Israel were overwhelmed by their unworthiness. They knew holy God would not tolerate their sin. Incredibly, God told the wayward Israelites, "You will be my kingdom of priests and my holy nation" (Exod. 19:6). God intended to transform the sin-prone, unreliable people into a holy nation and a kingdom of priests.

The task would not be easy. After the Israelites worshipped the golden calf, God declared: "Tell the Israelites: You are a stiff-necked people. If I went up with you for a single moment, I would destroy you" (Exod. 33:5). The entire book of Leviticus, though one of the less popular books in the Bible, is devoted to helping God's people understand how important it is for them to be holy. The psalmist warned: "For you are not a God who delights in wickedness; evil cannot dwell with you" (Ps. 5:4). Finally, God took on human form to demonstrate what holy living actually looked like (John 1:14). The apostle Paul urged Timothy to "train yourself in godliness" (1 Tim. 4:7). Holy living does not come naturally. Yet, if we are to take our divine calling seriously, a consecrated lifestyle must become our life's ambition.

Holiness is a prerequisite for worship that is acceptable to God. The psalmist asked, "Who may ascend the mountain of the LORD? Who may stand in his holy place? The one who has clean hands and a pure heart" (Ps. 24:3–4). The prophet Isaiah chastised God's people for assuming they could waltz into the temple and worship God when they had blood on their hands (Isa. 1:10–15). God declared: "Wash yourselves. Cleanse yourselves. Remove your evil deeds from my sight. Stop doing evil" (Isa. 1:16). The Old Testament deals at length with the perennial tension between the fact that God invites us to worship him and the reality that he will not accept worship, prayer, or service from people with sinful hands and evil hearts. We are slow to comprehend the fact that living sinfully all week nullifies our worship when we go to church.

Worship certainly is a Christian's highest calling. But we can often be as misguided as the ancient Israelites. In the modern church many people enjoy the worship experience because of what they receive. They appreciate the music. Hearing encouraging sermons makes them feel good. They like seeing their friends. People evaluate their worship by whether they "received" anything from the service. We are often assured that God loves us "just the way we are" and assume that, regardless of whether we cheated others at work that week or erupted in anger at home, or indulged in lust, greed, or unforgiveness, God is pleased that we came to sing his praises.

In our effort to make people feel welcome at our churches, we can inadvertently turn the focus of worship on our contentment rather than God's pleasure. The measure of successful worship is not whether it pleased us but if it satisfied holy God.

Jesus said if we came to worship him but had a broken relationship, we were to leave the place of worship and seek reconciliation. Then we could return and worship God properly (Matt. 5:23–24). If we allow sin to remain in our heart, he will not hear our prayer (Isa. 1:15; 59:1–3; 1 Pet. 3:7). The prophet Isaiah learned this firsthand. He went to worship God one day and was overwhelmed by the encounter. The first thing God revealed to him was that he had a sinful mouth (Isa. 6:5). It mattered not what offering Isaiah had brought or how much he was looking forward to hearing from God; God insisted that his mouth be cleansed before he continued to worship. God demands holiness from those who worship him (James 4:8–10). Being holy does not mean you are sinless or perfect. It does mean you take your sin seriously and you respect God enough to deal with your sin before you worship him. True worship can be at once deeply joyful, profoundly convicting, and spiritually healing.

Being holy does not mean you are sinless or perfect. It does mean you take your sin seriously and you respect God enough to deal with your sin before you worship him.

Relating to Others in Holiness

Are we, as New Testament believers, exempt from the holy standards God laid out in the days before Christ? Many Christians seem to think so. They say we now live by grace rather than the Law. Absolutely, we live by grace, but that does not mean God has redefined holiness. The apostle Peter said, "But as the one who called you is holy, you also are to be holy in all your conduct; for it is written, Be holy, because I am holy" (1 Pet. 1:15–16). God is full of grace now as he has been throughout history; nevertheless, he still expects Christians to conduct their lives in a godly way.

When Samuel was nearing the end of his life, he called the elders of Israel together and challenged them to identify anything he had done over his long life that was unethical (1 Sam. 12:1–5). Not one person could bring a charge against him. That is holy living. That was in the Old Testament, but what about today? The Bible continues to challenge us to live blamelessly (Phil. 2:15; 1 Thess. 3:13; Titus 1:6). Paul urged overseers to be "above reproach" (1 Tim. 3:2). We should strive to live like Samuel, in such a way that no aspect of our behavior dishonors Christ. A good prayer for us to adopt was penned by David: "May the words of my mouth and the meditation of my heart be acceptable to you, LORD, my rock and my Redeemer" (Ps. 19:14).

In our day there seems to be an epidemic of scandal among prominent Christians and church leaders. Perhaps that is because we have often focused more on outward "results" and neglected inward character. Pastors have grown large churches but then have been exposed as adulterers. Christian leaders have written popular books but later been revealed to use unethical practices or to abuse their staff. Some Christians lead large institutions, but they are notorious for their pride or anger. The same person who sings beautiful solos in church can simultaneously be living a secret life of perversion. Christian politicians have lied in order to win votes. If anything has been obvious of late, it is that despite a wide and even adoring following, God will eventually expose and discipline hypocrites (Matt. 12:33–36; Gal. 6:7).

Christians sometimes assume that if they are fighting for a good cause, such as orthodoxy or an ethical issue, the end justifies the means. Church history has been plagued with individuals who mistakenly assumed that all manner of unChristlike behavior was acceptable if they did it for the cause of the church.

Between 1414 and 1418, the Catholic Church convened the Council of Constance in Germany. Church leaders sought to bring an end to discord that had divided its ranks. Jan Huss was a reformer in Bohemia who preached against corruption in the church and called for people to return to Christ. The church viewed him as a heretic and troublemaker. The Holy Roman emperor, Sigismund, promised Huss that he would not be harmed if he attended the council and discussed the issues with church authorities. Nevertheless, ecclesiastical leaders eventually arrested Huss and threw him in prison where he suffered greatly. When Sigismund protested, recalling that he had given his word to Huss, the prelates assured him that promises to heretics were not binding. At his trial, Huss was ordered to recant his beliefs. Huss offered to recant if he was shown, from Scripture, where he was incorrect. His accusers refused because, of course, they could not comply. On July 6, 1415, Huss was burned alive at the stake. One hundred years later Huss's story would inspire Martin Luther to take up his mantle and attempt to reform the church.

Examples abound where people, professing to be Christians, excused their unchristian behavior because they were protecting the church. Lies and broken promises have been explained away. Violence has been rationalized. People's characters have been slandered and misrepresented. Those taking upon themselves the defense of the church often exude anger, pride, hatred, and disdain for their perceived enemies.

Still today, pastors will troll and slander other pastors in their sacred "defense of God's name." Believers will maliciously malign someone else's character and distort their words because they hold opposing political or theological positions. Make no mistake, it matters not how noble, orthodox, or missional your cause, God will not condone unChristlike behavior, even if you are ostensibly doing it for him. God considers how you do something to be as important as what you do (Num. 20:11–12). Many well-intentioned Christians have discredited their efforts because they attempted to serve God in a carnal or worldly manner. To serve God in a way that honors him, extends his kingdom, and glorifies his name, requires holiness. The way we treat others is an accurate gauge for the true condition of our heart.

Conclusion

Maintaining a close relationship with a holy God can appear daunting. The writer of Hebrews warned: "For we know the one who has said, . . . The Lord will judge his people. It is a terrifying thing to fall into the hands of the living God" (Heb. 10:30–31). In fact, apart from Christ's working in our life, it is impossible for us to walk closely with him (Heb. 4:16). But we can take heart. If sin has made its way into our life and disrupted our walk with holy God, he has provided a way of cleansing and return. James, the brother of Jesus urged: "Draw near to God, and he will draw near to you. Cleanse your hands, sinners, and purify your hearts, you double-minded" (James 4:8). It matters not how terribly you sinned in the past. You can begin a journey today, with God's help, to return to him on a highway of holiness (Isa. 35:8).

Questions for Reflection/Discussion

1. What thoughts and feelings do you experience when you consider God's holiness? Are they positive or negative?

2. Are you comfortable speaking to holy God? Are you at peace hearing holy God speak to you?

3. Are you trying to relate to God with an unholy life? What areas of your life are not as pleasing to God as they should be?

4. Are you relating to people in a godly way? What, in your life, is currently misrepresenting Christ to others? How could you change that?

5. Are you serving God using ungodly ways? How are you trying to do God's work, the world's way? What adjustments could you make in the ways you are serving him?

CHAPTER 4

GOD'S WAYS ARE LOVING

God is love.
(1 John 4:16)

We love because he first loved us. If anyone says, "I love God," and yet hates his brother or sister, he is a liar.
(1 John 4:19–20)

I was blessed to grow up in the home of a loving mother. When my dad was a mission pastor in Canada, our household income was extremely modest. To help make ends meet, mom took a menial job as an aide in a nursing home, after having spent many years as a stay-at-home mom. It was not an easy job, but she did not complain. Mom wanted each of her five children to have an opportunity to see the world. When I was nineteen, my parents cobbled enough money together to send my brother Tom and me to Vienna, Austria, so we could experience Europe with our uncle and aunt. But there were also numerous small ways she consistently sacrificed for my sake. At one time, I had a commitment that forced me to leave my house once a week at 4:30 a.m. My mother would rise at 4:00 a.m. to cook eggs and homemade biscuits so I kept up my strength! In college I played on a church hockey league. At times our games were played past midnight. My mother was often there and invariably the loudest fan in the stands. She has been my lifelong cheerleader. I cannot imagine what my life would be like without her steadfast love. Nevertheless, as enthusiastic as her affection for me has been, it has not always been faultless. As loving as she was, I felt at times that she treated me unfairly or was distracted by her own problems. In truth, although she would go to great lengths to show her devotion to me, she could sometimes be inconsistent and arbitrary in how she expressed it.

It is difficult for us to understand God's love because everything we might compare it to, even the love of a devoted parent, pales in comparison. The most caring people on the earth are still tainted by sin. Their love can be misguided and selective. Because we use the word *love* to describe a new outfit, our favorite dessert, or our mother, we can mistakenly assume we understand what it is. In fact, we can presume we are qualified to judge God's love, based on our own limited experience. It is crucial that we understand, as best we can, what God's love is like. Otherwise, his behavior will invariably confuse us.

God not only does things that are loving; he *is* love (1 John 4:8, 16). He is love's source, its standard, and its sustainer. Everything God does is an expression of perfect love. For God to act unlovingly would be to deny his fundamental nature.

People may question God's love when they experience deep pain, tragedy, or loss. The problem of evil has often been cited as Exhibit A in charges that God is unloving. There is no easy answer to this perplexing issue. Some of the most brilliant minds in history have grappled with it. While love describes God's ways, love does not encompass all that God is. God's love, though central to his nature, perfectly syncs with his other traits. God is loving, but he is also holy, sovereign, and just. People sometimes accuse God of being unloving because he did not grant them the marriage, job, family, or health they asked for. God's love is not merely a sentimental, softhearted grandfatherly affection that doles out whatever people desire. God will always act lovingly toward you, but he will never sacrifice his other divine traits to do so.

God's love is not merely a sentimental, softhearted grandfatherly affection that doles out whatever people desire. God will always act lovingly toward you, but he will never sacrifice his other divine traits to do so.

A. W. Tozer noted: "From God's other known attributes we may learn much about His love. We know, for instance, that because God is self-existent, His love has no beginning; because He is eternal, His love can have no end; because He is infinite, it has no limit; because He is holy, it is the quintessence of all spotless purity; because He is immense, His love is an incomprehensibly vast, bottomless, shoreless sea before which we kneel in joyful silence and from which the loftiest eloquence retreats confused and abashed."[14]

The Way God Loves

It is impossible, with the limitations of human language, to adequately describe the way God expresses love. We do not have sufficient tools to do so. A beginning point might include these key aspects.

God's Love Takes the Initiative

People often love others reciprocally. We are willing to match the love others express toward us. If our spouse behaves selflessly, we may act in kind. But if not, we are sorely tempted to withhold our affection. If our friend won't apologize after a disagreement, we won't either. If our sibling refuses to take steps toward reconciliation, neither will we.

But that is not the nature of God's love. God never withdraws and waits for us to make the first move. God's love always takes the initiative. Long before you decide to reach out to God, he has already been reaching out with tender concern toward you (Ezek. 36:16–38; Hosea 11:8–9). The apostle John wrote, "We love because he first loved us" (1 John 4:19). The world tends to keep a record of grievances and aims for a fifty-fifty relationship. If we apologized first the last time, it is our friend's turn this time. Not so with God. Though he has taken the initiative in every encounter we have ever experienced with him, he will still take the initiative the next time. God doesn't keep a balance sheet on who has invested what in our relationship with him. He is more than willing to give far more than we could possibly offer him in return.

God Loves Uniquely

The primary reason God's loving ways differ from ours is because there is a depth and quality to his love that far surpasses the ordinary affection people express toward one another. In the Old Testament this love was often identified as *hesed* love. A general translation is "covenant love" or "faithful love" (Ps. 13:5; 17:7; 36:7). It refers to the covenant God made with Abraham and his descendants. God initiated a covenant with his people in which he promised to love them and provide for them, and in return they would love and obey him. Nevertheless, the Old Testament provides the tragic tale of how God's people continually forsook him. God's love was called a "covenant love" because he was relentless and undaunted in his love for his people even when they committed abominations against him.

The prophet Hosea provides the ultimate example of God's *hesed* love. The righteous prophet was instructed to marry a prostitute named Gomer (Hosea 1:2). Gomer betrayed her godly husband, Hosea, and pursued other lovers. God claimed that his people's love for him was just as fickle as Gomer's. God claimed, "Your love is like the morning mist" (Hosea 6:4). He further charged: "Israel, do not rejoice jubilantly as the nations do, for you have acted promiscuously, leaving your God. You love the wages of a prostitute" (Hosea 9:1). Gomer might have told Hosea that she loved him, but her love was as fleeting as the morning mist. She did not express covenant love since she broke every term in the covenant.

In contrast, God's love led him to keep every promise he made. In fact, God's love was so robust that even when his people broke the terms of their agreement and deserved to be punished, God's love made him reluctant to do so. God exclaimed, "How can I give you up, Ephraim? How can I surrender you, Israel? How can I make you like Admah? How can I treat you like Zeboiim? I have had a change of heart; my compassion is stirred! I will not vent the full fury of my anger; I will not turn back to destroy Ephraim. For I am God and not man" (Hosea 11:8–9). God's *hesed* love is so powerful it continues to yearn for his people even after they have abandoned him and directed their affections elsewhere.

The book of Hosea demonstrates the profound nature of God's love by contrasting it with one of the most devastating of human experiences: adultery. Infidelity was so painful to the one betrayed that the Mosaic law made it the one acceptable reason for obtaining a divorce, since it seemed humanly impossible for people to continue loving someone who had inflicted such heartache. God claimed that when we forsook him, it felt to him like adultery. This is what makes God's love so unique. He is willing to suffer the most painful rejections imaginable and yet continue to endure, believe, and forgive. This is impossible for people to do but not for God. When our love reaches the end of its endurance, God's love keeps going.

When our love reaches the end of its endurance, God's love keeps going.

In the Greek New Testament world, God's love continued to be unique, but it was known by a different word. During Jesus's time, the Greek language used throughout the Roman Empire had three primary words for love. The first was *eros.* This is erotic, or romantic, love between a man and a woman. The Greek world was extremely familiar with this form of love. Hollywood is obsessed with it. It is sensual and powerful. It is an important part of marriage. It can also destroy a marriage when directed outside the relationship. The false gods of biblical times, since they were man-made, reflected this type of love, taking it to hedonistic extremes.

The second Greek term for love was *phileo.* The Bible often describes God's love with this word (John 5:20; 16:27; 20:2). *Phileo* typically refers to tender affection, as toward a friend or family member.

The third word for love is *agapao.* This term was rarely used in secular language. It came to be understood as the fundamental way God loves people. It is a far more durable, sacrificial, and active love than people commonly express. The apostle Paul offered one of the fullest descriptions of what *agape* love is like: "Love is patient, love is kind. Love does not envy, is not boastful, is not arrogant, is not rude, is not self-seeking, is not irritable, and does not keep a record of wrongs. Love finds no joy in unrighteousness but rejoices in the truth. It bears all things, believes all things, hopes all things, endures all things.

Love never ends" (1 Cor. 13:4–8). A depth and quality inhabit this love that the world cannot understand. Apart from God's enabling, it is impossible for people to practice it.

In both the Old and New Testaments, God expresses a love toward his people that is unique. People fall far short of it. Though there are many names for love and numerous expressions of it, God uses the highest form when he relates to us. We might assume we are like God because we experience love. However, the way God expresses love far surpasses the fickle and selfish way we apply it to others.

God's Love Is Steadfast

Human love grows hot and cold. We find it difficult to love others consistently, even when we truly care about them. That is because our love is emotion based. It fluctuates based on how people are treating us or responding to our love.

The entertainment industry has done incalculable damage to people's concepts of love. A plethora of movies portray couples falling in and out of love. Hollywood romances that were red-hot one moment cool off the next. Celebrity columns gush about the beautiful union of a Hollywood couple in one issue and relate the messy details of their split in the next. Human love burns brightly for a season but often wanes over time. Unkind words spoken during a holiday gathering can estrange friends or family members for years. But God's love remains fervent. Nothing discourages it. Nothing can diminish it.

Notice what God says about his love for his people: "Can a woman forget her nursing child, or lack compassion for the child of her womb? Even if these forget, yet I will not forget you. Look, I have inscribed you on the palms of my hands; your walls are constantly before me" (Isa. 49:15–16). We will inevitably disappoint God and depart from him, and he may discipline us, but he will never forsake us! Regardless of how we neglect and reject

God's love, he continues to care for us with the same tender concern he always has and always will. One of the prime ways to evaluate how your love compares to God's is to examine how steadfast your love remains when the going gets rough.

God's Love Is Sacrificial

God's love is action oriented. It is not a cozy, emotional, sentimental love he ponders while distantly ensconced in heaven. God's love is active, not relegated to the sidelines of human affairs. Paul observed: "But God proves his own love for us in that while we were still sinners, Christ died for us" (Rom. 5:8). God granted his creatures paradise, but they rebelled, demanding more. He offered them eternal life in his presence, but people opted for eternal separation from him. He invited them to enjoy close, personal fellowship, but humanity chose to be his enemies. Blinded by sin, people made the worst possible decisions imaginable. Through the ages, God has suffered all manner of insolent blasphemies and coldhearted rejection from his people, yet, rather than taking offense or nursing his rejection, God gives more.

God would have been thoroughly justified in waiting for humanity to come to its senses and ask for forgiveness. But he did not. He acted. He gave. He did not give sparingly or miserly. He sacrificed the most precious thing he had: his only Son. This is the nature of God's love. It acts, regardless of the cost. God never checks the price tag before choosing to love you.

Perhaps you know people who talk much but do little. They often tell you how much they care about you, but they never demonstrate their love with action. This is mere verbiage. If they really care, they will demonstrate it with deeds. Not so with God. Even before you finish verbalizing your prayer, God is marshaling his response (Dan. 10:10–12). Before you know your need, God's provision is already mobilized. Even while you are angrily shouting at God and rejecting his overtures, he has everything in place to respond with love.

God Loves with Eternity in View

The world's love is extremely conditional and transitory. Some people are downright difficult to love. They can be obnoxious, ungrateful, rude, and argumentative. We tend to give up on such people and consider them hopeless cases. Many marriages that were once loving, degenerate to a place of bitter coexistence or acrimonious divorce. Most people have a limit to what they are willing to endure from others in the name of love.

God's love has the unique dimension of an eternal perspective. When God looks on our life, he views it with the background of eternity. He not only sees what is; he sees what could be. Our natural response is to avoid that rude colleague at work who constantly offends us and to wish she would be fired. But God sees that same person with an eternal destiny waiting before her. That parent who harmed us in our childhood has an eternal soul that is presently lost and racing toward eternal separation from God. That friend who betrayed us—God loves him with an eternal love. If we saw people the way God does, we would find it in our heart to be much more loving and compassionate toward them.

God's love will never make sense to us if we do not understand that he loves us from an eternal vantage point. We only see the moment along with our current pain or pleasure. But God expresses his love from out of his eternal perspective leading up to this moment, as well as his eternal view beyond today and forevermore.

When we are healthy, have a great job, and enjoy a full life, we can easily believe God loves us. But how do we view God's love when we lose our job, or our spouse commits adultery, or we are diagnosed with a serious illness?

We must recognize that God does not love us temporally but eternally. His primary focus is not to make us comfortable this hour, or this year, but to prepare us to enjoy eternal bliss with him. His goal is not our happiness but our Christlikeness. Therefore, God expresses his love in terms of how it most effectively prepares us for eternity, not time.

I have known many instances where people were converted at a Christian's funeral. Though the deceased believer had witnessed to family members and friends numerous times over the years, it was not until their memorial service that their loved ones finally put their faith in Christ. Likewise, there have been many cases where people came to believe in Christ as they watched a Christian bravely battle an illness or face other hardships. People's eternal destinies have been radically altered because God allowed his saints to suffer. God does not cause our suffering, but he is adept at using our pain to alter the eternal trajectory of others.

One of the classic biblical examples of someone who grew to understand God's eternal love is Ruth. She was a young Moabite woman who wed a Jewish immigrant. We are not told what her parents thought of her marrying a foreigner who had many different customs from theirs. Ruth might have wondered if her Moabite god was punishing her because she was married for several years without having any children. This was a traditional sign of divine disfavor. Then her Jewish husband, brother-in-law, and father-in-law all died, leaving Ruth, Orpah, and Naomi as widows. Had Ruth considered whether God loved her at this point, she could not be blamed for assuming he did not. Her life had been devastated by hardship and loss. But, of course, that was not the end of her story.

Henceforth, Naomi, Ruth's mother-in-law, wanted to be called "Mara," which means "bitter," because she assumed God was dealing harshly with her (Ruth 1:13, 20). Ruth faced the most important decision of her life. Should she return to her family in Moab, like her sister-in-law Orpah had done? Or would she follow an older, miserable woman to a foreign land and devote the remainder of her widowhood to her care? This was an enormous test of character and devotion. Ruth chose to go with Naomi to her hometown of Bethlehem. She determined to make the best of a difficult life. Far from her own family, Ruth resolutely trudged into the fields daily, laboring long hours to provide for herself and her unhappy mother-in-law. Of course, her story is well-known. Boaz, a wealthy landowner, noticed Ruth's faithfulness and ultimately married her. They had a son named Obed. He had a son named Jesse, who had a son named David (Ruth 4:21–22).

What an enormous turn of events! Ironically, during the wilderness wanderings of the Israelites, Moabite women tempted Israelite men to worship their god, Baal of Peor (Num. 25:1–5). It was one of the most disastrous of the Israelite's many failures. Consequently, God forbade any Moabite from entering the sanctuary for ten generations (Deut. 23:3). How fitting that Ruth's descendant, Solomon, would one day construct the magnificent temple in which God was worshipped for centuries.

To understand God's love, we must view it from an eternal perspective. Ruth suffered pain and disappointment. But, by moving to Bethlehem, she was admitted into the people of God. Her eternal destiny was secured. David and Solomon and a long line of kings would be her direct descendants. And for the rest of eternity, she will worship God for his amazing love for her. God's love is always best understood through an eternal lens.

Responding to God's Loving Ways

Though God freely and generously expresses his love toward us, his desire is for us to embrace his love and reciprocate it in kind. It is perhaps the most unfathomable of universal mysteries that the Creator of all that is, should desire, even be jealous for, our love. God's people tend to happily receive his blessings but then ignore the one who lovingly provides them.

God will continually reach out to us in love, but he watches closely for our response. He once asked, through the prophet Isaiah, "Why was no one there when I came? Why was there no one to answer when I called? Is my arm too weak to redeem? Or do I have no power to rescue?" (Isa. 50:2). Incredibly, the Lord's creatures often reject his loving overtures.

In one of the most heart-wrenching scenes of Jesus's ministry, Jesus condemned those who had received much from God and yet refused to give their hearts to him. In some of the strongest language he ever used, Jesus declared:

> "Snakes! Brood of vipers! How can you escape being condemned to hell? This is why I am sending you prophets, sages, and scribes. Some of them you will kill and crucify, and some of them you will flog in your synagogues and pursue from town to town. So all the righteous blood shed on the earth will be charged to you, from the blood of righteous Abel to the blood of Zechariah, son of Berechiah, whom you murdered between the sanctuary and the altar. Truly I tell you, all these things will come on this generation.
>
> "Jerusalem, Jerusalem, who kills the prophets and stones those who are sent to her. How often I wanted to gather your children together, as a hen gathers her chicks under her wings, but you were not willing!" (Matt. 23:33–37)

In this devastating indictment of God's people, Jesus condemned them for ignoring and rejecting every messenger God sent to them to restore their broken relationship. No one had received more divine invitations than they, yet they refused to humble themselves and turn from their sin. God finally sent his only Son to them in the ultimate effort to draw them to himself, but they would have none of it. Instead, they cruelly nailed God's son, the Messiah, to a harsh cross. Though God's love is deeper than the ocean and greater than the heavens, his single greatest desire for us is simply that we respond to his love by loving him in return.

Since God's character and ways are always loving, how should we respond? The love we experience from God ought to radically impact two primary areas of our life: how we relate to God and how we treat others.

Loving God with All Our Heart, Soul, Mind, and Strength

When Jesus was asked what the greatest commandment was, he immediately responded: "The most important is Listen, Israel! The Lord our God, the Lord is one. Love the Lord your God with all your heart, with all your soul, with all your mind, and with all your strength" (Mark 12:29–30). God wants us to love him with every fiber of our being. Anything less falls drastically short of what God desires.

Jesus identified four major dimensions through which God's people can experience a love relationship with him. Not surprisingly, Jesus said first to love God with all our *heart.* This is the seat of our affections. We can love many things, to many degrees, but God desires for us to love him fully. Not just partially. This may have been part of Martha's problem. Mary, her sister, loved Jesus with all her heart. She enjoyed nothing as much as spending time with Jesus (Luke 10:38–42). Martha loved Jesus with her strength, expressing her love in her service to him (Luke 10:41–42). Nonetheless, more than our labor on his behalf, God wants us to love him with all our heart. It might surprise us how many pastors confess to spending too little time in prayer and communion with the Lord. They are so busy loving God with their mind and strength that they feel they are too overworked to love him with all their heart. However, when our heart is right with God, our actions naturally fall into place. My father used to say that if you are having difficulty obeying God, your fundamental issue is not an obedience problem; it is a love problem. If your heart truly belongs to God, you will obey him (John 15:14–15).

We can love many things, to many degrees, but God desires for us to love him fully.

Second, Jesus said God wants us to love him with all our *soul*. That represents our deepest spiritual dimension, and it takes our love for God to the innermost places of our being. We typically don't love people with all our soul. The average person rarely takes time to consider what is even taking place in their soul. We tend to live and love at a surface level. That is why there are always deeper and deeper levels in which we can love God. Our souls are a vast, largely untapped region that God wants us to fully devote to him.

God also wants us to love him with all our *mind*. If we *only* love him intellectually, our relationship with God will be heady, academic, and largely speculative. That is why it is best to begin with the heart. But our minds are powerful instruments that can greatly enhance our walk with God. Great thinkers like Isaac Newton, Blaise Pascal, and C. S. Lewis have blessed generations of people because they devoted their minds to God. To love him with all our mind involves reading about, studying, and learning all we can about God. The more we understand of God, the more of him we discover to love. This can involve reading deep, inspirational, and insightful books, or taking online Bible classes. We ought to continually stretch our minds to contemplate and understand more and more about infinite God. Some of the greatest thinkers in history were those who loved God with all their mind.

Finally, we are to love God with all our *strength*, which involves our service for him. Some people are content to read about God all day, loving him with their mind. Others enjoy worshipping God at church, loving him with their heart. Or perhaps they enjoy spending deep times of prayer with God, loving him with their soul. But they have no interest in loving God with their strength, or service. Brother Lawrence discovered the simple pleasures of loving God this way. Though a humble cook in a monastery, Lawrence found he could continually experience the loving presence of God. Rather than daydreaming, or longing for a loftier assignment, he expressed his love for God through the most mundane service.

> "In the way of God," he said, "thoughts count for little, love does everything. And it is not necessary," he continued, "to have great things to do. I turn my little omelet in the pan for the love of God; when it is finished, if I have nothing to do, I prostrate myself on the ground and adore my God, Who gave me the grace to make it, after which I arise more content than a king. When I cannot do anything else, it is enough for me to have lifted a straw from the earth for the love of God."[15]

It certainly is possible to serve God out of duty rather than as an expression of love. However, when our service becomes an act of devotion to God, it will matter not whether we do great things or small tasks for our King, nor will it be important if people thank us or despise us, for our efforts will be a doxology to God.

Loving Others

Jesus said, "We love because he first loved us. If anyone says, 'I love God,' and yet hates his brother or sister, he is a liar" (1 John 4:19–20). If we truly embrace God's amazing love for us, then we will be supremely motivated, even compelled, to express that same love to the people in our life.

It is the dilemma of countless Christians that they readily love Christ, but they struggle to love people! Yes, people, even our brothers and sisters in Christ, can be obnoxious and unkind (for that matter, so can we). But the mark of a Christian is love for others (John 13:35). We can *hear* about God's love and yet be unloving toward others. We can *believe* in God's love yet be unloving toward others. But it is unfathomable to truly *experience* the amazing, overflowing, unlimited love of God and yet disdain his people (1 John 4:20). What would it look like to love others with a God-like love? God's love for us is undeserved. It is infused with grace. It is undaunted by our most reprehensible behavior. It refuses to nurse hurt feelings. It keeps hoping for a breakthrough. How can we be enveloped in such love and then be stingy, harsh, or unforgiving toward others? (Matt. 18:21–35).[16]

Paul understood the power of God's love because he had experienced it. Paul took the gospel to those who mocked and persecuted him, just as he had once been a mocker and persecutor himself. He was repeatedly plotted against, lied about, and imprisoned, yet he never lost heart while ministering to others. He was unjustly and cruelly beaten and thrown into prison in Philippi, and yet he demonstrated love to his jailor and helped him and his household find salvation (Acts 16:19–34). How could Paul keep ministering despite the trials and opposition he regularly faced? He explained it this way: "For the love of Christ compels us, since we have reached this conclusion, that one died for all, and therefore all died. And he died for all so that those who live should no longer live for themselves, but for the one who died for them and was raised" (2 Cor. 5:14–15). Paul knew, perhaps better than most, that Christ's love had purchased him when he was totally undeserving. His life was no longer his own. He had no right to choose whom he would love and whom he would not. He had forfeited his right to determine the working conditions under which he served his Lord. Once an ardent enemy of Christ, now Paul considered himself a bondslave. There was no one he would not love. There was no place he would not serve. No assignment was beneath him. Christ's love settled that once and for all.

Conclusion

One of the primary ways God relates to people is by love. His love is unique. Though people occasionally reach noble heights in their affection for others, this does not come naturally. God's love is untainted by sin. It is unselfish. It readily takes the initiative. It is active. God's love paid the ultimate price to redeem us. God's love is undaunted, forgiving, and long-suffering. It goes the distance. It never gives up. It always seeks to give us the best, even when we yearn for something less. God's love works in perfect harmony with all his other attributes and ways. We will never understand God's ways if we do not comprehend the reality that everything God does in our life is motivated and characterized by love. As a result, everything we do and say ought to also be motivated and characterized by Christ's love (1 John 4:7, 19). How better to express our grateful love to God than by doing as he instructed and loving others.

Questions for Reflection/Discussion

1. How is God's love different from your love?

2. Reflect for a moment on God's love for you. When was a time God clearly expressed his love to you? How did he express his love to you this week? Today? How are you responding to his overtures?

3. Has an event in your life ever caused you to question God's love? If so, what was it? How did you process it?

4. Can you honestly say that you love God with all your heart, mind, soul, and strength? Which of those areas is the easiest for you? Which is the most difficult?

5. Do you have difficulty loving certain people? If so, why is that? How might God help you love them as he does?

6. How do you act unlovingly, making it harder for others to love you?

CHAPTER 5

GOD'S WAYS ARE FAITHFUL

Because of the Lord*'s faithful love we do not perish, for his mercies never end. They are new every morning; great is your faithfulness!*
(Lam. 3:22–23)

He who calls you is faithful; he will do it.
(1 Thess. 5:24)

My father simultaneously pastored two churches during the first two years our family lived in Canada. Every weekend dad would teach an adult Bible study, then preach at our home church. Then he would drive ninety miles north to Prince Albert and teach an adult Bible study and preach at our mission church. Then he'd drive ninety miles back home in time to preach at the evening service. Afterward, we would convene at a church member's home, and Dad would teach a discipleship class. Every Tuesday Dad would drive back to Prince Albert and lead a Bible study and prayer time. Winters in Saskatchewan could be brutal, with temperatures plummeting to 40 degrees below zero or colder. Our family had moved from Los Angeles. Many people warned him that he could not make that trip twice a week through the winter. It was too dangerous and would be too hard on his California vehicle.

One Tuesday, Dad was on the edge of town, about to head out on the highway for Prince Albert. He felt impressed to call home to my mother. He stopped at a gas station to call her. She was crying. She was struggling that day, home alone with five young children. Dad returned home to comfort my mom. Finally, she told him to go on. She would be okay. With a heavy heart, Dad drove the ninety miles to Prince Albert. Wouldn't you know it. Throughout the two years Dad made that trip, that was the only time *no one* showed up for the meeting. My dad drove home that night, praying to God and promising that even if no one else was faithful, he would be. Life is often filled with hardship and disappointments. We may fail to receive or experience all we hoped for. Yet the closer we draw to God, the better we will know his heart. The more experienced we become at recognizing his activity around us, the more convinced we will be of his amazing faithfulness. Many years later, my parents loved to visit over coffee in the mornings and celebrate how absolutely faithful God had been to them throughout the years.

God's love and faithfulness are inseparably linked (Ps. 25:10; 13:5; 17:7; 36:7). A faithless God would be an unloving God. For God to be faithful means he is entirely consistent, reliable, and predictable. God is never arbitrary. His ways always completely align with his character. He always keeps his word. What God says, he does. What God promises, he fulfills. Therefore, we know what to expect when we encounter him every single time.

For God to be faithful means he is entirely consistent, reliable, and predictable. God is never arbitrary. His ways always completely align with his character. He always keeps his word. What God says, he does. What God promises, he fulfills.

The Nature of God's Faithfulness

God is faithful in all his ways (1 Cor. 1:9; 2 Cor. 1:18). The following are four broad areas in which we experience God's faithfulness.

God Is Faithful to His Character

We often disappoint ourselves. Perhaps we are on a diet but succumb to a slice of our favorite cheesecake. Maybe we determine to speak only kind words but find ourselves criticizing a business colleague, or we lapse into an old addiction and are immediately smitten with regret and self-reproach. We know how we should live, but we regularly fail to live up to our values. To varying degrees, disappointing ourselves is a common experience for us all. This experience, however, is utterly foreign to God. He is entirely consistent in every area of his being. Because he is always true to himself, he can be faithful to you and me. God's faithfulness, just like his love, deeply impacts his other attributes. Because God is faithful, he is consistently and unvaryingly holy, loving, and powerful.

It is fine to be loving some of the time and even better to be loving most of the time. But there can be tragic ramifications when someone is not loving all the time. After decades of fidelity, a spouse, perhaps undergoing a midlife crisis, commits adultery in a one-night stand. That one choice will cause profound anguish to a family, destroy trust, and negate years of fidelity.

The same is true for holy living. One is not holy who behaves in a holy manner some or even most of the time. God's power is trustworthy because he is *always* powerful. At times people pray, "Lord, come in power!" But the truth is, that's the only way he ever acts! God never does anything powerlessly.

Can you imagine what it would be like to serve a god who suffered power lapses? Imagine David standing before Goliath, trusting in almighty God for victory. Then God awkwardly confessing to the teen that he was currently incapable of aiding him in battle. How could we confidently serve God if we were never certain of his power to do what he promised? How could we worship a god who was holy most of the time but not always? Could we trust God's guidance if we harbored doubts about his love? It is God's faithfulness in every situation that gives us confidence to trust his other attributes.

God Is Faithful to His Purposes

God makes no idle plans. God developed his purposes for humanity before time began. Every hour, week, and century, God's plans march toward their certain consummation. God said: "I declare the end from the beginning, and from long ago what is not yet done, saying: my plan will take place and I will do my will. I call a bird of prey from the east, a man for my purpose from a far country. Yes, I have spoken; so I will also bring it about. I have planned it; I will also do it" (Isa. 46:10–11). Nothing can thwart God's plans. Satan cannot stop God's intentions, try as he might.

People cast visions and make plans, yet their efforts often fail. Politicians make bold pronouncements, seemingly oblivious to the fact that their words have no bearing on reality. God alone is 100 percent true to his word. God would not be true to himself if he did not ensure that his every word came to pass. That is the beauty of the Old Testament prophecies, especially concerning the Messiah. Once God spoke through the prophets, his foretelling became an eventual certainty in Christ.

God's promises don't necessarily occur immediately, or even in our lifetime; but they *will* happen. Paul assured the Thessalonian Christians, "He who calls you is faithful; he will do it" (1 Thess. 5:24). If we do not remain steadfast, we may miss out on what God intended to do in our life. But our lack of allegiance does not alter God's faithfulness to his word. Paul assured his young protege: "If we are faithless, he remains faithful, for he cannot deny himself" (2 Tim. 2:13).

Sometimes we might wonder if God has been entirely faithful to do what he promised. But we can be confident that, regardless of what we see or do not see in our life, he continues to steadily work out his purposes. For example, Jesus announced: "Truly I tell you, anything you ask the Father in my name, he will give you" (John 16:23). You might respond, "That's not true. I have prayed for many things in Jesus's name that God has not granted to me." But praying in Jesus's name includes far more than hurriedly adding the phrase at the close of our prayers as if it were a magical formula. Jesus's name represents his character. Any request we make to the heavenly Father must be consistent with Christ's character. The Father will not honor prayers, no matter how fervent, that go against Jesus's character. Jesus's name also includes the Father's will. If we pray in faith, asking God to do something that is in Christ's will and in line with his character, the outcome is assured. If we are not seeing answers to our prayers, the reason is never that God has not kept his promise. It may be that we have not followed his instructions.

If we could see our lives from heaven's vantage point, we would recognize that God has been completely true to his promises down through the generations and in our life as well. It is imperative that we know God's purposes for us and for those around us. God has broad intentions for every person. He wants our lives to bring him glory. He intends for his people to be on mission with him to redeem a lost world (Matt. 28:18–20). God also has unique assignments for each person. God told the prophet Jeremiah that he had a purpose for him before he was born (Jer. 1:5). Saul of Tarsus discovered, to his amazement, that God had a plan for his life to be a missionary to the Gentiles. For the remainder of Paul's life, he strove to be true to God's vision (Acts 26:19). Since God has specific plans for your life, your children, and your church, you ought to do everything possible to learn what they are.

If you have ever held an infant in your arms, you cannot help but wonder what God's purpose for that child is. Lisa and I were blessed with three children. Our oldest child, Mike, almost died at birth. As the emergency birth unfolded, I was not allowed in the OR, so I wandered back to the waiting room and slumped into a chair in a daze. I was only twenty-four and all alone. All I could do was cry out to God and ask him to spare my wife and child. I prayed that if God saved my child, I would commit my life to helping him become everything God intended him to be.

When Mike was a little boy, we told him about God's love. Mike grew up in church, surrounded by faithful and godly people who invested in his spiritual life. At a young age, he embraced Christ as his Savior. When Mike began dreaming about what he would do with his life, one thing he knew he did *not* want to be was a pastor. Then at eighteen he discovered that he was a type 1 diabetic. He did not become angry at God. Just one day earlier, God had spoken to him during a worship service saying, "Do not fear what is ahead, for I am with you." Mike accepted his condition and trusted the Lord. When Mike was finishing college, he sensed God wanted him to go to seminary and earn a master's degree. He felt he was not smart enough to do master's work, but he enrolled in seminary. Several years later Mike was convinced God wanted him to enter a PhD program in Christian apologetics. Again he doubted his own ability, but again he put his trust in God. After Mike earned his PhD, he shared with us that he sensed God leading him to move his family from Atlanta, Georgia, to Victoria, British Columbia in Canada to plant a church in an area where, per capita, church attendance is at one of the lowest levels in North America. He would be almost three thousand miles away from family and friends. It was a brave move, but God had proven himself faithful this far, so Mike and Sarah were committed to seeing God's purposes accomplished, regardless of the cost.

Does this mean they never faced hardships or disappointments? Of course not. In the four years since they moved, there have been numerous setbacks—financial, emotional, and physical. The Covid pandemic hit their small congregation hard. Navigating the Canadian governmental restrictions was tricky, as different members of their church had opposing viewpoints on what the church should do. Hardest of all, last Christmas, on their son's third birthday, Finley suffered a severe respiratory infection that resulted in a thirty-minute seizure. He ended up on a ventilator in a two-week induced coma. He had to be airlifted to a hospital on the mainland. Little Finley suffered greatly before making a full recovery. Mike and Sarah can point to numerous ways God intervened at just the right time to spare Finley's life. With these and many other challenges along the way, it would be natural to grow discouraged. But Mike and Sarah had learned that God has a purpose for them and their family, and they had witnessed the Father's faithfulness time and time again. Today, God is blessing Mike's ministry. He has written several books and recently recorded new videos with me for the course, *Experiencing God.* His church is growing and changing lives. One of the greatest joys in my life is watching God's purposes unfold through all three of my children's lives. I often think back to that terrifying moment of Mike's birth and marvel at the Lord's faithfulness not just to me but to Mike.

God Is Faithful to His Pronouncements

God never speaks an idle word. He never makes a promise unless he is wholly committed to use every resource of heaven to ensure it comes to pass. God spoke through the wicked prophet Balaam, declaring: "God is not a man, that he might lie, or a son of man, that he might change his mind. Does he speak and not act, or promise and not fulfill?" (Num. 23:19). God spoke through the prophet Isaiah and declared: "For just as rain and snow fall from heaven and do not return there without saturating the earth and making it germinate and sprout, and providing seed to sow and food to eat, so my word that comes from my mouth will not return to me empty, but it will accomplish what I please and will prosper in what I send it to do" (Isa. 55:10–11).

Throughout history, people have suffered grievously when they treated God's Word lightly. The Scriptures abound with examples. The serpent assured Eve that God would not keep his word and allow her to experience death if she ate the forbidden fruit (Gen. 3:4). Humanity has endured the dire consequences ever since. God told the Israelites not to take any loot from Jericho, but Achan believed he could avoid the consequences of ignoring God's Word. He and his family paid dreadfully for his underestimation of God's Word (Josh. 7:24–26). God told King Saul to wait at Gilgal until Samuel arrived to offer a sacrifice. But when Samuel was delayed, Saul felt justified in disregarding God's Word. The aftermath was devastating (1 Sam. 13).

Conversely, Abraham took God's Word seriously, even when the thought of God granting him a son in his advanced years was humanly impossible (Gen. 15:6). Mary believed God's message to her through the angel Gabriel, and as a result, she became one of the most celebrated of all women (Luke 1:26–38). Jesus stood before Peter and Andrew and said, "Follow me, . . . and I will make you fish for people" (Mark 1:17). Everything in their lives hinged on how they responded to Jesus's word. Could they trust this itinerant rabbi? Was it worth walking away from their business and their plans for retirement? They could remain beside the beautiful Sea of Galilee and live safe, secure, and ordinary lives. Or they could trust Jesus. Sure enough, Jesus was true to his word, and God used those unsophisticated fishermen to change the world.

History is marked by people who believed God's Word was true. Martin Luther believed God would justify those who trusted in his grace to save them, and the Protestant Reformation swept across Europe as a result. Corrie ten Boom clung to God's Word even though she was held captive in a horrific Nazi concentration camp, and God brought hope and salvation to countless people through her life. Preachers such as George Whitefield, D. L. Moody, and Charles Spurgeon preached every word of Scripture as true and trustworthy, and God used them mightily. Fanny Crosby, though blind, clung to the hope found in God's Word and wrote eight thousand hymns. Songs such as "Blessed Assurance," "Pass Me Not, Oh Gentle Savior," and "Jesus Is Tenderly Calling You Home" were used regularly by Ira Sankey and D. L. Moody in their revival meetings, which saw many thousands of people come to faith in Christ. Billy Graham settled the matter as a young man that if God said it, he would believe it, and he became the greatest evangelist in history.

Scripture, as well as church history, proves that God is always true to his word. Those who trust God's Word will never be disappointed.

God Is Faithful to His Promises

As we have seen, God remains true to *every* word he speaks. His word never expires or grows out of date. Nevertheless, there are times when God chooses to explicitly make a promise so there is no mistaking what he intends to do for those who trust him.

The most famous of God's promises were his covenants. A covenant was a contract or commitment God made with people. This involved certain obligations by people, typically to obey God and to remain true to him. God in turn promised to protect, provide for, and bless his people. Sometimes God would make a promise without expecting anything in return. Such was his oath to Noah to never again destroy the earth with a flood (Gen. 9:8–17). At other times God made commitments to individuals who walked closely with him, such as with Abraham and David (Gen. 12:1–3; 15; 2 Sam. 7). As a result of Abraham's and David's faithfulness, their descendants received blessings as well (Gen. 12:1–3; 1 Sam. 7). Then there were covenants God made with his people, such as when he gave the law to Moses at Mount Sinai. These were binding on each generation. In every case, God always proved to be exceedingly more faithful to his commitments than were his people. Simply put by the writer of Hebrews: "He who promised is faithful" (Heb. 10:23).

Because of God's absolute faithfulness, he is meticulous about keeping his promises. Scripture declares: "Know that the Lord your God is God, the faithful God who keeps his gracious covenant loyalty for a thousand generations with those who love him and keep his commands" (Deut. 7:9). Sadly, people abrogated every covenant they ever made with God. Regardless of what God promised, his people abandoned their love and commitment to him every time. God, in turn, would follow through with his commitments. He would dispatch prophets and messengers to plead with the people to return to the covenant. When they refused, God would eventually enact the terms of the covenant and bring judgment upon his wayward people.

Perhaps you have dealt with someone who was quick to make a promise and yet failed to keep it. I have recently been the victim of such a person. I engaged a building contractor to build a sunroom on my house. He provided me glowing reviews of his work and assured me I would be extremely pleased. But once the agreement was made and a deposit paid, delays and excuses became routine. Excuse after excuse ensued for why no work was being done. In the rare instance when he could be reached, he would gush assurances and iterate new vows to complete the job. All to no avail. It became clear that my contractor was a liar who felt no qualms about making vows he had no intention of keeping. I suffered significant financial loss, but far worse was my great frustration and disappointment that someone could look me in the face and assure me I could trust him when, in fact, everything he told me was a blatant lie.

I eventually brought in a trusted Christian man who is a member of my church. He is a retired gentleman who has spent his life keeping his word. He did not effuse bold promises or elaborate plans. But everything he said, I was confident he would do. And he did. He is a man who values integrity. How refreshing it was to finally deal with someone I could trust!

In light of this experience, I have been reminded how wonderful it is to relate to a God who stands by every word he speaks. He certainly is under no obligation to do so. We routinely break our word and commitment to him. Yet for him to make a promise is to guarantee it will be done. There is no person in history who could ever successfully convict God of reneging on his word. God's timing is not always in sync with our own. However, if we wait upon the Lord, we will discover that in heaven's perfect timing, God is absolutely trustworthy. Not even the smallest, seemingly minor commitment is neglected or explained away. When God makes a promise, it is as good as done.

When God makes a promise, it is as good as done.

How should this affect the way we relate to God? It behooves us to identify and claim the divine promises he has made that apply to us. Peter declared: "His divine power has given us everything required for life and godliness through the knowledge of him who called us by his own glory and goodness. By these he has given us very great and precious promises, so that through them you may share in the divine nature, escaping the corruption that is in the world because of evil desire" (2 Pet. 1:3–4). Everything we need for a godly life has been made available to us through God's promises. How foolish it would be for us to remain ignorant of what they are. We can have confidence in every promise found in Scripture because, as the psalmist proclaimed: "For the LORD is good, and his faithful love endures forever; his faithfulness, through all generations" (Ps. 100:5).

Responding to God's Faithfulness

Be Faithful to God

How do we relate to someone who is entirely reliable? We must respond in kind. David declared: "With the faithful you prove yourself faithful" (2 Sam. 22:26). Jesus told the story of the master who went away on a long journey (Matt. 25:14–30). He entrusted five talents to one servant, two talents to another, and one to a third servant. The servants knew the character of their master and understood he would hold them accountable for what he had given them. This knowledge drove the first two servants to aggressively invest the talents entrusted to them. Upon their master's return, they had both doubled their holdings. The master responded with the cherished words: "Well done, good and faithful servant! You were faithful over a few things; I will put you in charge of many things. Share your master's joy" (Matt. 25:21, 23).

The first two servants knew their master's character. He was entirely predictable. In response, they conducted themselves in a manner they knew would please him. Sure enough, he commended and rewarded them. The third servant knew his master also, but he responded in fear, not faith. He was driven by dread of loss rather than by hope of gain. As a result, his master rebuked him and confiscated what he had entrusted to him. A faithful master expects faithfulness from his servants. It is important to note that God is the judge of our faithfulness. We are not. The third servant assumed he had been trustworthy because he had not lost anything. But that was not how the master measured faithfulness. The unwise servant used the wrong measuring stick to evaluate his faithfulness, and it led to his ruin.

If anyone deserves our supreme loyalty, it is God. The writer of Ecclesiastes warned, "When you make a vow to God, don't delay fulfilling it, because he does not delight in fools" (Eccles. 5:4). God is never pacified by our empty promises. Only obedience satisfies his desire for obedience.

Take an inventory of all God has entrusted into your hands. This may include possessions, positions, relationships, and skills. He will not hold you accountable for what he has not given you. But you can fully expect that one day he will demand an accounting for whatever he entrusted to you.

Be Faithful to Others

Christians ought to be the most reliable friends, family members, employees, and volunteers on the earth. For we are guided by an ever-faithful God. We should model God's faithfulness in our relationships with others. Scripture warns us to make sure our yes means yes and our no means no (Matt. 5:37; James 5:12).

We should never be careless with our words or commitments. We should be known for our integrity because we represent the Lord. It can be tempting to tell people what they want to hear. But believers should refrain from that temptation and only speak when we are fully prepared to act. Jesus told the parable of the father who had two sons (Matt. 21:28–31). He asked them both to go and work in his vineyard. The first refused. Later, however, the son had a change of heart and went. The second son told his father he would go, but he never did. Jesus made clear that God is unimpressed with our words. He desires action. Too often we sing words of commitment to God in worship, but then we leave the church and never follow through with deeds. God would rather have one act of obedience over ten thousand words of promises! Christians ought to be known not for the promises we make but the commitments we keep.

Conclusion

God's ways are unlike our own. Though we have good intentions, our faithfulness is nowhere near the same degree or quality as God's. His is the gold standard while ours is a low-grade substitute. His faithfulness is undaunted and unwavering. How wonderful it is to relate to a heavenly Father who is entirely trustworthy in every way. Oh, that we would honor God by proving ourselves faithful to him and to others!

Questions for Reflection/Discussion

1. What is one way God has been faithful to you?

2. On a scale of one to ten, with ten being perfectly faithful, how would you rate your faithfulness to God?

3. How are you responding to God's purposes for your life, your family's life, and your church? Do your actions demonstrate an assurance that he will keep his word to you?

4. What promise of God are you currently claiming and watching for its fulfilment in your life?

5. How reliable are your words and promises? How certain are people that you will follow through on what you say?

6. What most often causes you to be unfaithful to God? What causes you to break your word to people?

CHAPTER 6

GOD'S WAYS ARE POWERFUL, SOVEREIGN

"Do you not know? Have you not heard? Has it not been declared to you from the beginning? Have you not considered the foundations of the earth? God is enthroned above the circle of the earth; its inhabitants are like grasshoppers. He stretches out the heavens like thin cloth and spreads them out like a tent to live in. He reduces princes to nothing and makes judges of the earth like a wasteland. They are barely planted, barely sown, their stem hardly takes root in the ground when he blows on them and they wither, and a whirlwind carries them away like stubble. 'To whom will you compare me, or who is my equal?' asks the Holy One. Look up and see! Who created these? He brings out the stars by number; he calls them all by name. Because of his great power and strength, not one of them is missing."

(Isa. 40:21–26)

"All authority has been given to me in heaven and on earth. Go, therefore, and make disciples of all nations, baptizing them in the name of the Father and of the Son and of the Holy Spirit, teaching them to observe everything I have commanded you. And remember, I am with you always, to the end of the age."
(Matt. 28:18–20)

It is one of literature's greatest understatements to write that God is powerful. His might dwarfs that of any other monarch, president, prime minister, or dictator. Because God is all-powerful, he exercises undisputed sovereignty over every atom of creation. Since no one comes close to matching his strength, nothing can prevent him from accomplishing his will. Because God is supremely powerful, he always achieves his purpose, regardless of how impossible it may appear from a human perspective.

God Is Powerful

It is impossible for mere humans to grasp the vastness of God's strength. We have nothing to compare it to. We cannot fathom someone who can speak and bring a universe into existence. It is incomprehensible that someone could conceptualize, create, and sustain the earth along with its vast array of plants and animals. It is beyond our comprehension to understand an eternal spiritual being, let alone one who is omniscient, omnipotent, and omnipresent.

Scripture provides glimpses into the wonders of God, but they strike us as more poetic than existential. We often find God's power comforting but tend to overlook how supremely practical it is. The prophet Habakkuk declared:

> God comes from Teman, the Holy One from Mount Paran. His splendor covers the heavens, and the earth is full of his praise. His brilliance is like light; rays are flashing from his hand. This is where his power is hidden. Plague goes before him, and pestilence follows in his steps. He stands and shakes the earth; he looks and startles the nations. The age-old mountains break apart; the ancient hills sink down. His pathways are ancient. (Hab. 3:3–6)

Such might vastly surpass our experiences. We may know of powerful figures in history and in our current day, but they are pathetically impotent compared to God. Alexander the Great was the mightiest king and conqueror of his day. Yet at the age of thirty-two, he grew seriously ill, perhaps from poisoning or malaria, and lay helpless in the ancient city of Babylon while his loyal soldiers filed past to bid him farewell. Julius Caesar was the dominant leader of his time, yet twenty-three dagger blows quickly reduced him to a bloody corpse. Napoleon dominated Europe for over a decade, yet during his final six years he languished on the prison island of Saint Helena until his death at age fifty-one. In 1939 Adolph Hitler believed he had launched a war that would usher in a thousand-year rule. In the ensuing six years, millions of soldiers, as well as innocent civilians, died before the führer committed suicide at the age of fifty-six. Joseph Stalin terrorized the Soviet Union throughout his murderous rule. Perhaps twenty million people were killed and twenty-eight million deported, of whom an estimated eighteen million toiled as slaves in the Gulag. Yet, when he suffered a debilitating stroke, his lieutenants were so terrified of him that no one initially dared to call a doctor. For many hours Stalin lay helpless while his bewildered aides fretted over doing something that might upset him. In each case, these prominent world leaders died feeble and helpless. Each inevitably came to their ignoble end. With no minions to command, no armies to mobilize, no resort to arms remaining, they surrendered to death, as all humans inevitably do. There is no potentate strutting across the world stage today who will not eventually be dismissed to the grave to stand before the judgment seat of almighty God to give an account for his actions (2 Cor. 5:10). No one in history or in our present day begins to compare with the infinite power that is eternal God's alone.

King Hezekiah witnessed God's strength dwarf that of the world's greatest superpower. In the fourteenth year of his reign, the Assyrian army invaded Judah with a seemingly invincible force. The Judean forces could do nothing to resist the Assyrian onslaught except withdraw into their few remaining fortified cities. Sennacherib, king of Assyria, boasted that he had King Hezekiah shut up like a bird in a cage. He sent a messenger to warn Hezekiah that no other nation on the earth had withstood his might, and no other god could match his deity's power.

In response, God sent word through the prophet Isaiah:

> "Have you not heard? I designed it long ago; I planned it in days gone by. I have now brought it to pass, and you have crushed fortified cities into piles of rubble. Their inhabitants have become powerless, dismayed, and ashamed. They are plants of the field, tender grass, grass on the rooftops, blasted by the east wind."
>
> "But I know your sitting down, your going out and your coming in, and your raging against me. Because your raging against me and your arrogance have reached my ears, I will put my hook in your nose and my bit in your

> mouth; I will make you go back the way you came." (Isa. 37:26–29)

These were audacious words to speak to a king who had cruelly destroyed entire nations in his path to world conquest. Yet almighty God does not enter negotiations or sue for peace. He issues decrees!

One night, as the Assyrian army encircled Jerusalem, an angel of the Lord struck the Assyrian camp and killed 185,000 soldiers (Isa. 37:36). God only had to dispatch one out of his legions of angels to destroy the seemingly invincible army. Sennacherib was forced to beat a hasty retreat to Assyria. Upon his return, while he was worshipping his god, two of his sons murdered him. The kings of the earth had dreaded Sennacherib, but once Almighty God spoke, the Assyrian monarch was summarily dismissed from this life. There is no political leader, military dictator, business tycoon, or cultural icon who begins to compare with God's infinite might.

God Is Sovereign

Because God is all-powerful, he is sovereign. He is the king of the universe who expects his will to always be done. When a small child stamps his foot and declares he is *not* going to bed, he has a sorely skewed perception of who is in charge. He can protest all he wants and make any pronouncement he chooses, but the parents have the final say. Likewise, many people have grand dreams of what they would do, if only they were elected to office or promoted into management. They may have impressive plans, but they lack the wherewithal to make their dreams a reality.

God, however, has all the power and resources necessary to ensure his every wish comes to pass. No undertaking is too expensive. No problem is too difficult. No opponent is too menacing, that he cannot accomplish his will every time.

In John Milton's epic poem, *Paradise Lost,* he describes a convocation of fallen angels after they are expelled from heaven. The evil spirit Molech argues that they should launch a counterassault upon heaven to try to conquer it. Belial asserts that to attack heaven could lead to even greater woe. Better to make the best of hell and hope to get used to it in time, he argues. Finally, Beelzebub presents a third option. He acknowledges the futility of directly assailing heaven's battlements. He notes: "His captive multitude: for he, be sure in height or depth, still first and last will reign. Sole King, and of his kingdom lose no part by our revolt, but over Hell extend His empire, and with iron scepter rule us here, as with golden those in Heav'n."[17]

Beelzebub then suggests they look for a new theater in which to wage war against God so they might not be so disadvantaged. He suggests the newly created Earth. The demonic horde delights in the proposal of virgin territory over which God's rule might be usurped. Though Milton used his imagination for much of his epic poem, it is clear from Genesis onward that, commencing with the garden of Eden, Satan and his minions appear to have won a decisive victory. For centuries sin and death hold humanity in its iron grip. Scripture even refers to Satan as the "ruler of the power of the air" (Eph. 2:2). But then God sends an invasion force of his only Son into the midst of sinful humanity. Satan's evil forces, deeply entrenched throughout the earth, desperately strive to overcome him but to no avail (John 1:5).

It is not surprising that the Gospels recount Jesus performing numerous exorcisms throughout his ministry. Satan's underlings had established strongholds in all strata of society. Evil spirits influenced the decisions of kings and nations, as well as possessing hapless individuals. At the outset of Jesus's ministry, he entered a synagogue in Capernaum. A man was present who was inhabited by an evil spirit (Mark 1:21–26). We are not told how often this man attended the synagogue or how long he had been demon possessed. However, when Jesus entered the building, the evil spirit immediately became agitated. Whenever light enters a room, darkness is disturbed. The evil spirit cried out, "Leave us alone! . . . Have you come to destroy us? I know who you are—the Holy One of God!" (Luke 4:34). Clearly, the demonic forces recognized that Jesus had the power to obliterate them. Jesus rebuked and silenced the demon and commanded it to depart from the man. Onlookers were amazed at Jesus's power and authority (Luke 4:36).

It is evident from the Gospels that whenever Jesus encountered a demon in control of someone's life, he always drove it out. Even when a legion of demons had erected a seemingly impregnable stronghold in a man's life, they were no match for God's Son (Mark 5:1–20). There is no record of Jesus ever being thwarted, outmatched, or fooled by a demon. Jesus was victorious every time. Though Satan's forces presumed they had finally gained mastery over Jesus at Calvary, they soon discovered, to their horror, that instead, they had just suffered their most devastating defeat. Though Satan won some early skirmishes with humanity, he would learn that on Earth, as in heaven, God's rule is supreme. Though brutal regimes outlaw Christianity within their borders and totalitarian states threaten gruesome death to Jesus's followers, and though hostile governments pass all manner of oppressive legislation against the church, yet there is no place on Earth over which God does not reign supreme.

Responding to God's Sovereign Power

Implications to God's sovereign power are many. These include the following:

All-powerful God Grants Free Will to His Creatures

Numerous Scriptures exalt God's sovereignty. For instance, we read in Isaiah, "I declare the end from the beginning, and from long ago what is not yet done, saying: my plan will take place, and I will do my will. I call a bird of prey from the east, a man for my purpose from a far country. Yes, I have spoken; so I will also bring it about. I have planned it; I will also do it" (Isa. 46:10–11).

The above passage and many others make clear that God's will is certain to come to pass. No plan of God can be thwarted. No divine purpose is ever annulled. Yet, although God's sovereignty is evident throughout the Bible, theologians have endlessly debated the issue of whether God's sovereignty negates people's free will. On the one hand are those who hold that, for God to exercise sovereignty over the earth, he must have predetermined everything that will happen. On the other hand, there are those who maintain that God can be perfectly sovereign while still allowing people autonomy to make their own choices.

We touched on determinism in chapter 1, but let's explore it in more depth here, as it pertains to people's free will. A school of thought insists that God has decreed everything that will happen; therefore, it matters not what we choose to do. Since God's plans are certain to be accomplished, our actions are irrelevant. If God intends for our best friend to become a Christian, he will ensure that she is converted in due time, regardless of whether we share the gospel with her. If God intends for us to become spiritually mature, it makes no difference whether we study our Bible or rise early for prayer. We will grow in our faith because God has predetermined that we would.

There are many problems with this approach. First, we cannot ignore the numerous biblical instances wherein God invites his people to choose. "Follow me. . . . Come to me. . . . But to all who did receive him" (Mark 1:17; Matt. 11:28; John 1:12), to cite just a few. Would God offer people a choice even though he had already predetermined exactly how we would respond? Such a conclusion makes a farce of God's invitation since people are, for all practical purposes, unable to freely accept or reject God's invitation. We are left with only the illusion of choice.

Some hold that if God grants us freedom to choose, it must diminish his sovereignty. Such thinking leads to blasphemous conclusions. While God certainly *is* sovereign over human affairs, the deterministic view in fact makes God a deceiver and a trickster, for he commands people to do things for which they have no ability. It also makes God unjust, for he condemns people for doing the things he predetermined them to do.

If God has determined everything we do, then he must also be responsible for our sin and disobedience. If we have no choice, then God has made that choice on our behalf. Giving his creation free will does not, in fact, diminish God's sovereignty. The truth is that God is fully in control of every aspect of creation. He exercises dominion over all nature and humanity. He makes the rules. For instance, he has declared that whoever believes in Christ shall have eternal life and those who do not believe will perish (John 3:16). Every person has a choice. Nevertheless, regardless of what they choose, they are entirely subservient to God's rules. His will shall prevail.

The problem is that some have an all-or-nothing mindset. They are uncomfortable with ambiguity. They cannot reconcile how God can grant us freedom to choose without simultaneously lessening his own power.

A second issue involves that of responsibility for wrongdoing and motivation to do right. God holds us responsible for our sins. The Scriptures are filled with warnings that we will one day give an account for our actions (2 Cor. 5:10; Rev. 20:12). But, if we have no freedom to choose, we should bear no responsibility for our choices. If we lie, steal, cheat, or abuse others, this was part of God's plan. If whatever happens was meant to happen, what motivates us to make our lives better? If we are obese, God must have planned for us to be overweight. If world hunger and poverty are part of God's plan, why give to feed or clothe the less fortunate? In philosophy there is a phrase, "Ought implies can." If God holds us accountable for our sinful actions or rewards our righteous deeds, then we must have the capacity to do them.

If we are not free to choose, then God is behind each act of greed, selfishness, or violence. Why resist committing adultery with your neighbor if you were predetermined to do so? The words of Jesus to the woman caught in adultery to go and sin no more ring hollow if she were powerless to do so.

The Scriptures are filled with God's instructions, telling us to: care for our bodies, for they are God's temple (1 Cor. 6:10–20); work diligently (Col. 3:23); be ministers of reconciliation and be peacemakers (2 Cor. 5:18; Matt. 5:9); and care for the poor and hungry (Matt. 25:31–46). Throughout Scripture, God makes his will clear. Then he invites us to obey and enjoy the fruit of obedience (John 14:15; 15:14).

In every encounter God has with humanity, he acts as an all-powerful sovereign. He is continually working out his eternal purposes. Nevertheless, he grants us the freedom to make certain decisions. We can willingly follow guidance from his Word and thereby experience the promised rewards. Or we can reject his word and suffer the prescribed consequences. God's purposes will surely be accomplished, but we will forfeit much that would have been ours had we chosen wisely. God grants people choice precisely because he *is* sovereign.

God's Power Ensures His Purposes Are Achieved

God declared: "I act, and who can reverse it?" (Isa. 43:13). Though people throughout the ages have attempted to thwart God's plans, no one has succeeded. Roman emperors and government officials attempted to intimidate the church and sent many of its leaders to prison and death. Yet even the fiercest persecution could not squelch God's work. Tertullian observed: "The blood of the martyrs is the seed of the church."

Based on our current situation, it can sometimes be difficult to believe God will be victorious. There are pastors who earnestly desire God to revive their church, but the congregation continues to squabble and resist the Spirit's work. Parents pray fervently for their prodigal child to return, but he continues to drift. People long for their nation to return to God, but the country continues to reject God's Word and descends into depravity. In a world that appears to grow increasingly dark and secular, it can seem as though evil is triumphing over God's plans.

It is important to understand that God does not promise to ensure that *our* plans come to fruition. He is committed to achieving *his* will. At times individuals, churches, and nations choose to forfeit the good God would have done had they followed his lead. Nevertheless, God can achieve his purposes in multiple ways.

Jonathan Edwards was one of the most influential Christian leaders and writers in American history. He served most famously as the pastor at Northampton Congregational Church from February 15, 1727, until October 1751. During his tenure he participated in the First Great Awakening in America and witnessed several revivals sweep over his congregation. He became friends with many of the leading Christians of his day, including George Whitefield. Yet he ultimately lost favor with his parishioners. Edwards set a high standard for church membership where applicants had to demonstrate evidence of their conversion. Edwards's opponents believed this was unnecessary and judgmental. He was eventually dismissed as pastor. Though he was highly respected in Europe and across America, Edwards ultimately accepted a humble post in Stockbridge, ministering on the frontier to native Americans. For many it seemed inconceivable that one of the most respected pastors in America could be unceremoniously fired for attempting to lead his church according to biblical standards. Though Edwards trusted fully in God's power and sovereignty, God did not prevent his people from releasing their famous pastor and forcing him to look elsewhere for employment.

When evaluating Edwards's experience, it might appear that Satan achieved a stunning victory by humiliating and removing one of the greatest revival leaders in the world at that time. One can wonder why God would allow such a travesty to occur in a church shepherded by the author of "Sinners in the Hands of an Angry God." Yet we must ask what God's purposes were for Edwards. Was God focused on ensuring that his faithful servant never experience unemployment? Was God determined that Northampton Church always enjoy world-class preaching, regardless of whether they valued it? Was God's priority to ensure that Edwards secure a healthy retirement income?

It is worth noting that, by relocating to Stockbridge on the American frontier, Edwards was granted more time to focus on his writing and study, enabling him to produce some of his most influential works. The world also witnessed how fallen human nature can be exposed to excellent teaching and yet resist its sanctifying powers. The once proud Northampton Church was humbled and cast aside, no longer a major influence in American religious life. In many ways Edwards's faithful trust and service for God, even in modest circumstances, raised him higher in people's estimation. Ultimately, many of his opponents acknowledged their wrongdoing. Edwards was eventually called as president of Princeton University. History has decisively sided with Edwards, and the names of his antagonists have largely been forgotten. To this day people study and learn from Edwards's life and continue to be enriched by his brilliant thought. Were God's purposes accomplished? Certainly.[18]

The key is for us to understand God's purposes. We have our wishes, but they do not always align with God's will. At times God may choose to discipline a church that refuses to repent of its sin rather than revive it as we have prayed. God may allow our prodigal child to sink further into the depths of sin, so their eventual restoration brings greater glory to God. God's purpose for us is that we bring him glory, and he knows how to achieve maximum glory from every circumstance in our life. We might pray for national revival, while God intends to humble our nation as a graphic deterrent to other nations tempted to forsake God's standards. When history comes to an end and the veil is finally drawn back from heaven, we will learn, to our delight, that every purpose of God, throughout the often turbulent and confusing world in which we lived, was accomplished to the letter.

God's Power Leads People to Revere and Obey Him

The psalmist wrote: "Let the whole earth fear the LORD; let all the inhabitants of the world stand in awe of him. For he spoke, and it came into being; he commanded, and it came into existence" (Ps. 33:8–9). If you have ever stood at the rim of the Grand Canyon, or gazed into the heavens on a clear night, or looked upon the majestic Rocky Mountains as they meet the sky, you may have felt a peculiar awareness of God's magnificence. God's love is a powerful motivator for people's worship, but so is his power.

When the Pharisees told Jesus that if he would perform a miracle for them, they would believe in him, he declared, "An evil and adulterous generation demands a sign, but no sign will be given to it except the sign of the prophet Jonah" (Matt. 12:39). Rather than displaying his power to a skeptical audience, Jesus claimed that their only evidence would be when he died and was buried for three days.

Yet there were other times when God was pleased to work in power among his believing followers. Jesus told Peter and his fishing partners, seasoned fishermen, to cast their nets into the sea after they had fished all night and caught nothing. Peter knew better than to fish at that time of day or in the same location where there had been no fish, yet they followed their Rabbi's instructions. To their amazement, the two boats filled up with fish until they were in danger of sinking. Peter exclaimed, "Go away from me, because I'm a sinful man, Lord!" (Luke 5:8).

Later, Jesus took his disciples to a tearful funeral. The deceased had been dead four days. All hope of recovery was long since passed. Yet Jesus stood in front of the somber grave and commanded, "Lazarus, come out!" (John 11:43). To everyone's utter amazement, he did.

God is sovereign over when and where he chooses to exercise his power. Early in Jesus's ministry, he returned to his childhood home in Nazareth. However, the townspeople knew Jesus's family and could not believe anyone from their small community could be the Messiah, especially when his father had merely been a local craftsman. Scripture says, "He was not able to do a miracle there, except that he laid his hands on a few sick people and healed them. And he was amazed at their unbelief" (Mark 6:5–6). Clearly we cannot summon God's power at our whim. At the same time, our faith (or lack of it) can determine how God chooses to work through us. Shortly after Jesus was transfigured on the mountain, nine of his disciples were unable to cast a demon out of a boy, even though Jesus had earlier granted them the power to do so. When they asked why they had failed, Jesus replied: "'Because of your little faith,' he told them. 'For truly I tell you if you have faith the size of a mustard seed, you will tell this mountain, "'Move from here to there,' and it will move. Nothing will be impossible for you'" (Matt. 17:20). Clearly, God chooses to exercise his power in our lives in accordance with our faith.

God is sovereign over when and where he chooses to exercise his power.

God's Power and Wind

I served for thirteen years as president of a seminary in Cochrane, Alberta, Canada. Early in my tenure, God set in motion an amazing opportunity to more than double our academic floor space by having volunteers, mostly from Texas, raise money for materials and provide volunteer labor to construct it. I was a young man at that time and had never been responsible for such a major project. More than four hundred volunteers were needed during the summer, and over $1.5 million needed to be raised.

Early in the process I flew to Texas where my father Henry was speaking at a conference center. I met with Bob, our primary contact for the building project. He told me that God had put a particular wealthy Christian woman on his heart who might be willing to provide some initial money to commence the project. However, he had been unable to connect with her despite numerous attempts. Bob asked me to pray for an opportunity to talk to her about the project. As we concluded our meeting, we could hear people lining up just outside our conference room door for lunch. When Bob opened the door, he suddenly turned pale. He found himself staring into the face of the woman we had just prayed for him to meet! We had no idea she had chosen to attend the conference that day. In shock, Bob explained to her that we had been discussing a building project in Canada. In response, the woman took my hand in hers and said, "Richard, I feel like this may be a divine appointment!" I am still in awe when I recall that encounter.

We did embark on the project the following summer. We would often have only enough funds to complete the current phase of construction. One Monday we were to hang trusses for the roof. We had rented an expensive crane and were being charged by the hour for its use. The seminary is in the foothills of the Rocky Mountains, and that morning the winds were blowing fiercely. People's hats were blown off their heads. Our volunteers clearly could not work in those conditions. But neither could we let the crane sit idle, or our remaining funds would soon be exhausted.

Two dozen men met that morning in my office building for their daily morning briefing and prayer. It was a somber gathering. Everyone knew we faced a crisis. Finally, a grizzled retired man looked at me and said, "Well doc, it looks like you need to pray and ask God to stop the wind!" Everyone stared at me. I had never had my prayer life put to the test like that before. Over the years I had prayed many "safe" prayers, but I had never been asked to do anything so audacious as to ask God to bring peace to a windstorm.

So I prayed. I tried to muster all the faith I could. This time I did not try to cover my bases by adding, "If it be your will." We all knew God wanted us to build the building. We had no time to lose. When I finished entreating the Lord, no one moved. I suspect no one wanted to go outside and discover that the winds were still howling. At last the man who asked me to pray announced, "Well, it's time to get to work!" With that, he put on his hat and walked toward the door. That man was an ordinary working man, but that was one of the greatest acts of faith I'd ever witnessed. Other men followed him. In a few moments, I began hearing people shouting. "Praise the Lord!" "Hallelujah!" I hurried to the door and stepped outside. There was an eerie calm.

Not a trace of wind! The men fired up the crane and commenced working. Two days later, as the last two trusses were being hung, the wind returned. As the nails were driven into the final truss, the wind was just as strong as it was Monday morning. Everyone knew we had experienced a miracle.

I will be forever grateful I was able to experience God's awesome power early in my life. It is one thing to read about God working mightily in Bible times or on the mission field. It is quite another to have a front-row seat when he chooses to demonstrate his power to an ordinary group of people.

Almighty God Protects His Glory

Because God reigns supreme throughout the universe, he alone is worthy of all praise and adoration. It was jealousy of God's glory and coveting it for himself that led to Satan's epic downfall. The first test humanity faced was when Adam and Eve opted to disobey God so they could become like God (Gen. 3:5). Our greatest temptation is to covet what belongs to God. Our human tendency is to desire to be our own god rather than to submit to the true God. Imagine the audacity for creatures of dust to be jealous of the one to whom we owe our existence.

God's glory is the praise, recognition, and exaltation due him. God declared: "I am the LORD. That is my name, and I will not give my glory to another or my praise to idols" (Isa. 42:8). "I will act for my own sake, indeed, my own, for how can I be defiled? I will not give my glory to another" (Isa. 48:11). Satan was dissatisfied being subordinate to God. He wanted the adulation that belonged to the Creator. God would have none of that and cast him from heaven. Thereafter, Satan has been deceiving people to believe that life is about them rather than God—to make much of ourselves rather than much of God.

God's ways ultimately point back to him. When we achieve something God's way, he receives the recognition. When we accomplish something the world's way, we receive the accolades. When Nebuchadnezzar grew conceited as the most powerful man in the world, God humiliated him with an unusual disease (Dan. 4). It is a dangerous thing to touch God's glory.

We glorify the Lord when we wholeheartedly submit to his will. When Saul became king, he came to view the throne as his own, not as a gift on loan from God. As a result, Saul became paranoid over anyone who might take what he saw as his. He launched a deranged campaign to kill David, to whom God had promised the throne. For several years it appeared that Saul would prevent God's will for David from becoming a reality. At David's lowest ebb, he wrote: "God, be exalted above the heavens; let your glory be over the whole earth" (Ps. 57:11). Ultimately, having failed to commit suicide, the egotistical and insecure Saul was reduced to begging servants and passersby to kill him (1 Sam. 31:4; 2 Sam. 1:9). David would indeed ascend the throne, as God had declared, and lead his nation to its greatest heights. Though God's enemies may strut and boast and threaten for a time, God's purposes will inevitably come to pass, and all glory will come to him, where it rightly belongs.

God Is Sovereign over Every Nation

Countless wars have been fought as nations and kingdoms asserted their sovereignty over disputed territory. During World War I, thousands of young men died horrific deaths to gain patches of territory the length of a football field. In every generation there have been nations whose pride compelled them to dominate others at any cost.

In an age where totalitarian governments outlaw Christianity and threaten death for anyone possessing a Bible, it can appear as if there are regions of the world where God is outlawed. Some nations have spent generations under the domination of cruel, godless tyrants. Churches have been abolished, pastors imprisoned, and Christians persecuted; yet, when the veil is occasionally lifted from such oppressive regimes, it has often been revealed that those places are where Christianity is growing the fastest. Though it might seem impossible to believe that God is working out his purposes in some of the darkest locales spiritually, almighty God's sovereignty is in no way restricted to nations with governments friendly to the Christian cause.

Notice how God views the earth and its nations:

> Heaven is my throne, and earth is my footstool. (Isa. 66:1)
>
> God has spoken in his sanctuary: "I will celebrate! I will divide up Shechem. I will apportion the Valley of Succoth. Gilead is mine, Manasseh is mine, and Ephraim is my helmet; Judah is my scepter. Moab is my washbasin. I throw my sandal on Edom; I shout triumph over Philistia." (Ps. 60:6–8)
>
> Why do the nations rage and the peoples plot in vain? The kings of the earth take their stand, and the rulers conspire together against the LORD and his Anointed One: "Let's tear off their chains and throw their ropes off of us."
>
> The one enthroned in heaven laughs; the Lord ridicules them. Then he speaks to them in his anger and terrifies them in his wrath. (Ps. 2:1–5)

God is never inhibited by a dictator's decree or a United Nations' resolution. He continues to majestically carry out his purposes around the world. At the close of the book of Isaiah, God revealed his intent: "Knowing their works and their thoughts, I have come to gather all nations and languages; they will come and see my glory" (Isa. 66:18). God has made clear that history is moving toward a crescendo where people from every nation and language on the earth will draw near to him in worship and ascribe to him the glory due him.

Jesus's final command was to make disciples of all nations (Matt. 28:18–20). When we invest in making disciples throughout the earth, especially in difficult places, we are joining God's work of the ages that will ultimately bring history to a close (Matt. 24:14). Christians generally do well to follow world events less and to join in God's activity far more.

During the Cold War between the United States and the Soviet Union, Romania, led by the dictator Nicolae Ceausescu, was the most oppressive nation in Eastern Europe. Many Romanians attempted to flee the country to escape the brutal regime. Numerous Christians faced persecution and intimidation as they sought to honor God under an atheist government. In 1985, Billy Graham spoke in six cities across Romania. Churches were packed, and thousands of people gathered outside the churches to hear the evangelist. People were desperate for God to work mightily in their nation.

Then, in December 1989, a Hungarian Reformed pastor named Laszio Tokes, was dismissed from his church in Timisoara for having criticized the government. Church members and supporters surrounded his home and refused to allow government authorities to evict the pastor. Eventually, the army was called in, and the revolution rapidly spread across the country. When the army finally turned against the Ceausescus, the couple attempted to flee the country but were arrested. They were quickly tried and condemned, then executed on Christmas Day, 1989.

I have, since that time, had the privilege of ministering in Romania. It is fascinating to hear from Christians who lived through that era and how they trusted God even when their circumstances suggested that the government was all-powerful. Governments may pass oppressive laws and threaten Christians with prison and death, but God's ultimate purposes for each nation will be achieved, nonetheless.

God Is Powerful to Save

We see God's awesome might evident in nature, whether it is through studying the trillions of stars and galaxies or in analyzing the brilliant complexity of the human body. Yet God's most amazing display of power is demonstrated when he refashions sinners into saints and washes away a lifetime of sin. The Bible says people are spiritually dead in their sins (Eph. 2:1). To transform a dead person into a living one requires enormous power. The psalmist declared: "With power you redeemed your people" (Ps. 77:15).

Many people today equate becoming a Christian with merely uttering a formulaic prayer or being baptized so their name is duly added to the church membership roll. But something far more magnificent than that occurs at conversion. It involves a total rebirth, not just an adoption of a new worldview. Jesus told Nicodemus that the only way to achieve eternal life was for him to be born again. The esteemed Pharisee immediately recognized the impossibility and asked, "How can anyone be born when he is old?" (John 3:4). Of course, Jesus referred to a spiritual rebirth. Only God can remake someone into an entirely new person (2 Cor. 5:17).

If you have ever witnessed firsthand the transformation of a sinner into a saint, you understand the magnitude of this miracle. I have had the opportunity to minister in maximum security prisons. I have walked down death row at the Louisiana State Men's Prison at Angola, Louisiana. The crimes the men were convicted of were horrific. One man was facing execution for the rape, murder, and mutilation of nineteen women. Yet, in that ghastly environment, one could also witness what God's grace and power had done in the lives of some of America's most heinous criminals. The difference was evident. Several now serve as pastors of churches within the prison. Some volunteered to go as missionaries to other prisons. I worshipped with the inmates and watched them praise God with all their hearts, even though they knew they would probably never leave that prison. It takes a miracle to transform into a saint someone who is spiritually dead.

Over the course of my travels, I have been privileged to meet a fourth-generation alcoholic who now serves as a beloved pastor of a large congregation. I have met formerly angry, bitter people who now radiate the peace of Christ. I know several men and women who were once drug-addicted felons, but now they hold responsible jobs and are godly, loving parents. I have talked with many who attempted suicide because they felt so hopeless but who are now filled with the joy of the Lord. God's power to transform a life is truly a marvel to behold.

Responding to God's Powerful, Sovereign Ways

We must live with a constant awareness that God will *always* relate to us with power and authority. We must keep in mind that there is *nothing* he cannot do. He has assured us, "The eyes of the Lord roam throughout the earth to show himself strong for those who are wholeheartedly devoted to him" (2 Chron. 16:9). God's desire is to demonstrate his strength to a watching world through the lives of his people. Those inhabited by the Holy Spirit have access to God's mighty power. As Jesus prepared to ascend to heaven, he declared, "But you will receive power when the Holy Spirit has come on you, and you will be my witnesses in Jerusalem, in all Judea and Samaria, and to the ends of the earth" (Acts 1:8). God's power is always expressed for a purpose. When God, the king of the universe, grants power to people, it is so they can do his will and bring him glory. Sadly, many Christians talk about how powerful God is, but they don't live as if this is true. The apostle Paul declared, "For the kingdom of God is not a matter of talk but of power" (1 Cor. 4:20). To live your life God's way is to live victoriously.

God's power is always expressed for a purpose. When God, the king of the universe, grants power to people, it is so they can do his will and bring him glory.

I remember when my father was a pastor and then a denominational missionary in Canada. He believed with all his heart that he served a mighty God. At first glance you might have questioned his judgment. Dad moved our family to a small church in Saskatoon, Canada. There were only about twenty-five people on our first Sunday. The building was arguably the ugliest church facility in the entire city. I remember listening to my father preaching each week about almighty God. I would look around at our modest congregation and wonder what he was talking about. It wasn't as if everything we did was miraculous. Yet incredible changes occurred. Lives were radically transformed. Scores of people felt called into the ministry. That little church kept starting new congregations even though we had no funds. Over the years I noticed something interesting. When other pastors witnessed the unusual way God worked in our church, they responded in various ways. Some eagerly spoke with my father and tried to learn how they, too, could experience God's power in their life and ministry. Others, however, seemed sensitive that God's activity was not as evident in their ministry as it was in my father's. Some pastors made excuses. Others tried to discount and explain away what was happening. When you relate to the most powerful being in the universe, you should *expect* to experience his might.

God's sovereignty insists that we treat him as the supreme king that he is. Many tried to negotiate with Jesus. The rich young ruler wanted to inherit eternal life and yet still retain his wealth as his god, but Jesus said no. Some promised Jesus they would follow him but only after their father had died and they had given him a proper burial, but Jesus said the dead could bury the dead. Jesus was the most loving person on the earth, yet he was also the Lord of the universe. He fully expected his will to be done to the letter.

Some people like to model themselves after Jacob who wrestled with God (Gen. 32:24–32). Many believers claim they know what God wants them to do, but they have been "wrestling" with God about it, as if it is natural to combat God over his will. Yet Jacob's experience is never used as a biblical example for God's people to emulate. In fact, Jacob walked with a limp for the rest of his life after his divine wrestling match. It may well have served as a painful reminder that when you hear from God, he expects instant surrender, not resistance.

God is sovereign. He is king. He taught his followers to pray in this manner: "Your will be done on earth as it is in heaven" (Matt. 6:10). How is God's will followed in heaven? Perfectly. Instantly. Joyfully. Jesus taught his disciples to pray every day that God's will would be carried out in their life in the same way. If we, as believers, settle in our mind that God, not we, sits on the throne—that God is all-powerful and we are frail and sinful creatures—our daily life will reflect these truths, and God *will* be glorified through us.

Conclusion

God is the supremely powerful king, reigning majestically over all that exists. He speaks with absolute authority. He is undaunted by world rulers. His will is unstoppable. His resources are unlimited. His power is unfathomable. His purposes advance, undaunted, to their certain conclusion. When God reveals his will to you, he always does so with the full conviction that his purposes can and will be done. Serve him with total confidence and instantaneous obedience and bring glory to your king.

Questions for Reflection/Discussion

1. How have you experienced God's power in your life?

2. How are you currently seeing God systematically working out his purposes in the world around you?

3. Is God's sovereignty clearly evident over every area of your life? If not, what do you still need to surrender?

4. How is your life presently bringing glory to God? What areas of your life are not yet honoring to God?

5. How does the way you are living convey your confidence that God's purposes will be accomplished in your community and your church?

6. Are you confident that God will achieve his will in your nation, regardless of what the government might do? How does your life reflect that confidence?

CHAPTER 7

GOD'S WAYS ARE TRUE (AT ALL TIMES AND IN ALL PLACES)

The entirety of your word is truth, each of
your righteous judgments endures forever.
(Ps. 119:160)

Lord God, the Almighty; just and true are your ways.
(Rev. 15:3)

Is anger a sin? Is it justifiable in some cases? How angry is "too angry"? Paul exhorted the believers at Colossae, "But now, put away all the following: anger, wrath, malice, slander, and filthy language from your mouth" (Col. 3:8). While most people would view such things as slander and filthy language as sinful and to be condemned, anger has somehow come to be viewed as acceptable. But consider the context of Paul's exhortation. He said, "For you died, and your life is hidden with Christ in God" (Col. 3:3). Therefore, he went on, believers should "put to death what belongs to your earthly nature" (Col. 3:5).

I recall a Bible study where I made a comment that sparked an animated discussion. I said, "If you are a person who regularly gets angry, you are an angry person." Immediately several people became visibly perturbed. Everyone began speaking at once. Some argued that certain people have difficult, painful lives, and therefore, they struggle with anger. Others noted that some people are more emotional or expressive than others so anger is how they communicate their feelings. Some grew up with angry fathers. Others had stressful lives. Who was I to judge those who wrestled with controlling their "passion"? Of course, there were those who mentioned Jesus cleansing the temple (although interestingly, Scripture doesn't say Jesus was angry). Nevertheless, I stood my ground. The Bible would not tell us to put away our anger unless it were possible for us to do so. We must resist the temptation to evaluate biblical instruction based on our experience or wishful thinking.

One woman in that tense Bible study was extremely agitated. She insisted that it was not easy for people like her to simply "put away" anger. She, for one, had a difficult life and had suffered a painful past. She had been plagued with anger since her childhood. The following week she shared that she had gone home after the class imploding at the suggestion that her anger was not justified. But as the week wore on, she felt increasingly convicted about her attitude. Anger had been so much a part of her life that she couldn't imagine simply asking God to take it away from her. Finally, she cried out to God and pled for him to free her from the anger that was consuming her life.

Suddenly she felt an enormous load lifted from her shoulders. She was overcome with joy. Days later her teenage son asked her if she had changed her medication, since her mood was so improved. This woman had heard God's truth for most of her life, yet she remained in bondage. It was not until she believed it and obeyed it that she finally experienced true freedom.

God's Word Is True

Jesus declared: "I am the way, the truth, and the life" (John 14:6). Jesus does not merely *tell* people the truth; he *is* the truth. Truth defines the essence of his being. This means that Scripture, which is God's Word to humanity, is perfectly true as well. Paul declared: "All Scripture is inspired by God and is profitable for teaching, for rebuking, for correcting, for training in righteousness" (2 Tim. 3:16). The Psalms announce: "The entirety of your word is truth, each of your righteous judgments endures forever" (Ps. 119:160).

Jesus does not merely *tell* people the truth; he *is* the truth.

Many claim that God's Word may have been applicable at the time he spoke it, but due to the passage of time, many of his pronouncements and commandments are outdated or irrelevant today. Some argue that the Old Testament truth was superseded by New Testament teaching. Yet God's Word, like his person, is eternal. It has no expiration date! God's truth in the New Testament built on and fulfilled truths presented in the Old Testament. Culture changes. Technology advances. Social issues can become increasingly complex, yet God's Word stands the test of time. Its truth transcends every age and culture.

Today people claim to have their own truth. They adamantly pronounce, "That's my truth!" or "I have my truth and you have yours." Clearly there cannot be multiple, contradictory truths. God's truth is supreme over all human opinion. Though the entire population on the earth were to reach 100 percent consensus on a particular matter, their collective conclusion would still only be valid as far as it aligns with God's truth.

The key to knowing the truth of your situation is to be in proper relationship with Christ. When the twelve disciples were caught in a violent storm at night on the Sea of Galilee, they concluded that the truth of their situation was that they were going to die (Mark 4:37–38). But, as my father likes to say, on that night, Truth was asleep at the back of the boat. These seasoned fishermen had spent their lives sailing on that sea. All their experience and knowledge led them to conclude they were going to perish. But they had not yet heard from Jesus. Jesus was not intimidated by the fierce wind and immense waves. He knew perfectly well how the night was going to end.

Today there are panels of experts, prominent psychologists, and best-selling authors who confidently extol what they believe to be the truth on a wide array of issues. And, though they are lauded for their education, popularity, and erudition, time routinely proves many of them to be wrong. However, through the ages, those who have based their lives on God's Word have found it leads invariably to abundant life.

The Father of Lies

Our great challenge is that we have a mortal enemy who desperately wants to destroy us and who is fiendishly skilled at deception. Jesus claimed that Satan was a "murderer from the beginning" and that "there is no truth in him. When he tells a lie, he speaks from his own nature, because he is a liar and the father of lies" (John 8:44). Just as God's character makes him an absolute truth teller, so Satan, by his evil nature, continually utters falsehood.

The first time Satan appears in Scripture, he is questioning the truth of God's Word. He asks Eve, "Did God really say, 'You can't eat from any tree in the garden'?" (Gen. 3:1). From the beginning, Satan has been planting seeds of doubt in people's minds about God's Word. Of course, God had *not* said that. In fact, God told Adam and Eve they could eat from *all* the trees in the garden except one. One rule was all God gave them; only one item was off limits. Yet Satan twisted God's Word in a manner that made God sound like a miserly Scrooge. It is one of the most oft-used techniques of the devil to skirt the truth by attacking the character of the truth teller. Distort what the person said. Then create a straw man that appears harsh and unfair.

Next, Satan denied God's Word, exclaiming, "No! You will certainly not die" (Gen. 3:4). Satan moved from questioning God's Word to blatantly contradicting it. This is the battle that continues to wage fiercely today. God has spoken clearly about what is right and wrong: true and false, good and evil. The author of lies uses cultural influencers, secular psychologists, pundits, and false prophets to challenge and mock what God has clearly said.

Finally, Satan offered his own false narrative: "In fact, God knows that when you eat it your eyes will be opened and you will be like God" (Gen. 3:5). This was the greatest of all lies and the most seductive. Adolf Hitler claimed that the larger the lie, the easier it was to believe. Satan told a creature of dust that by eating a piece of fruit, made by God, she would become just like the one who made the fruit (and her). The lie of becoming one's own god has seduced millions of people through the ages. Satan is finding that this falsehood has lost none of its appeal over the years. It is in large part what drives people to be atheists and agnostics. If there is no God, then we can be our own deity. We can make our own rules, establish our own truth, and be the final judge of our own life. It is seductive to think we are not answerable to anyone but ourselves. Yet, sadly, we have not the power or wisdom to be a god. We cannot change reality to reflect our narrative, regardless of how we feel. We cannot give ourselves life. We cannot perform miracles. To become our own god is to greatly diminish our life's potential.

It is trendy today to back up a viewpoint with, "I choose to follow the science." In fact, two people with radically opposing views can both make this claim. The fact is, science can be misinterpreted or manipulated to support a bias. Human knowledge, though it has grown exponentially, is still finite. The reality is that people choose to believe what they want to believe. Our beliefs tend to follow our feelings. We feel that no one has a right to challenge "our truth." While we are free to choose what we believe, there is only one truth and it is God's. Satan convinced Adam and Eve to believe their own version of truth, that they were gods. However, as fervently as they might have believed it, it was pathetically, tragically, and obviously not true.

The apostle Paul wrote to the church at Ephesus, "And you were dead in your trespasses and sins in which you previously walked according to the ways of this world, according to the ruler of the power of the air, the spirit now working in the disobedient" (Eph. 2:1–2). Paul acknowledged the dreadful reality that the world was dominated by Satan's evil influence. World systems have been corrupted by his sinister deception through the ages. Satan is masterful in his ability to mislead. He may use a half-truth, a misdirection, or an outright lie. He may exaggerate the situation or minimize God's truth. His goal is to lead you to question, doubt, and discard God's Word.

The apostle John wrote that in the beginning was the Word (John 1:1). "In him was life, and that life was the light of men" (John 1:4). God's Word, his truth, enlightens people and gives life. And, though the powers of darkness have desperately tried to quench the light, they have been repeatedly foiled (John 1:5). We live our lives in the middle of a fierce battleground between truth and falsehood. We must cling to God's truth, regardless of how appealing Satan's deception may appear.

Responding to God's Truth

God's nature dramatically affects the way we should respond to him. Because he is spirit and truth, we must worship him in Spirit and truth (John 4:24). We cannot fully worship or relate to God while simultaneously believing things that are untrue. To experience the closest relationship with God possible, we must embrace the truth about God and ourselves. Inaccurate views of God inevitably lead to sinful acts and a dissatisfying relationship. If we mistakenly assume God is not all-powerful, then we will expect less of him. If we accept the lie that God tolerates sin, we will fail to repent of our transgressions, thereby remaining estranged from him (1 John 1:9). But knowing the truth about God and his ways leads to wholeness. Acknowledging that we are children of the King in need of his grace leads us to seek God for whatever we need (Luke 18:9–14). If we overestimate our spiritual condition or underestimate our need, we will be unable to love God with all our heart and mind. We cannot serve God in a manner that glorifies him when our service is built on falsehood. Knowing the truth about God and ourselves frees us to authentically worship God as he is.

Grace and Truth

Fortunately for us, Christ embodies both truth and grace (John 1:14). God's way is to always speak truth. At times truth is painful and difficult to accept. Some people take great delight in proclaiming hard truths to others. I recall hearing a preacher say one time, "I love preaching on sin!" God certainly delights in truth, but he dispenses it with grace. When God confronted Adam and Eve about their sin, he was telling them a devastating truth. But grace led him to make clothing for them and not strike them dead (Gen. 3:21). God told Ahab, the wickedest king of his age, the truth that he was sending a devastating judgment upon his family, yet when Ahab humbled himself, God showed grace and delayed his wrath for a generation (1 Kings 21:17–29). Jesus told Peter the truth when he foretold Peter's denial of him, but Jesus showed grace by giving him a second chance, assuring Peter he would recover and ultimately strengthen his friends (Luke 22:31–32).

It is human nature to balk at discomforting truths. We dislike being told that God views our attitudes or behavior as sin. We do not want to hear that we must give up a habit or addiction we enjoy. We chafe at the thought that we are at fault in a broken relationship.

It is common for people trapped in sin to stop attending church or to quit reading their Bibles to avoid "hard" truth. People will pull out of Christian fellowship rather than make a course correction.

A family in my church had a daughter they adored. In their eyes she could do no wrong. This young lady became engaged to a man who claimed to be an atheist. Her parents assured everyone that they viewed his spiritual condition as "progress" because he had formerly been a member of a religious cult! This family desperately needed their church family to walk with them during this crucial time.

Their daughter had grown up in church, and she had professed Christ as her Lord. But now, enamored with her fiancé, she was being enticed to surrender her values and beliefs. Her parents should have asked for prayer. They should have asked the pastor to meet with their daughter or to share Christ with her potential groom. Instead, they abruptly left the church because they assumed the pastor would not perform the wedding.

The parents had no interest in talking with their pastor or explaining why they were leaving the church. They could not bear to be told that what they were doing contravened God's Word. They were determined to do whatever their daughter wanted, even if it meant walking away from a church in which they had been members for many years. They found someone willing to officiate the wedding, but the marriage lasted less than a year. The young couple endured a painful divorce, and the bride turned her back on God. The family was now estranged from the people who would have lovingly and compassionately walked with them through their pain. Embracing God's truth would have saved them much suffering. God's truth is not always easy or comfortable. It can be the last thing we want to hear. But it will save us much grief and regret.

Three years ago my thirteen-year-old niece, Jasmine, developed some unusual bruises. Her mother took her to the doctor. On Friday afternoon they were told horrific news. Jasmine had leukemia. Doctors wanted to admit her to the hospital the following Monday morning and immediately begin extensive chemotherapy. She would have to drop out of school for the remainder of the year. The family was in shock. Jasmine was a vibrant, beautiful teenage girl who loved God and her family. She and her family had to quickly decide how to respond to the earth-shattering truth they had been told.

Her church family immediately mobilized to help. That Sunday evening, they threw a hair-cutting party where she shaved her long, beautiful hair. Several friends and relatives (including her grandmother) shaved their own heads in solidarity. Jasmine underwent devastating chemotherapy treatments over the next several months. Her mother had to take leave from work to stay with her at the hospital. It was grueling for the family as they watched this once active teen suffer from the painful, exhausting treatments. Her body grew so weak she could not get out of bed. Her already tiny frame became skeletal. But much good also occurred. Some of Jasmine's friends at school, who were not Christians, began reading their Bibles and praying. Many were inspired by her faith in God. Ultimately, her treatments were successful. Today she is a healthy young woman, full of life with a strong faith in God.

Jasmine and her family received a harsh truth. The choice of response was theirs. To accept the truth would involve the most pain and discomfort they had ever known. But it would also bring renewed life and a deeper walk with God. Had they been unwilling to walk through the valley of the shadow of death, Jasmine would not be alive today. Out of love God will always tell us the truth. But he will never force us to accept it. That decision is always ours.

Truth Sets People Free

We never need to fear when God speaks truth into our life. It may humble us, embarrass us, frighten us, or cause temporary pain or discomfort. But it will invariably set us free. Whenever you encounter someone in bondage, look for the lie that led to their captivity. Falsehood leads to bondage. Perhaps you can lovingly help them see the truths revealed in the Bible, so God's truth sets them free (John 8:32).

Only heaven knows the enormous carnage that lies have caused through the ages. A successful businessperson with a beautiful family bought into the lie that a one-night stand with a colleague would be an exciting adventure that was never discovered. A gifted college student concluded that occasional drug use would lift her spirits but not become addictive or interfere with her life. A child growing up was continually told he was stupid and incompetent. Now as an adult, he battles crippling feelings of insecurity and worthlessness. A cursory look at society today reveals large swaths of the population that have been grossly deceived. They have believed lies, and now they are paying an enormous price.

Whenever you encounter someone in bondage, look for the lie that led to their captivity.

Truth, on the other hand, has set untold millions of people free over the years. Martin Luther was haunted by his sin and the looming judgment of holy God. Then he learned the truth that God makes people righteous by grace, through faith, and the world felt the enormous impact of that profound truth.

Several years ago my father was speaking at a church. A retired soldier approached him. He had served in active combat in Vietnam. Having seen so much death and destruction, his heart had grown calloused and hard. He had closed off his emotions. It was destroying his marriage and family. He desperately wanted to be free from his condition, but it seemed as if something within him had died and left him with a heart of stone. My father referred to the truth in Ezekiel 11:19 where God promised to remove hearts of stone and replace them with hearts of flesh. As my father prayed, the man began to cry out, "It's gone! It's gone!" His hardened heart was gone. He was set free. Years afterward, whenever the veteran saw my dad, he would tell him, "I'm still free!" Truth sets people free.

Tell the Truth

How should we relate to a God who always speaks truth? We should embrace and speak the truth as well. In an age dominated by lies, this can be difficult. I recently heard of some Christian students who were attending a state university. On their exams they were asked what they thought about current social issues. The students knew their professor actively championed a popular, unchristian view. They knew that if they voiced an opposing perspective on their exam, they would not receive a high grade.

They confessed to giving the answer the professor was looking for, even though it was not their personal viewpoint. They needed a good grade in that class so they could continue receiving a scholarship. The students were not receiving an education. They were learning how to lie effectively.

There are numerous times when Christians often face the dilemma of whether to tell the truth. In countries where the government restricts the practice of Christianity, people face serious danger if they tell the truth. I have ministered in communist as well as Muslim countries. Local Christians agonized over whether they should be completely honest with the government, lest it bring harm or even death to fellow believers.

In the book, *The Hiding Place,* Corrie ten Boom relates how she strongly disagreed with her sister Nollie about being honest in all circumstances. Nollie believed Christians should always tell the truth. Yet her family was hiding Jewish refugees to protect them from being arrested by the Nazis and sent to concentration camps. One day the secret police arrived at Nollie's house where she was harboring a Jewish woman named Annaliese. The police pointed to their guest and asked Nollie if she was a Jew. Nollie answered honestly, that she was. Both women were arrested. Nollie knew the police were shipping Jewish people to concentration camps in Germany and Poland. However, Nollie sincerely believed that "no ill will happen to Annaliese. God will not let them take her to Germany. He will not let her suffer because I obeyed him."[19] Of course, we know that people have suffered grievously for obeying God. History has produced a long list of martyrs. Nevertheless, within the week an attack was carried out on the prison where Annaliese was held. She and forty other prisoners were freed. Nollie was eventually released as well and reunited with her husband and six children. Corrie ten Boom struggled throughout her time in concentration camps over whether the God of truth expected her to be entirely honest with her Nazi captors. Is it wise, given the evil world in which we live, to always tell the truth?

Today's world produces extremely complicated situations where people could suffer greatly if someone told the truth. Winston Churchill once declared: "In wartime, truth is so precious that she should always be attended by a bodyguard of lies." Nevertheless, God never faces this dilemma. He is never pressured to stretch the truth or tell a half-truth. God never obscures the truth to gain new converts or to convince someone to obey him. When Jesus was teaching his disciples, he stated: "If anyone wants to follow after me, let him deny himself, take up his cross, and follow me" (Matt. 16:24). Jesus could have stated his requirements in many ways so they were more attractive to potential disciples. He could have told would-be followers that all they would be healthy and wealthy if they followed him. But Jesus never compromised the truth to build his church. Rather, he spoke the truth and then watched to see who was being convinced by his Father to believe it (Matt. 16:17). Beware the temptation to compromise the truth to further the cause of God. You will never build the kingdom of truth with tools of falsehood.

God never obscures the truth to gain new converts or to convince someone to obey him.

Christians are called to be truth tellers, though it is especially difficult in places where falsehood predominates. This has traditionally been the role of the prophet. Nathan exposed the deceit of King David when he attempted to cover up adultery and murder. How exceedingly difficult it must have been for Nathan to look into the eyes of the giant-killing king and pronounce, "You are the man!" (2 Sam. 12:7). When King Ahab called on his religious officials to support his planned assault against the king of Aram, four hundred prophets dutifully told the king what he wanted to hear. Only the prophet Micaiah had the courage to tell the monarch the truth, that if he proceeded with his plans, he would be killed (1 Kings 22:1–28). For that he was thrown in prison. When the high priest Jehoiada lived, King Joash heeded his wise counsel. But after Jehoiada died, his son, Zechariah, told the king the truth about his nation's apostacy, and for that the king had him stoned to death (2 Chron. 24:15–22). When the prophet Jeremiah delivered God's message to the king, he was charged with treason and thrown in jail (Jer. 37–38). Yet every word Jeremiah said was true.

This does not necessarily mean that every Christian is called to speak "truth to power." It does mean that we are not to accept falsehood, even if the government is promoting it, celebrities are endorsing it, and the media are propagating it. Christians ought to be the one group of people who refuse to deviate from the truth, regardless of how unpopular their stance is. Our Lord and Savior lived out perfect truth, and for that he was crucified.

God Judges Falsehood

The psalmist David declared: "For you are not a God who delights in wickedness; evil cannot dwell with you. The boastful cannot stand in your sight; you hate all evildoers. You destroy those who tell lies" (Ps. 5:4–6). One of the signs that a society is corrupt is when it forsakes truth and false narratives abound. The prophet Isaiah declared: "Justice is turned back, and righteousness stands far off. For truth has stumbled in the public square, and honesty cannot enter. Truth is missing, and whoever turns from evil is plundered" (Isa. 59:14–15). Jeremiah charged the prophets and priests of his day, saying: "They have treated my people's brokenness superficially, claiming, 'Peace, peace,' when there is no peace. Were they ashamed when they acted so detestably? They weren't at all ashamed. They can no longer feel humiliation" (Jer. 6:14–15). The NKJV translation says, "Nor did they know how to blush." The righteous prophets condemned a society that treated the truth as an inconvenience and in which no one was ashamed to tell a brazen lie. When society tolerates falsehood as commonplace and acceptable, it stands on the brink of God's righteous judgment.

Mark Twain claimed you didn't need a good memory if you always told the truth. For those who promote falsehood, God promises that judgment will be certain. Jesus warned: "There is nothing covered that won't be uncovered, nothing hidden that won't be made known. Therefore, whatever you have said in the dark will be heard in the light, and what you have whispered in an ear in private rooms will be proclaimed on the housetops" (Luke 12:2–3). Though the father of lies currently exercises vast influence over people and nations, God is determined to expose every deception. Rarely does a week go by without news of a pastor, businessperson, or government leader who is exposed for their immoral acts. They have been presenting a façade to the world and hoping their exploits will never be discovered. Businesspeople cheat and lie to customers yet vainly assume their deception will remain hidden. Politicians are regularly exposed for the seamy side of their life that negates what they have been pronouncing in public. And it is not just public speakers who are deceitful.

At times liars take their dark secrets with them to the grave. But even then they are not beyond the reach of justice. God will one day hold us accountable for every lie we ever told (2 Cor. 5:10). In that day God will finally expose the enormous deceptions that held sway over large portions of the world's population. Many world religions as well as Christian denominations will be astonished to discover the falsehood they accepted as truth. Evil people who manipulated and exploited others with their twisted narratives will give an account for every deceitful word.

Falsehood will be exposed. Truth will be vindicated. On that day, how blessed will be those who based their lives and their conduct on God's truth!

Conclusion

God's ways are always based on truth. He never resorts to deceit or faulty information to accomplish his purposes. God knows the truth about every person and circumstance, and he always acts accordingly. You may not like what God is saying, but you can be certain it is the truth. Don't be afraid of the truth. It will set you free. The only way to relate to God in an intimate, fruitful, and glorifying manner is to do so in total truth.

Questions for Reflection/Discussion

1. How comfortable are you with people telling you the truth?

2. How comfortable are you with God telling you the truth?

3. How serious are you about always telling the truth?

4. How are you protecting yourself from the falsehoods that abound today?

5. How are you combatting falsehood?

6. How are you working to set people free with God's truth?

CHAPTER 8

GOD'S WAYS ARE ETERNAL

Before the mountains were born, before
you gave birth to the earth and the world,
from eternity to eternity, you are God.
(Ps. 90:2)

Do you not know? Have you not heard?
The LORD is the everlasting God.
(Isa. 40:28)

A provocative and often posed question is, "If you only had one day left to live, how would you spend it?" The assumption is, time being limited, we would focus on our highest priorities. But what if the opposite were true? What if our time were limitless? What if we had existed from eternity past and would continue to exist for eternity into the future? How would that affect what we did and how we did it?

This reality dramatically underscores why God's ways vastly differ from ours. He has always existed and always will. Not only does God know what will happen in the future, but he also has unlimited time to prepare for it. When a major crisis unexpectedly strikes a nation, its leaders hurriedly meet in closed-door sessions to study the situation and develop a rapid response. Because the issues they face are urgent, their decisions can vary widely in wisdom and effectiveness.

Not so with God. What may have caught you by surprise is something God has been preparing for since before time began.

God Takes the Long View

The saying goes, "Life is short. Eat dessert first!" Time is limited so some decisions and actions are often rushed. But God never hurries. He moves majestically from age to age, perfectly in control of every situation.

Sam Andrews was an inventor and entrepreneurial businessman in the late nineteenth century. Like many entrepreneurs of the Gilded Age, he wanted to strike it rich. In 1870 he garnered 10 percent ownership of a new company. However, he often disagreed with the business decisions of the company president and majority owner. Andrews wanted to be paid large dividends each year, while the president sought to reinvest company profits to expand the business. Over time this infuriated Andrews who resented the fact that his domineering partner always got his way. Finally, in 1878, when the president announced a 50 percent dividend on its stock, Andrews exclaimed: "I wish I was out of this business!" "What will you take for your holdings?" his partner asked. "I will take one million dollars," Andrews replied. The next day Andrews received a check for one million dollars. Ecstatic, he boasted that he had finally bested his partner and received an exorbitant return for his shares.

In truth, he had just made one of the costliest mistakes in business history. For his partner was John Rockefeller, and the company shares he had just sold were for Standard Oil. Rockefeller promptly sold Andrews's shares to William Vanderbilt for $1.3 million. Standard Oil would become legendary in American business, eventually growing so powerful the

American government forced it to subdivide into thirty-four smaller companies. Some of those lesser companies included Exxon, Mobil, Amoco, Chevron, Conoco, and British Petroleum. Had Andrews kept his shares, he would have owned 10 percent of each of those companies, and by the 1930s, he would have been worth $900 million. Instead, he constructed a massive five-story home in Cleveland with more than one hundred rooms that required more than one hundred staff to maintain. Andrews spent the remainder of his life bitterly complaining that Rockefeller had cheated him. He had taken a short-term perspective, and it cost him and his heirs. Rockefeller's long-term approach made him mythically wealthy.[20]

Investors have long known that impulsive or reactionary decisions can have disastrous consequences. During the 2000s, Warren Buffet was often criticized for not jumping on the dot-com bandwagon. People were becoming millionaires overnight by starting and selling their technology company. Yet Buffet shrewdly observed that the companies were grossly overvalued, and he knew time was the great leveler. Sure enough, many people lost fortunes when the market corrected itself while Buffet became one of the wealthiest people in the world.

Taking a long-term view is typically good for business, as well as many other professions. If you dream of being a professor one day, you must be willing to invest the time and effort to first earn a PhD. Becoming a medical doctor requires years of intense training. A promotion into upper management typically follows a period of effective work in the lower ranks. It is easier to make sacrifices today if you understand where those efforts will lead tomorrow.

The parable of the prodigal son is the classic tale of someone whose impatience led to disaster (Luke 15:11–32). In his desire for immediate independence, he forsook his father and alienated his brother. Then he foolishly squandered his entire inheritance as if there were no tomorrow. Finally coming to his senses, the young man realized he had lived extravagantly for a brief time and now was doomed to live his remaining years in poverty. Only the gracious forgiveness of his father spared him the squalid life he deserved.

People who take a long-term mentality generally act more prudently, fruitfully, and wisely than those who do not. If patience is a virtue in our business, careers, and families, it is even more so in our relationship with God. God views every person and situation with eternity as the backdrop. Every act of God has eternal ramifications.

Predestined and Prophesied

God is never caught by surprise. He never makes rash decisions. Because of our limited perspective, we can be enticed by the glitter of dazzling opportunities and seduced by short-term gains. God, however, views every situation in our lives both from eternity past and eternity future.

The Bible indicates that God has been working out his purposes on Earth since before time began. Paul declared: "He predestined us to be adopted as sons through Jesus Christ for himself, according to the good pleasure of his will. . . . In him we have also received an inheritance, because we were predestined according to the plan of the one who works out everything in agreement with the purpose of his will" (Eph. 1:5, 11). One of the more controversial Christian doctrines is that of predestination. The fundamental truth addressed by it is that God began working out his purposes for our lives long before we were born. When God intends to work through your life today, he begins preparing years, or generations before. God has had the benefit of eternity past to ensure he has everything in place so you can successfully accomplish his will today.

When God first spoke to Moses, he said, "I am the God of your father, the God of Abraham, the God of Isaac, and the God of Jacob" (Exod. 3:6). In part God was assuring Moses that the same God who worked mightily through previous generations was now prepared to work in his life as well. But God was also inviting Moses into the activity he had commenced centuries before through Abraham, Isaac, and Jacob. Moses did not need to be afraid of the assignment God was giving him. Every detail in heaven and on the earth was in place for Moses to fulfill his divine purpose.

Jesus, of course, had a special calling as the Messiah that is unlike ours. Nevertheless, we learn much about God's ways as we examine how the Father prepared for his Son's ministry on the earth. When did God the Father first know that his Son would come to the earth to die for humanity's sins? He understood that from all eternity. Consider Mary and Joseph, Jesus's parents. It is unlikely that as the first century commenced, God began searching throughout Israel to find a suitable Jewish woman to bear his Son. Just as God knew his plans for Jeremiah and David before they were born, so God knew his purpose for Mary and Joseph before the universe was formed (Ps. 139:13–18; Jer. 1:5). Joseph did not play a role in procreating Jesus, but he was responsible for rearing him and protecting him from Herod, the paranoid king who wanted the child murdered. God prepared Joseph so when the crucial day arrived, he would believe his fiancée when she told him she had become pregnant by the Holy Spirit. What typical Jewish man would have left his business and fled to Egypt to protect a child that was not his and a wife who, in the world's eyes, had betrayed him? (Matt. 2:13–15). God chose this amazing, ordinary couple as the perfect parents to nurture and teach his only Son.

Even as God created Adam and Eve, he knew that one day two of their distant descendants, Joseph and Mary, would be tasked with bringing up and protecting the world's Savior. Consider what a miracle it was that Joseph and Mary were ever born. God launched the human race through Adam and Eve, from whom Joseph and Mary would come. But the human population was obliterated in a catastrophic flood. Yet Joseph and Mary's ancestry came through Noah and Shem, two of only six people to survive the deluge (Luke 3:36). Through the centuries, the land of Israel was constantly invaded. Entire cities were destroyed or taken into exile. Joseph and Mary's ancestors survived when thousands of others were killed or lost to history. Joseph and Mary's ancestors overcame the Babylonian exile and returned to Israel so this couple would be in place for the birth of the Messiah.

You might find the genealogical tables in the Bible rather boring (Matt. 1:1–17; Luke 3:23–38), but they represent many fascinating stories of how God worked through generation after generation until Joseph and Mary were in position to parent the baby Jesus. Consider one of the most bizarre accounts in the Bible. Both Mary and Joseph traced their lineage through Judah. When God saw that Jacob loved Rachel but not Leah, God had compassion on Leah and initially granted her four sons (Gen 29:31–35). Then she stopped bearing children for a time. Judah was the fourth son. Judah's first son was Er. He married Tamar. Er was so evil that God struck him dead (Gen. 38). In that culture, a surviving brother was obligated to marry his brother's widow and help her conceive a child who could care for her in her old age. Judah's second son, Onan, married Tamar. He was so wicked that God struck him dead too. Imagine! God planned to make Tamar one of the ancestors of the Messiah, yet God killed her first two husbands because they were so wicked. Judah was understandably leery of having his third son, Shelah, marry Tamar, so he delayed fulfilling this obligation. Mary and Joseph's existence hinged on Tamar's having a child, yet it seemed increasingly unlikely.

This is when the story gets even stranger. Judah's wife died. He went to Timnah to shear his sheep. Hearing of this, Tamar dressed as a prostitute and waited beside the road for Judah to pass. Thinking she was a prostitute, he propositioned her and slept with her. As a result, Judah impregnated his daughter-in-law. She ultimately gave birth to twins, Perez and Zerah. It is through Perez that the Messiah would trace his earthly lineage. In one of Scripture's most baffling moments, had Tamar not seduced her father-in-law, Joseph and Mary would never have existed.

Consider some of the other colorful individuals in Jesus's family tree. There is Rahab, perhaps a prostitute, living in Jericho, a city designated to be destroyed, leaving no survivors. Yet God determined to have Rahab as a part of the lineage that produced the Messiah (Josh. 2:1–24; 6:22–25; Matt. 1:5). Had she alerted the authorities when the two Jewish spies approached her, she would never have joined the Israelites and survived their assault. What if, in the melee of Jericho's walls falling and Hebrew soldiers pouring into the doomed city, an overly enthusiastic Hebrew soldier had struck her with a sword? What if no self-respecting Hebrew man were willing to marry a former prostitute from Jericho? Joseph might never have been.

Consider the fact that King Solomon was an ancestor of Jesus. Solomon's mother, Bathsheba, was an adulteress (2 Sam. 11–12:25; Matt. 1:6). Mosaic law prescribed death for such sins. At the very least, holy God could have commanded David to choose a different, more respectable son to succeed him as king. Solomon's older brother died as an infant, but Solomon survived. What if Solomon's older half brother, Adonijah, had been successful in usurping the throne for himself when he sought to claim it as the oldest son of the king (1 Kings 1)? What if the prophet Nathan and the warrior Benaiah had sided with Adonijah instead of Solomon? Perhaps Solomon, rather than Adonijah, would have met a grisly end (1 Kings 2:13–25).

Or what of Ruth and Boaz? Had Ruth's first husband not died, and had she not chosen to return to Bethlehem with her widowed mother-in-law, Joseph and Mary would not have been born (Ruth 4:18–22).

Manasseh was arguably the most wicked king ever to rule Judah (2 Kings 21:1–18). He would inflict so much evil upon Judah that even the godly king Josiah could not overcome the damage that was done (2 Kings 23:26–27). But Manasseh is also in Jesus's family tree. His father, Hezekiah, was one of the better kings of Judah. One day the prophet Isaiah informed Hezekiah to get his house in order for he was going to die soon. Hezekiah pled with God to spare his life and grant him more time. God graciously extended Hezekiah's life by fifteen years (Isa. 38). During those years Hezekiah's wife gave birth to Manasseh. Had God not extended Hezekiah's life, Jesus's family tree would have been disrupted. Bible scholars have mused over why God granted Hezekiah bonus years when he knew it would produce such grave harm to the nation. Yet for God to fulfill his plan for Mary and Joseph to care for the Messiah, Manasseh's birth was necessary. Joseph and Mary could take pride in ancestors such as Abraham and David. Others, such as Manasseh, may have been genealogical "placeholders," necessary so the line of descendants continued and key members of the family tree were born.

These are some of the most obvious "chances" of history that had to occur for Joseph and Mary to be born and entrusted with Jesus during the first century. But there are many other events in history that God would have to providentially oversee if his choice of Joseph and Mary was to eventually occur. We can't know the large number of variables—a freak accident, a potential fatal illness, a near miscarriage, an epidemic, food poisoning, or a stray arrow in battle—that, had these situations gone slightly differently, would have caused a crucial ancestor to die prematurely.

For God to accomplish his eternal purposes upon the earth, countless details must align perfectly. Key people must survive until they give birth to a specific child. Certain couples must meet and marry. Individuals must survive plagues, battles, and violent crimes. God planned, before he ever created the earth, that Mary and Joseph would care for his Son. He perfectly orchestrated events throughout history to bring his plan to fruition.

Family Trees

If you ever need to be reminded of how much you owe to God, consider how many factors had to be just right for you to be born. We all have unique and varied lives. Some come from a strong Christian heritage while others are first-generation believers. Nonetheless, God has a purpose for every life. In one way or another, he has presided over events so you could be alive to read these pages.

I, like you, have a divine purpose. I have discovered some of that purpose over the years, but I suspect there is more. I am not sure if God intends for me to do anything particularly noteworthy. I may be primarily destined to be a placeholder for one of my grandchildren. But it is humbling to consider some of what God has done just so I could have my brief moments on the earth. For example, my mother became gravely ill and went into a coma when she was five years old. Doctors told my grandmother that if her daughter ever regained consciousness, she would suffer debilitating brain damage. My paternal grandfather, Gerald Richard Blackaby, fought in many of the major battles of the First World War. He was wounded twice. One day he was summoned to his officer's quarters. Upon returning to his post, he found a crater where he had previously been stationed. An enemy artillery shell had struck moments before. On another occasion his unit was ordered to advance across no-man's-land. As he began to climb out of the trench, he realized his machine gun was malfunctioning. His best friend, Jack, offered to take his place so he could repair his weapon. Jack was killed moments later. I am keenly aware that, but for the slightest change in my grandfather's circumstances, I would never have been born. Those are just two instances from my mother's and father's families. But I have no way of knowing the many occasions, through the generations, where one of my relatives was spared almost certain death. Should I learn the untold times when God protected an ancestor of mine, I'm sure I would fall to my knees in wonder at the goodness and omniscience of God.

Of course, God does not always prevent people from dying. There were millions of young men who died during World War I, even as my grandfather was spared. I cannot know the sovereign mind of God on those matters. However, you are alive and reading these pages, so God also protected your family tree until this moment.

Your life, like mine, has been largely influenced by decisions many people made in preceding generations. You may have had a grandfather who launched out and started a business. Now you may work for that company and, as a result, have opportunities to serve God. You may have a great-grandparent who lived a saintly life, and your generation is still blessed by that faithfulness. I often wonder how much our lives are impacted by the prayers of relatives we never met.

I have a businessman friend named Brett. His father was also a businessman who had no time for the Christian faith. But after coming to his own faith, Brett was drawn to participate in various Christian causes and ministries and is currently employed in mission work to the business community. A few years ago, he opened a box he had inherited. It was filled with sermon notes from messages his great-grandfather had delivered seventy years earlier. Brett was surprised to discover that his great-grandfather had been an itinerant preacher. One man had minimized his father's Christian influence, but that influence, nevertheless, made it to the fourth generation.

I am aware of a few decisions my relatives made that have greatly impacted me. My grandfather sensed God's leading him to emigrate from England (a country he loved and to which he was deeply loyal) to Canada. Therefore, my father and his brothers, as well as their children, grew up in Canada rather than England. (I have always regretted not growing up with a British accent!) My grandfather loved books. He wrote several poems that were published. Perhaps his interest in writing contributed to my father, Henry Blackaby, ultimately authoring *Experiencing God*.[21] All five of my parents' children have written books. All three of my children have been published. But perhaps the writing that has been prevalent in my family tree is merely preparation for a Christian classic my great grandchild will pen one day.

We must recognize that God's work in our life did not begin with us. God has been active through each generation. Knowing this gives our life a larger perspective than merely focusing on the present. God may have saved your great-grandparent from a potentially lethal farming accident because he intended to use your life to make a significant contribution to his kingdom one day. You may be a first-generation Christian. You don't have a Christian legacy. Perhaps God, in his grace, desired to change the trajectory of your family. He pursued you and loved you until you accepted his gift of salvation. Now you are the first Christian in your family. You can't know what effect that will have on your great-grandchildren. Will your future descendants look back on your life as the turning point in their family tree? Will a great champion for the faith arise from your descendants because you infused a godly influence into your children?

Since God is eternal, he never merely looks at your life. He views your life in the context of all he has done in your ancestors and all he will do in your descendants in the generations to come. The God who works in your life is eternal; therefore, your life is part of something far larger than you know.

The God who works in your life is eternal; therefore, your life is part of something far larger than you know.

Our Response to God's Eternality

God did not make us primarily for time. He made us for eternity. The world is enamored with the moment. God looks beyond the present into eternity. Scripture declares: "The Lord is the everlasting God" (Isa. 40:28), and "From eternity to eternity, you are God" (Ps. 90:2). God's ways are fundamentally different from ours because only he has always been. Conversely, there was a time when humanity did not exist. God created people to live forever. We need to live our lives with this truth always before us.

Scripture affirms: "He has made everything appropriate in its time. He has also put eternity in their hearts" (Eccles. 3:11). We are eternal souls dwelling in temporal bodies. A. W. Tozer observed: "To be made for eternity and forced to dwell in time is for mankind a tragedy of huge proportions. All within us cries for life and permanence, and everything around us reminds us of mortality and change."[22] People have an innate longing to experience immortality. Many are convinced there must be more to their current life than what they observe. C. S. Lewis wrote:

"If I find in myself a desire which no experience in this world can satisfy, the most probable explanation is that I was made for another world."[23] Although we inhabit mortal, time-constrained bodies, our souls were designed to last forever. We are constantly being tempted and distracted by temporal concerns, yet God seeks to focus us on the eternal. Several eternal realities ought to consume our attention.

Eternal Relationship with God

Our earthly relationships can vacillate over time. Our best friends may change through the years. Married couples may experience varying degrees of intimacy. Colleagues at work come and go. Neighbors move away. Even our children grow up and leave the nest. Nevertheless, our relationship with Christ continues and will only deepen into eternity. God declared to his people: "I have loved you with an everlasting love" (Jer. 31:3). The psalmist announced that God's faithful love endures forever (Ps. 136:1). The way God loves us today is identical to the way he will love us a hundred million years from now. Our relationships with people, however, vacillate over time. It is tragic, therefore, when we allow people who temporarily pass through our life to harm or distract our walk with God. We will not always have that person in our life, but God remains forever.

God's Eternal Word

Because God is eternal, so is his word. The prophet Isaiah wrote: "The grass withers, the flowers fade, but the word of our God remains forever" (Isa. 40:8). The words of politicians, scientists, businesspeople, and well-meaning friends fade over time but not God's Word. It is just as powerful and relevant today as when he first spoke it. That is why, when modern psychological or sociological theories contradict Scripture, we should always cling to God's Word. It will still be standing strong long after formerly popular theories are consigned to the garbage bin as out-of-date.

Eternal People

One of the reasons people matter to God so much is because they are eternal. Houses, money, fame, and power are not. Jesus made clear that after the final judgment every person will either spend an eternity with him in heaven or suffer an eternity apart from him in hell (Matt. 25:46). Every person we encounter, whether it is our sweet four-year-old daughter or the rude customer service representative behind a counter, has an eternity stretching out before them. This ought to dramatically affect how we view, treat, and invest in people. Loving people is one of the greatest investments we can make. Those we encounter each day are not just people; they are eternal souls.

Eternal Purpose

Just as it is wise to invest in that which is eternal, it is also prudent to pursue our eternal calling. God sits upon his throne forever (Ps. 9:7). The destiny of every child of God is to one day bow before that throne and worship him (Phil. 2:9–11). Our ultimate purpose in life is to glorify God. Our calling is to live lives of worship. The apostle John described magnificent scenes in heaven. In one he wrote: "After this I looked, and there was a vast multitude from every nation, tribe, people, and language, which no one could number, standing before the throne and before the Lamb. They were clothed in white robes with palm branches in their hands. And they cried out in a loud voice: Salvation belongs to our God, who is seated on the throne, and to the Lamb! All the angels stood around the throne, and along with the elders and the four living creatures they fell facedown before the throne and worshiped God" (Rev. 7:9–11).

Every person has a rendezvous with eternity. Those who are Christians have a spot reserved in the heavenly choir. Eternity will not be sufficient for us to worship God to the degree he deserves. In heaven our adoration will have no end. In this life we worship imperfectly. One day our exaltation of the Savior will reach levels only possible in paradise. In this life we are often distracted, criticized, opposed, and persecuted for our desire to glorify Christ. But a day is coming when we will be free to do so with abandon. Paul testified: "Even though our outer person is being destroyed, our inner person is being renewed day by day. For our momentary light affliction is producing for us an absolutely incomparable eternal weight of glory. So we do not focus on what is seen, but on what is unseen. For what is seen is temporary, but what is unseen is eternal" (2 Cor. 4:16–18).

Though we cannot yet see our final, eternal home, it surely awaits us. Throughout our earthly sojourn, we progress steadily toward our ultimate calling.

Obedience with Eternal Results

To relate to an eternal God, we must adjust to his perfect timing. From God's perspective the span of a thousand years is like a day (Ps. 90:4). Yet he sees the eternal consequences of every act of obedience or disobedience. Adam and Eve viewed their eating of the fruit of one tree as an isolated and momentary indiscretion. God, however, saw the eternal destinies of all humanity forever changed because of that one sin. Likewise, one act of obedience can dramatically impact eternity for good. Consider, for instance, the well-known example of Edward Kimball. When his church, Mount Vernon Church, in Boston, held a series of revival meetings, Kimball felt led to visit one of the young men in his Sunday school class to make sure he had experienced salvation. When he arrived at Holton's Shoe Store where the student worked, Kimball began to have second thoughts. He later confessed:

> I started down to Holton's shoe store. When I was nearly there I began to wonder whether I ought to go just then during business hours. And I thought maybe my mission might embarrass the boy, that when I went away the other clerks might ask who I was, and when they learned might taunt Moody and ask if I was trying to make a good boy out of him. While I was pondering over it all I passed the store without noticing it. Then, when I found I had gone by the door I determined to make a dash for it and have it over at once.[24]

D. L. Moody became a Christian during Kimball's visit. He would become the greatest evangelist of his age. It has been estimated that over a million people entered heaven due to his speaking ministry. Only God knows the eternal ramifications of just one act of obedience. That is why he takes our obedience so seriously. He knows what is at stake!

Conclusion

We cannot understand God's ways if we do not view them in eternal terms. His love is constant. His power is unending. His rule is everlasting. Praise God there is no tumult so catastrophic, no evil so destructive, and no enemy so fierce that God ceases to do what he has always done. God is working in our life and world today. He is preparing us to spend the rest of our days enjoying and worshipping him throughout all eternity.

We must keep this reality in view as we go about our day. When we are angered by the obnoxious behavior of a colleague, we should consider eternity before we respond. In deciding to tithe or spend the money on a luxurious cruise, we ought to place eternity in the backdrop. When a married colleague at work flirts with us, we must keep eternity in mind. God does nothing in our life without considering the eternal ramifications. We should do likewise.

Questions for Reflection/Discussion

1. How does the knowledge that God is eternal affect how you trust him and respond to him?

2. Knowing your actions have eternal consequences, how does that affect how you behave?

3. How does the reality that every person you encounter has an eternal soul affect how you treat them?

4. What percentage of your time and money is invested in eternal things?

5. How does an eternal mindset affect how you view current events in your nation and in the world?

CHAPTER 9

GOD'S WAYS ARE SEQUENTIAL

I declare the end from the beginning, and from long ago what is not yet done, saying: my plan will take place, and I will do all my will.
(Isa. 46:10)

When the time came to completion, God sent his Son.
(Gal. 4:4)

I, like most fathers, was totally inexperienced at child-rearing when my wife and I became parents. We were, therefore, completely unprepared one Texas winter's day when our eighteen-month-old son Mike developed a fever. During his afternoon nap I heard a strange sound coming from the nursery. I rushed into the room and witnessed my son undergoing a febrile seizure. Holding my baby while he convulsed in my arms was the most terrifying moment I had ever experienced. We raced to the emergency room of the nearest hospital.

In our haste to get our child medical attention, I neglected to do several important tasks which I would later regret. For one, I had not taken time to put my shoes on, so I drove our standard transmission vehicle with bare feet. I had also not sought anyone's advice. Had I done so, they most likely would have suggested I remove Mike's outer clothes and give him Tylenol. I could have saved $800 in medical expenses since that is exactly what the emergency medical staff did. Had I prepared, I might have brought food and drink, so we were not famished while waiting to see a doctor. We had responded in haste, which often leads to regret.

God always acts in a planned, effective, methodical manner. This is one of the ways in which God is highly predictable. His ways are sequential, not random. God takes no shortcuts, is not impulsive, and never panics. Understanding the sequential way God acts will greatly enhance our ability to recognize and anticipate his work in and around our life.

God always acts in a planned, effective, methodical manner.

God Acts Sequentially

Everything God does today is based on what he has done before and what he intends to accomplish tomorrow. Each act of God builds on what has gone before. He steadily and methodically progresses with his eternal purposes on the earth. This is evident in several ways.

Messiah

When God created humanity, he knew full well what it would ultimately cost him. He understood that Adam and Eve would sin and the only remedy would be the death of his Son. Undoubtedly, creation was one of God's most loving acts, for it cost him the ultimate sacrifice.

Long before God created the universe, he already had a redemptive plan in place to restore his fallen creatures. Even as he fashioned Adam and Eve, he knew how he would redeem them from their future rebellion. After the couple sinned, God first spoke of the future Messiah (Gen. 3:15). God was fully prepared to respond the moment his creatures sinned. We might ask, "Could God have sent Jesus to die on a cross for Adam and Eve in the garden? Could the first church have been established in paradise?" Clearly God deemed preliminary steps to be necessary before he provided the ultimate salvation for sinful humanity. Adam would live to be 930 (Gen. 5:5). His descendants would also experience longevity, such as Seth (912 years), Kenan (910 years), Mahalalel (895 years), Jared (962 years), Methuselah (969 years), and Lamech (777 years). Centuries passed, but the Messiah did not come.

Rather than sending a Savior, God dispatched a cataclysmic flood. Humanity had degenerated into sin and debauchery to the extent that God determined to judge the earth. Only Noah's family was spared. Yet, even though Noah was the most righteous man on the earth, he and his children soon demonstrated their propensity to sin (Gen. 9:18–27). Generations came and went without the advent of the Messiah. Then one day God approached a shepherd named Abram and told him he was going to make a mighty nation from his descendants (Gen. 12:1–3). Though Abram was seventy-five at that time, the Lord waited an additional twenty-five years before he granted the patriarch his promised child. Abraham lived to be 175. Isaac lived to be 180. Jacob died at 147. Yet, after these patriarchs passed from the scene, their descendants remained in Egypt for four hundred years. Century after century passed. It appeared as if God had forgotten his promise to Abraham.

Finally, God approached a fugitive named Moses as he was tending sheep in the backside of the desert. Through Moses,

God launched a massive rescue operation of his people from slavery in Egypt. God gave his people the law. He established clear standards for holy living and acceptable sacrifice. With the law, sin was clearly identified and sacrifices for sins spelled out. For over a thousand years, God's people observed the law, albeit often poorly. Many centuries after Moses, God promised that King David would always have a descendant upon the throne, and this came to be seen as the promise of a coming Messiah (Ps. 89:3–4, 27–29, 35–37; 132:11–12; 2 Sam. 7:16; Mic. 5:2). A millennium would pass after King David ruled before the Messiah finally arrived. During that time God dispatched many prophets, including Isaiah and Jeremiah, to urge God's people to repent of their sins and return to God. When they refused, God sent enemies and crises to humble them. Then they would cry out to him for deliverance. Eventually, God removed the entire northern nation of Israel into captivity at the hands of the Assyrians, yet God's people descended even further into apostacy. God used the Babylonians under King Nebuchadnezzar to destroy Jerusalem, along with the temple, and take the remaining Israelites into exile for seventy years. Even after their return, God's people often chose a form of religion over an authentic relationship with God. Eventually, God stilled the voice of the prophets for four hundred years until, suddenly, John the Baptist appeared on the scene, proclaiming the Messiah's coming was at hand. Soon thereafter Jesus of Nazareth commenced his public ministry. He performed astonishing miracles and drew large crowds, yet the religious leaders hated him and plotted to murder him. After many thousands of years of preparation, God's plan appeared to be tragically thwarted when the Roman governor Pilate ordered Roman soldiers to crucify Jesus. Nevertheless, God had designed all along for his Son to die so humanity might be saved.

Jesus's disciples might have assumed that, after his resurrection, Christ would establish his earthly kingdom. Instead, Jesus ascended to heaven and launched the church. For two thousand years Jesus's disciples have spread the gospel around the world. The church has often lost its focus or became corrupt, yet God revives it and draws his people back to himself. Though often splintered and distracted, the church, God's people, continues to be God's means of spreading the good news of salvation to each new generation that populates the earth. For two millennia God could have brought history to a close at any moment. He could have vanquished every rebel and banished Satan and his minions to the lake of fire. Yet he continues to steadily work out his purposes throughout the centuries.

God is never in a hurry, according to human standards. To him a thousand years is as a day (Ps. 90:4; 2 Pet. 3:8). He allows centuries to pass while he puts everything in place for his will to be done. He will take as long as necessary to ensure that each one of his purposes is accomplished, just as he intended.

Preparation

God is masterful in his preparation. Before God works through people, he works in them. God called Abraham to be the father of God's people. Then God took twenty-five years to prepare him. Not only did Abraham need to learn to *be* a patriarch; he had to learn how to *raise* a patriarch. God had Moses trained in the greatest leadership schools in Egypt for forty years. Then God trained him in the wilderness for the next forty. At age eighty Moses was finally ready to guide God's people. God anointed David to be the king of Israel and took him from tending sheep to shepherding God's people. But first David spent years running for his life from King Saul. During that time David grew in stature with God and with people (and wrote the lyrics to some amazing music!) before eventually becoming the greatest king in his nation's history and an ancestor of the Messiah. When Jesus called his twelve disciples, he took three and a half years to teach them before he issued the Great Commission. Paul met the risen Christ on the road to Damascus but then spent years in obscurity, studying and honing his message before commencing his missionary journeys.

God is infinitely powerful. If he so chose, he could fully equip people to serve him the instant he called them. But God's preferred method is to take time to prepare his servants before he uses them. At times people are unaware God is readying them for a divine assignment. For years Peter, Andrew, James, and John invested themselves in the fishing business. They would learn that God can take our past training and experiences and use them for an entirely new purpose (Mark 1:16–17). As a youth David learned to be a shepherd. He could not have imagined that God was preparing him to shepherd the nation of Israel (Ps. 78:70–72). Every life experience can be used by God as preparation for what he intends to accomplish through us next.

Babies: God's Work Often Begins Small

When we experience a crisis, we naturally want God to rescue us immediately. However, God's way has often been to send a baby. It seems counterintuitive. Why send a baby when we need a full-grown deliverer? Yet God often wraps his answers to our prayers in small packages. When God announced to Abram he would build a nation out of his descendants, Abram was seventy-five years old and childless. He would wait, in faith, for twenty-five years for the promised infant (Gen. 12–21). When the Hebrews were toiling under the oppressive subjugation of the Egyptians, God sent a baby named Moses and then miraculously preserved his life when it easily could have been extinguished (Exod. 2:1–10). When the Philistines were severely oppressing the Hebrews, God sent a baby named Samson (Judg. 13). When the religious leaders under Eli became corrupt, God honored

Hannah's pleas and Samuel was born (1 Sam. 1:19–27; 3:19). When the time drew near for the Messiah to come, God sent a baby to Elizabeth (Luke 1:5–25).

Most spectacularly, of course, was when God chose to send the Messiah, the world's Savior. He did so by granting a baby to a poor, engaged couple, Joseph and Mary, causing no small scandal. The infant arrived while the couple was away from home, in Bethlehem, and they had to resort to a stable in which to give birth.

Imagine the numerous steps the baby Jesus had to progress through before he could assume his role as Messiah. He had to learn to eat solid food, crawl, and then walk. He learned to talk and read. Surely, God could have sent a fully grown Messiah to Earth had he chosen to, but that was not his way. We wonder what Joseph taught his son as he was growing up in his home. How many times did the child Jesus witness someone come to his family home with something broken they needed Joseph to fix? How often did someone stop at Jesus's house to ask Joseph to build something new? When did young Jesus realize he could build and repair people, not just tables and chairs?

Bible scholars estimate that Jesus was approximately thirty-three years old when he began his public ministry. The eternal Son of God, the world's Savior, lived in obscurity as an ordinary human being for over three decades. For centuries people have speculated about what his childhood was like. When did he realize he could perform miracles? When did he first understand he was the Messiah? What did he think when he read Isaiah 53? The Bible is silent on such matters. Jesus grew up in humble circumstances. His father was an ordinary working man who lived in a nondescript village in a backwater region where nothing of historical significance had ever occurred. Jesus did not commence his public ministry until he was fully prepared for the undertaking.

When God initiates a major work, he often begins with something small. Jesus declared that the kingdom of God was like a miniscule mustard seed or like leaven, both of which grow exponentially over time (Matt. 13:31–33). The world is mesmerized by enormous and grandiose efforts. God cautioned people not to despise small things (Zech. 4:10). Jesus warned that unless people assumed the attitude of a small child they could not enter God's kingdom (Matt. 18:1–5). Why would the Creator of the universe, the one who measures the heavens by the span and weighs the mountains in a scale, do anything in a small way? (Isa. 40:12). Why would the most powerful being in the universe delight in small things?

Arthur Wallis, in his book *In the Day of Thy Power,* notes that the beginning of the eighteenth century was a spiritual low point for England.[25] Material prosperity was rising because of trade with the colonies. Secular philosophers such as Hobbes and Locke had challenged many traditional beliefs. David Hume and Edward Gibbon denied cherished Christian assumptions. Crime and immorality were rampant. The church was at a low ebb. Many devout Christians prayed earnestly for revival. God answered their supplications by sending three babies. In 1703, John Wesley, Gilbert Tennant, and Jonathan Edwards were born. Though people desperately longed for immediate revival, these three infants, along with others, had to grow up, be educated, be converted, and respond to God's call before they were ready to be God's instruments for revival. Wesley would launch a revival movement across England that may well have spared it from the violent revolution that engulfed France. Tennant and Edwards would be used powerfully to fan the flames of the First Great Awakening in America. The birth and maturation of a child reflects God's long-term perspective and timing. You must wait for children to mature before they exert their maximum effect.

God recognizes the enormous significance of that which is small. So should we.

Seasons

The writer of Ecclesiastes sagely observed: "To everything there is a season" (Eccles. 3:1 NKJV). God designed nature to follow a predictable, progressive pattern. He established laws that govern the earth's seasons. Likewise, the Christian life can be compared to the unfolding of nature as God designed. Spring is a time of beginnings. What you plant in spring determines what you harvest in fall. Paul observed: "Don't be deceived: God is not mocked. For whatever a person sows he will also reap" (Gal. 6:7). Summer is a period of maturing and growth. You cannot plant seeds one day and expect a harvest the next. Summer's heat must first do its ripening work. Fall is harvest time, that yields the reward for planting in spring and maturing in summer. Winter is a season of decline and endings. In nature's economy God designed a season in which growth ends and death results. Yet, regardless of winter's severity, spring inevitably returns. God established nature to follow a predictable pattern. The earth is generally not random or arbitrary.

To experience the kind of life God intends, we must align ourselves with God's timing and spiritual laws. Just as each season has a particular characteristic and function, so our life flows through seasons.[26] What you sow into your life is what you will eventually reap. If you work hard early in your career, you will reap the benefits when you are older. Couples who invest in their marriage will enjoy a rewarding family life. Conversely, if you quit when you face adversity or avoid hard work or preparation, you will inevitably be unprepared when opportunities come. If you invest in your walk with God, you will harvest much spiritual fruit.

Movies sometimes promote the illusion that we can decide something one morning and be reaping spectacular results later that afternoon. Yet God has established processes by which life's possibilities eventually become reality. A summertime of heat, water, and maturation must first take place. Paul exhorted: "Let us not get tired of doing good, for we will reap at the proper time if we don't give up" (Gal. 6:9). One of life's sinister temptations is to become impatient with God's timing and processes. The world offers numerous "shortcuts" to God's purposes for our lives, but they generally prove disappointing.

We must make countless decisions in terms of how we will invest our time, energy, and money. The choices we make can produce divergent results.

- Do I rise earlier to spend time in prayer and Bible study, or do I try to get more sleep?
- Do I participate in a Bible study at my church or use that time to catch up on tasks around the house?
- Do I spend more money on a larger house, or do I purchase a less expensive home and use the money saved to go on creative mission trips with my family?
- Do I keep working through the evenings or play board games with my children?
- Do I watch television or read a book?
- Do I exercise or play video games?
- Do I go to bed early or stay up late surfing the web?

God has built systems, principles, and seasons into the fabric of creation. He has determined that we reap what we have sown. His desire is to produce a bountiful harvest in and through us. He is willing to take all the time necessary to help us grow and mature for this to happen. For us to embrace God's will for our life, we must follow God's prescribed order for living.

Responding to God's Prescribed Order

If life's success and blessings depend on living in sync with God's ways, it is essential to understand them so we know what to expect and how to live. Consider the following suggestions:

View Life from God's Perspective

Many of God's greatest accomplishments have involved ordinary people. God launched a nation through one elderly, childless couple named Abram and Sarai. God took a remnant of exiles from Babylon and reestablished his people in Jerusalem. Jesus gathered a handful of ordinary people and launched a worldwide movement. When the church was birthed in the first century, it was dwarfed by other religions. The mighty Roman Empire dominated the known world. Yet Christianity would eventually become the official religion of the empire and ultimately the dominant religion worldwide. History is filled with examples of nondescript Christians, groups, churches, and faith-based organizations that grew to become a major force in their day.

On January 6, 1850, a snowstorm struck London. The minister of the Primitive Methodist Chapel on Artillery Street in Colchester, Essex, was unable to make it to the church building. A tall, thin uneducated layman with a feeble voice filled the pulpit in place of the stranded minister. He delivered an impromptu, simple sermon based on Isaiah 45:22, to the fifteen people who made it to the service that day. Unbeknown to the speaker, a fifteen-year-old, visiting the church, gave his life to Christ that blustery day. The teenager was Charles Spurgeon, who would become the greatest preacher of his day.

On September 23, 1857, Jeremiah Lanphier started a prayer meeting in New York City. Its inaugural gathering drew six people, but it was soon attracting tens of thousands throughout the city, and within a year one million people across America were converted.

In 1904, a twenty-six-year-old coal miner named Evan Roberts asked his minister in Loughor, Wales, if he could address the Monday night prayer service to share what God had laid on his heart. The minister was unwilling to allow Roberts's time in the scheduled service but informed those gathered that Roberts would speak to whomever chose to remain after the prayer service concluded. Seventeen people lingered to hear him. Soon revival had come to Wales and one hundred thousand people were converted in the span of six months.

In April 1970, a young minister by the name of Henry Blackaby moved his family to Saskatoon, Saskatchewan, Canada, to become the pastor of Faith Baptist Church. The congregation had dwindled to fewer than a dozen people and was considering selling its property and disbanding. Over the next twelve years, dozens of new churches were started, a Bible college established, and more than one hundred people called into ministry. Blackaby would eventually write what he learned in *Experiencing God: Knowing and Doing the Will of God*. Millions of people worldwide would be challenged and revived through the truths taught in that study.

God is certainly capable of initiating great works in large and dramatic fashion. He could send a comet across the skies to announce a revival or dispatch an angelic choir to proclaim a spiritual awakening. But typically, God chooses to commence his work in unspectacular, humble ways.

God's people must learn to recognize God's hand in the midst of ordinary circumstances. When the prophet Elijah prayed for God to send rain to end a three-and-a-half-year drought in Israel, he commissioned his servant to watch the horizon to see if God's answer was coming. The prophet prayed seven times. Each time the servant reported that nothing of significance was occurring. On the seventh time, the servant reported, "There's a cloud as small as a man's hand coming up from the sea" (1 Kings 18:44). Elijah instantly knew what this meant. He understood that God could take a mere wisp of a cloud and create a torrential downpour, thus ending a devastating drought. What seems small to us can have an enormous impact in the hand of God!

View Life as a Divine Process

Growing up in Western Canada, I struggled to learn French in high school. However, it was a requirement for my university hopes so I gave it a valiant effort. My French teacher spoke only French in class and expected us to "pick it up." I did not. One day I gave a particularly cringeworthy answer to a question, and her exasperation got the better of her: "Richard Blackaby, you have a fungus for a brain!" she intoned. At that moment I realized I was not destined to be the ambassador to France. I also did not bother to enroll in French for my final year of high school, assuming I was not smart enough to learn the language or attend university.

Nonetheless, I was admitted into university as a history major where, thankfully, I was no longer required to take classes in French, chemistry, or algebra. University prepared me for seminary, where I earned a master of divinity degree. Now I was focusing on theology and church history. These subjects were in my wheelhouse, and eventually I was encouraged to consider pursuing PhD studies.

Initially, I was intoxicated with exhilaration at the dizzying academic heights I had reached on my educational odyssey, until I read the requirements for entrance into the PhD program. Two years of German and one year of *French*. My heart sank. There was no way. A voice echoed from the past, "Fungus brain!" I had to decide whether my life was fixed in time or God was moving me to a different stage. Would I always find learning foreign languages to be impossible? Could God lift me up out of previous failure and do a new work in my life?

I applied to the PhD program. I was fortunate enough to have a compassionate, gifted French and German professor who was determined to help me succeed. Looking back on all the opportunities that having a PhD have afforded me, I am so thankful God works steadily and progressively in our lives.

God does not intend for anyone to be stuck in the same place, as if serving a perpetual life sentence. Your father may have declared that you would never amount to anything, but God can free you from that curse and do beautiful things in your life. You may have suffered from a painful divorce, but God can bring love and joy into your life once more. You may have failed in your effort to serve God, but he can raise you up from the ashes and do an amazing work through you. Satan will lie to you and pronounce that there is no more to your life than your present, or past, experience. But with God there is always another chapter to your story (Isa. 43:18–19)!

Jacob was a manipulator who cheated his brother and deceived his father. Yet God had far more in store for him than his scheming. Jacob would eventually take his place as a revered patriarch of his people and give his name, Israel, to his descendants. Moses was a murderer and a fugitive. Yet God would raise him up to be one of his mightiest servants. David was the youngest of eight sons, the baby of his family. His own father could not imagine God using his life in any significant way (1 Sam. 16:11). Later, David was a fugitive, fleeing from the crazed and jealous King Saul. Castigated by the king and declared public enemy number one, David spent years in a frustrated and perilous limbo. Later, as king, David would make several serious mistakes that drew dire consequences. Yet in each case that was not the end of the story. God had great plans for David. Zacchaeus had been given a name by his parents that meant "righteous one" or "innocent." Nevertheless, he had tarnished his name so terribly it seemed impossible for him to reclaim it. Yet one encounter with Christ transformed years of compromise, greed, and deceit (Luke 19:1–10). Mary Magdalene descended so far into the depths of evil she was occupied by seven demons, yet Jesus set her free and gave her a significant role among the early disciples (Luke 8:2; Mark 15:40–41; John 19:25–20:18).

The Christian life is a progressive journey. Along the way we may endure great pain and suffering, as well as success and advance. However, until we enter heaven's gates, we always have new opportunities for growth. Our current situation, whatever it may be, is not the end of our story. It is merely the next chapter as God steadily and intentionally works out his eternal purposes in our life. We must remain alert and expectant. God still has another chapter in our story to come.

The Folly of Taking Shortcuts

One of Satan's most diabolical deceptions is tempting us to take shortcuts. He tried to trap Jesus this way (Matt. 4:1–11; Luke 4:1–13). "Do a miracle to gather an instant following," or "Worship Satan and have numerous followers handed to you and bypass a painful death on a cross." But with God, how we do something is as important as what we do. Sarah grew weary of waiting on God to provide her a child, so she capitulated to an accepted local practice and gave her maid, Hagar, to her husband. Yet God refused to allow Abraham and Sarah to cut corners on the miracle he intended. Moses attempted to deliver some fellow Hebrews by killing an Egyptian taskmaster, but that effort cost him forty years herding sheep in the wilderness. When

Moses finally followed God's way, the entire Egyptian army was destroyed, Pharaoh was humbled, the Egyptians were looted, and not one Hebrew life was lost.

Finding a fast track to do God's will can be extremely alluring. We can have the sincerest of motives. Many seminary students have lept at the opportunity to enter ministry immediately, so they quit school, only to find they are woefully unprepared for the hitherto unknown challenges of ministry. How many couples wed in haste, under the spell of infatuation, and spend years regretting their impulsiveness?

As we have seen, one of God's ways is that he works *in* people before he works *through* them. An impatience for the various steps God intends for us to take may reveal a character issue. This might show up in an unwillingness to be faithful in a little before asking God for more. Or perhaps we overestimate our own ability. Preparation may seem to be a waste of time if we "feel ready" now. In truth, we may simply be unwilling to pay the price required to become the kind of servant God uses mightily. Perhaps we sense God wants us to further our education or get in shape or upgrade our skills, but we don't want to put in the effort required. We may suffer from character issues that need to be addressed but be reluctant to expose our flaws to a leadership coach or counselor. As a result, we are not prepared for God to work through us as he might.

God's purpose for our life will inevitably involve pain, growth, and patience, yet it will lead to the greatest fruitfulness and joy. If we want to experience all God intends for us, we must be willing to follow his lead, one step at a time.

Trust God's Process

Ron Dunn once commented that, with God, "timing is more important than time."[27] If there is an area wherein people can struggle with Christ's lordship, it is in God's timing. It is not surprising that mortal beings, with a life span like a vapor, would struggle to relate to an eternal being. Nevertheless, one aspect of surrendering our wills to God is our acceptance of his time schedule.

Scripture is filled with exhortations to wait on the Lord. David wrote: "Wait for the LORD; be strong, and let your heart be courageous. Wait for the LORD" (Ps. 27:14). This is not always easy! Single adults, waiting on God's provision of a spouse, can grow impatient, even desperate. People suffering illness, while waiting on God's healing, can grow fainthearted. Leaders with a vision for a preferred future can become discouraged when progress appears to lag. Parents praying for a prodigal's return can begin to doubt that God will ever act. Though we loudly proclaim our trust in God, our worry and impatience negate our assertion. When we trust God and his ways, it means we accept his timing.

Jesus once told Peter: "Where I am going you cannot follow me now, but you will follow later" (John 13:36). Peter responded: "Lord, . . . why can't I follow you now? I will lay my life down for you" (v. 37). Jesus was preparing to go to the cross and undertake the greatest assignment in history. Peter assumed he was ready to go wherever Jesus went. He was wrong. Even as Peter boasted of his loyalty, Jesus warned he was on the precipice of his greatest failure. However, Jesus also assured Peter that a day was coming when Peter could indeed walk the same path as his Master.

God's timing is unfailingly accurate. He knows our capacity as well as our limitations. He will not grant us more than we are prepared to handle, despite our protestations that we are ready. If we will trust God with the care and direction of our life, we will discover that one step always leads to the next until we have ultimately experienced everything he intends.

The world's ways are not like God's ways. Modern culture is characterized by "instant" and "quick." The world tempts us with the least demanding, minimally sacrificial approach. The world encourages the young to sow their wild oats. The Bible cautions that we will not play with fire without suffering the consequences (Prov. 5; 6:27). The world frowns on delayed gratification and, instead, promotes indulging ourselves with pleasure now (Isa. 22:13; Luke 12:19; 1 Cor. 15:32). The world behaves as if this life is all there is, but Christians know better.

Even believers are not immune to a short-term mindset. The church often downsizes God's commands in its haste to obey him. Jesus commissioned his followers to make disciples (Matt. 28:19). This command is straightforward. Yet many churches have substituted Christ's command with their own reasoning. Making disciples takes time and requires effort, so the path of least resistance can prove too alluring for many churches to pass up. They bypass making disciples and, instead, merely gather church attenders. The Church Growth Movement promoted numerous methods for drawing a crowd, but it typically failed to equip believers to make disciples. Churches focused on attracting people to attend their church services, but the newcomers were not disciples. They did not follow Jesus wherever he led. They were not in a close, loving relationship with him. They did not do what Jesus commanded. In short, theirs was a shallow faith, too easily attained. Church leaders congratulated themselves on the growing attendance at their services. This was satisfactory until a church conflict arose or a more exciting church in the community launched services. Then a mass exodus would inevitably occur.

It is far easier to add church attenders than to make disciples. Offer Broadway-type music, entertaining sermons, and a flashy children's program, and people will show up. Disciple-making, however, is not as attractive. Discipleship asks people to deny themselves, take up their cross, and follow Christ (Matt. 16:24). This involves surrender of control and selflessly loving others. It is not a popular request to make. So many churches ignore Christ's command and engage in Madison Avenue marketing instead. The results come more quickly, but they are fleeting. Of course, the world's methods produce worldly results. Operating God's way, in his time, brings lasting, heavenly reward.

Conclusion

If you do not understand God's ways, you will regularly be confused by his will. While not everything God does is easy to understand, certain ways of God are consistent throughout the ages. We can expect that God will relate to us in a sequential and progressive manner. He takes time to do his work the proper way. He is never in a hurry. He refuses to take shortcuts. He does not leave important steps out. His way may take longer, but it produces the greatest long-term results.

If you have followed the world's ways in the past, you cannot go back in time and change that. However, God is masterful at taking us from where we are and wisely and progressively moving us forward to where he intends for us to be. Commit yourself afresh today, to live your life God's way in God's time.

Questions for Reflection/Discussion

1. Do you sense God leading you toward a specific goal? Are you willing to accept the steps required, or are you impatient for God to move more quickly?

2. What shortcuts have you been tempted to take in your service for God?

3. Are you comfortable with the small things God is doing in and around your life, or are you impatient for God to do a larger work?

4. What is God preparing you to do? Are you willing for God to take as long as he wants until you are ready?

5. Have you unconsciously downsized a work God wants to do in your life so it is something you can more easily accomplish?

CHAPTER 10

GOD'S WAYS POINT TO THE CROSS

"If anyone wants to follow after me, let him deny himself, take up his cross, and follow me."
(Matt. 16:24)

For the word of the cross is foolishness to those who are perishing, but it is the power of God to us who are being saved.
(1 Cor. 1:18)

On September 18, 1807, nineteen-year-old Adoniram Judson delivered the valedictorian address during his graduation ceremony at Brown University. Though his father was a Congregational minister, Judson had fallen under the skeptical influence of a college friend named Jacob Eames. Eames was an avowed Deist who rejected Scripture and denied that God, if he existed, had any interest in people. Judson eventually confessed to his parents that he did not share their religious beliefs. He set out to pursue a career in theater in New York City. One evening he came to a roadside inn to spend the night. The innkeeper warned him that in the room next to his was a young man who was dying. The noises in the night might be disturbing. Sure enough, all night long Judson heard sounds of people's voices, footsteps entering and departing the room, and a man's groaning. Throughout the night Judson was haunted by the thought that he, like the young man in the next room, would eventually die too. Was he prepared for that day? His secular philosophy offered him no assurances.

The next morning Judson learned, to his astonishment, that the young man who had died in the room next to his that night had been none other than Jacob Eames, the person who had encouraged him to abandon his faith in God. Judson surrendered his life to Christ. He completed a seminary degree at Andover and then set sail in 1813, along with his wife Anne, to be missionaries in Burma. The Judsons were brilliant, gifted, and dedicated to Christ. They gave their lives so the Burmese could hear the gospel.

Their first child died in a miscarriage en route to Burma. The Burmese people seemed largely indifferent to the gospel message. In the first twelve years of the Judson's labor, they only gained eighteen converts. During war with the British, the Burmese government imprisoned Judson and forced him to endure unimaginable horrors. Anne gave birth to a baby girl named Maria while Adoniram languished in prison. Eventually he was released, but Anne was so enfeebled that she could not nurse her baby. Judson had to go around to various nursing mothers begging them to share some milk with their baby. Eventually Anne succumbed to her illness, and later so did Maria. So distraught was Judson at his losses that he dug a grave and sat beside it, contemplating his own death.

Judson eventually married a widowed missionary named Sarah. Together they had eight children, five of whom survived to adulthood. Sarah ultimately died of disease, and Judson married Emily Chubbuck. At age sixty-one, suffering from a severe lung disease, Judson sailed for home after serving in Burma for thirty-seven years. He had only taken one trip home during that time. He died during the voyage.

Despite years of suffering and loss, Judson translated the Bible into the Burmese language. He started several churches and won many converts. Today he is honored as the spiritual father of Burmese Christians. Judson was a model of lifelong devotion and service to Christ. Yet much of his life was characterized by intense suffering and loss.[28]

The Way of the Cross

The Cross Appears as Foolishness

One of the most remarkable aspects of God's ways is that he often calls for sacrifice and suffering to accomplish his work. This is incomprehensible from a human perspective. Why would the all-powerful Creator and Sustainer of the universe require suffering from his servants to achieve his purposes? Even more unfathomable is why God would commission his only Son to undergo a tortuous death on a cross to fulfill his eternal plan.

Paul observed, "For the word of the cross is foolishness to those who are perishing, but it is the power of God to us who are being saved" (1 Cor. 1:18). For those who do not understand God's ways, willingly submitting oneself to death on a cross appears absurd. We understand how people might accept suffering to achieve their desired end. A mother will endure labor pains for the joy of embracing her child. Firefighters will risk their lives to save someone from an inferno. Soldiers will pay the ultimate sacrifice to defend their country. But why would an all-powerful God require his Son or his people to suffer when he has the power to achieve his will countless other ways? We cannot imagine King Nebuchadnezzar of Babylon or Queen Victoria at the height of their powers willingly sacrificing their own child to win a victory over their enemies. So, why does God choose suffering?

We instinctively recoil from pain. It is unpleasant. It connotes failure or even God's displeasure. It is for the vanquished, not the victor. When Jesus told his disciples he was destined to suffer many things in Jerusalem, Peter rebuked his rabbi, saying, "Oh no, Lord! This will never happen to you!" (Matt. 16:22). Who would stand by and let their friend suffer? Who would want to be a part of a movement where the leader was tortured and put to death? In any other setting, that would constitute an abysmal failure.

Yet Jesus's response was, "Get behind me, Satan! You are a hindrance to me because you're not thinking about God's concerns but human concerns" (Matt. 16:23). Peter's rebuke of his Lord was audacious. What drove him to act in such a disrespectful manner? Peter could not imagine any value or purpose to suffering and certainly not for their leader. Jesus, however, declared that to keep him from the cross was to be in league with Satan.

Christ was by no means diminishing the horrors of what was to come. In the garden, Jesus prayed, "My Father, if it is possible, let this cup pass from me" (Matt. 26:39). The cross was the Father's plan. Jesus went to the cross because his Father willed it. In his flesh Jesus recoiled at what awaited him at Calvary. He would have welcomed any reprieve his Father granted. But none came. Surely, had there been any other way to achieve the forgiveness of sins, the Father would have done so. But God, the Father, deigned that the supreme way to satisfy his holiness and also provide redemption for humanity was the horror of crucifixion. We must conclude, therefore, that there are times when God's perfect will can only be achieved through suffering. If God would not spare his own Son when suffering was required, then we cannot assume he will exempt us from it either if it is necessary (Matt. 16:24).

If God would not spare his own Son when suffering was required, then we cannot assume he will exempt us from it either if it is necessary.

Countless philosophers and theologians have speculated whether a loving God could have created a pain-free world. Presumably he could have. Yet, for God to make people in his image, they must have free will. Without freedom to choose, people might not be capable of committing adultery, murder, or waging war, but neither would they experience the ecstasy of freely loving, communing with, and worshipping God. God considered the benefits of freedom to outweigh the evil that would inevitably result from that freedom.

The only way to create a world without pain would be to create a world without freedom, which would lead to another form of hardship. And so, by allowing people to freely choose their actions, God made hardship inevitable. As a result, even as God fashioned the first creatures in his own image, he also signed a death sentence for his Son.

The Cross Embodies God's Ways

Holiness

The cross is the ultimate and clearest symbol of God's ways. One of the most important ways of God, vividly demonstrated at Calvary, is holiness. If you ever wonder how seriously God views sin, picture the cross. View the battered, scourged body of Jesus. Watch the blood pouring from his head, hands, and feet. Listen to his anguished cry, "My God, my God, why have you abandoned me?" (Mark 15:34). Read the prophet Isaiah's words: "Yet he himself bore our sicknesses, and he carried our pains;

but we in turn regarded him stricken, struck down by God, and afflicted. But he was pierced because of our rebellion, crushed because of our iniquities; punishment for our peace was on him. . . . Yet the LORD was pleased to crush him severely" (Isa. 53:4–5, 10). God treats his holiness with utmost gravity.

If you ever wonder how seriously God views sin, picture the cross.

To watch God pouring out his wrath upon his perfect, sinless, obedient Son should forever convince us of how vehemently God hates sin. As God's only Son was paying the full price for our iniquities, God the Father withheld none of his righteous wrath. Today many Christians delight in decorative crosses in their churches, artwork, and jewelry; yet the harsh truth is that crucifixion was the ghastliest form of capital punishment practiced by the Romans. It was so brutal, in fact, it was illegal for Roman citizens to be executed in such manner. If you are ever tempted to make light of your sin, return to the cross and cast your gaze upon your bloodied Savior. The cross loudly exclaims: God is holy! There is nothing trite, humorous, or excusable about sin.

Love

Even as we shudder at the horrific, unthinkable price Jesus paid at Calvary, we are overwhelmed at the magnitude of love demonstrated at that desolate place. The Bible says, "But God proves his own love for us in that while we were still sinners, Christ died for us" (Rom. 5:8). Though God's holiness demanded full payment for sin, his love compelled him to satisfy the astronomical price himself. Holiness and love are both perfectly displayed at Golgotha.

My parents served God faithfully for many years in three churches and later as denominational missionaries in Canada. Amid their frenetic schedule, they learned that their only daughter, age sixteen, had cancer. Doctors had found a spot on an X-ray two years earlier but had not followed up on it. Now the cancer had spread, and the prognosis was grim. My sister immediately began undergoing extensive chemotherapy and radiation treatments. She suffered terribly. During that time people wondered if my father's view of God's love had changed. My parents had faithfully served the Lord all their lives. It seemed that a loving God should have spared their teenage daughter the ravages of cancer. Yet my father declared: "I have stood before the cross and watched my Savior dying for me. I settled the matter at that moment: God loves me! Nothing can change that. No circumstance in my life can alter that fact. God, at the cross, forever settled the question: Does God love me?"[29]

Eternal

The cross also reveals how God's actions reflect his eternal perspective. The most beloved Scripture verse reminds us, "For God loved the world in this way: He gave his one and only Son, so that everyone who believes in him will not perish but have eternal life" (John 3:16). Even though this is sometimes viewed as a simple child's verse, it is deeply profound. What did Jesus mean when he used the word *perish*? If we could fully grasp the horror of that word, we would be forever grateful for God's mercy and grace. Biblically, to perish does not mean that you cease to exist. Rather, it describes an eternity separated from God in perpetual torment. Hell is an eternal place designed to punish Satan and his followers. Those who reject God will be consigned to that awful place forever. The reason God was willing to pay such an enormous price at the cross is because only he knew how immense the cost would be if he did not.

The verse goes on to say that those who place their faith in Christ will have eternal life. Eternal life entails far more than living forever. It is a quality of life in which people enjoy unending personal fellowship with God. The contrast is breathtaking; what hinged in the balance at the cross was an eternity apart from God or an eternity spent with him. That is why God was willing to forfeit so much.

Sin, Satan, Death, and Hell

There have been many watershed moments that forever altered history: Julius Caesar crossing the Rubicon, Napoleon's defeat at Waterloo, the Allied forces invading Europe on D-Day. Battles such as these changed the course of history. Yet no one passing by Jesus's cross that day could have imagined how his death would alter history (and eternity). Though people were accustomed to the gruesome sight of people being crucified along the roadside, no one had ever witnessed a death like this before. Every sin committed by anyone in history was nailed to that cross. Satan, who supposed he had successfully destroyed God's creation, would learn that sin now had an antidote and he had suffered a catastrophic defeat. In three days death, humanity's most sinister nemesis, would lose its vice grip. Hell would be robbed of countless millions of people because of one man affixed to a cross. Humanity's most diabolical foes were resoundingly vanquished at the cross. Though crucifixion was considered the most humiliating death imaginable, God would use it to achieve history's most glorious victory.

Beautiful

There was nothing attractive about watching someone bleeding and desperately gasping for breath, nailed to a sinister instrument of torture and death. Yet, to millions of people around the world, the cross holds a majestic, breathtaking beauty, for it represents the greatest story ever told.

It is the most tragic irony of the ages that creatures living on the brink of the abyss put to death the only one who could save them. The Romans designed the cross to terrify criminals and to dispense judgment. God transformed it into a symbol of grace and forgiveness. A crude device reserved for the worst of sinners, God used it to transform people into saints. There is no other story in literature that equals this. It is breathtaking in scope. The cross addresses every major issue of life. It answers humanity's fundamental questions. It offers hope to every person in every culture under every circumstance. Therein lies its beauty.

Relational

The Bible reveals God's relational character in a multitude of ways. That he desires a relationship with us cannot be questioned. The cross was his greatest expression of this truth. The cross demonstrates God's unwillingness to give up on his wayward people. It represents the highest price ever paid and for people who were entirely undeserving.

The prophet Isaiah wrote one of the most exalted books of Scripture. Through sixty-six chapters God continually exhorts his people to turn from their sin and to return to him. God looked to a day when fellowship would be restored with his people. He declared:

> I was sought by those who did not ask; I was found by those who did not seek me. I said, "Here I am, here I am," to a nation that did not call on my name. . . . For I will create new heavens and a new earth; the past events will not be remembered or come to mind. Then be glad and rejoice forever in what I am creating; for I

> will create Jerusalem to be a joy and its people to be a delight. I will rejoice in Jerusalem and be glad in my people. The sound of weeping and crying will no longer be heard in her. . . . Even before they call, I will answer; while they are still speaking, I will hear. (Isa. 65:1, 17–19, 24)

From Genesis to Revelation, we read that God is seeking to restore fellowship with his sinful people (Rev. 21:1–4). The cross was God's ultimate means of doing so.

Standing before the cross was Jesus's mother, along with other women who were devoted to him. John, possibly the youngest disciple, was there as well. Even as Jesus's life ebbed from his body, he took time to ensure his widowed mother was cared for (John 19:25–27). Perhaps he was also blessing his faithful disciple by entrusting to him a precious gift—his own mother. While enduring the most excruciating pain imaginable, Jesus ministered to a dying criminal and invited him into eternal fellowship with himself (Luke 23:39–43). Lest we ever be tempted to treat relationships in our life casually or carelessly, the cross reminds us that God takes them extremely seriously.

Joyful

On the surface the cross bears no resemblance to anything joyful. It was an instrument of enormous suffering, anguish, and shame. Yet, through the centuries, it has become a gateway to unquenchable joy. The writer of Hebrews noted: "For the joy that lay before him, he endured the cross" (Heb. 12:2). The scourging and crucifixion were in no way joyful for Jesus, but the reward on the other side of the cross was immeasurable. Jesus could, therefore, encourage his disciples, saying, "So you also have sorrow now. But I will see you again. Your hearts will rejoice, and no one will take away your joy from you" (John 16:22). On the other side of the cross is inexpressible joy!

Imagine the joy Jesus experienced as he returned to the right hand of his Father, having carried out, to the letter, God's eternal plan of salvation for the ages. Think of the heavenly reception and celebration that occurred! Only God can transform tragedy into rejoicing. Through Jeremiah, God promised: "I will turn their mourning into joy, give them consolation, and bring happiness out of grief" (Jer. 31:13). The psalmist David wrote: "Weeping may last overnight, but there is joy in the morning" (Ps. 30:5).

There certainly was much weeping at the foot of the cross. Mary, Jesus's mother, Mary Magdalene, and others, surely shed bitter tears at seeing their Lord and Savior treated so unjustly and cruelly. But their sorrow was short-lived. Just as their grieving had been intense, their elation three days later was greater still. Had Jesus not endured the cross, every one of his friends would ultimately have spent an eternity in anguish. God is not indifferent to our pain. However, he knows that some things can only be accomplished through suffering. He understands that the temporary agony of a cross cannot compare to the heavenly joy to be gained for eternity.

God is not indifferent to our pain. However, he knows that some things can only be accomplished through suffering.

Responding to God's Way of the Cross

We must never treat the cross lightly. To see the Son of God willingly and lovingly surrender his precious life to purchase forgiveness for the people spitting in his face is a scene too ghastly, yet majestic, to adequately describe. God did not merely inconvenience himself to obtain our salvation; he plunged into the deepest, darkest place imaginable. God did not pay our debt with pocket change; he forfeited heaven's most valuable treasure. He could have restricted the gift of salvation to those creatures most worthy and least sinful. Instead, he freely offered redemption to the worst of scoundrels and outcasts. There are so many dimensions to the cross. Only eternity will reveal all that God accomplished on that hallowed Easter weekend.

Had Christianity been nothing more than a fanciful invention of Jesus's disciples after his death, the cross would never have played such a prominent role in its doctrine. What religion makes dying on a cross a central tenet as well as an entrance requirement? How could a movement like Christianity ever succeed when it made such formidable demands upon its followers?

Deny Yourself, Take Up Your Cross, and Follow Me

Just as the cross played a central role in Jesus's life, so he fully intends for it to be pivotal in our life. He told his disciples, "If anyone wants to follow after me, let him deny himself, take up his cross, and follow me" (Matt. 16:24). This admonition was not intended for his twelve disciples alone. It is not restricted to church leaders or the spiritually mature. Jesus made clear that *no one* can be his disciple unless they follow this threefold stipulation.

Jesus first commanded his followers to deny themselves. He knew that no one would take up their cross if they remained self-centered. In the first century, when you saw someone literally carrying a cross, you immediately knew several things about them. First, life as they knew it was over. Criminals were forced to carry their cross to the site of their execution. It was one of the final humiliations inflicted upon the condemned. To see a man carrying his cross through public streets alerted you of his impending demise. Whether it was a baker, a farmer, or a carpenter, his career pursuits were at an end. It was inconsequential if they intended to retire by the Sea of Galilee or if they had built a retirement home near their grandchildren. Their future was no longer their own. Their plans mattered not. Neither did their possessions. Every detail of their life was dominated by the one pervasive reality of their life: they were carrying a cross.

Numerous people down through history have wanted to be disciples of Jesus, but they would not pay the price. Many today want to pray a sinner's prayer but have no desire to relinquish their plans or aspirations. They seek salvation but resist consecration. They feel certain that God would never ask them to make a sacrifice, and they are resentful if he leads them into a period of suffering.

To truly take up our cross, we *must* surrender our desires. The prosperity gospel is clearly false, for it proclaims that God wants to grant us all our desires. Rather than being our Lord, it makes him our servant. Yet Jesus's goal is not to make our dreams come true.

To truly take up our cross, we *must* surrender our desires.

Modern society adamantly rejects Jesus's message. Rather than denying ourselves, psychologists urge us to affirm ourselves. Rather than thinking of ourselves less, we are encouraged to be self-absorbed and to assiduously avoid anything that appears demeaning. The concept of being anyone's servant, let alone a bondslave, is anathema.

It is tempting to conclude our crucified Savior does not expect us to take up our cross. But Jesus told his would-be followers that we must not only surrender our pride and selfishness; we must also take up our cross. This is not something someone can do for us. Yet, once we accept our cross, others can help us carry the load as Simon of Cyrene helped Jesus (Mark 15:21). This is one reason true followers of Christ naturally band together in local congregations. Bearing a cross is burdensome and is best done within a community of fellow crossbearers.

The Christian life is a crucified life. It is impossible to only crucify a portion of yourself. You cannot have your fears crucified but not your greed or unforgiveness. When you are crucified, every part of your old self is buried (Rom. 6:1–7). Paul asserted, "I have been crucified with Christ, and I no longer live, but Christ lives in me. The life I now live in the body, I live by faith in the Son of God, who loved me and gave himself for me" (Gal. 2:20). You cannot be born again and continue being the same person you have always been. The church today, however, is filled with uncrucified people. There are countless church attenders who have never fully surrendered themselves to Christ's lordship. They are unwilling to place their lust or greed or pride on the cross so their sins can be decisively put to death. Yet it is impossible for uncrucified people to behave like their crucified Savior.

Dietrich Bonhoeffer wrote: "When Christ calls a man, he bids him come and die."[30] To deny ourselves and take up our cross means there is no place we will not go, no sacrifice we will not make, and no command we will not obey. Our goal is not to save ourselves but to serve our Lord.

To deny ourselves and take up our cross means there is no place we will not go, no sacrifice we will not make, and no command we will not obey.

There once was a small church that committed itself to do whatever the Lord told it to do. Over time God led them to start many Bible studies and plant churches in the surrounding communities. They supported numerous ministries, sending many from their own membership to serve. Their willingness to give themselves away for God's kingdom became widely known, and many churches and individuals felt inspired to send money and volunteer their time to support the church's efforts. Eventually, the pastor of the church was called to a new assignment. The congregation began looking for its next minister. They landed upon a candidate who informed the church leaders that if he became their pastor, he would make it a priority to care for the church's needs, and when it was strong enough, he would lead them to continue their "outside ministries." He noted that if the mother church was weak or overextended, then she could not properly care for her daughter congregations.

Sure enough, upon the pastor's arrival, he focused on preserving what they had rather than on giving it away. He spoke much about "wise stewardship." Before long, partner congregations realized the church was no longer seeking to start new churches so they discontinued their financial support. Soon the church's own mission giving was curtailed. Members, many of whom had found Christ through this church, were unaccustomed to this self-preservation mindset, and many moved on to congregations where they could continue serving as they had been taught. Within a few years, the church could no longer afford to pay its own bills, and it had to drastically reduce its ministries. The congregation ultimately declined to the point that it was perilously close to having to sell its building just to meet basic financial obligations. Then the pastor abruptly resigned and left the ministry altogether. When the church gave itself away for God's kingdom, they always had enough to do what God told them to do. The moment they began trying to "save" themselves, they entered a steep decline.

The cross is a graphic reminder that the power for a Christian comes not in being self-centered but in being Christ centered. The moment we focus on preserving ourselves, we cease to receive God's provision. Paul warned, "Everything that is not from faith is sin" (Rom. 14:23). The cross reminds us that God's calling on our lives is impossible apart from his power and provision. When we have been crucified, neither our fears nor our desires rule over us any longer. Our strengths and our weaknesses become inconsequential. Our will is no longer front and center.

History demonstrates that those God has used most powerfully have not typically been those most skilled but those most surrendered.[31] The Christian life is not modeled after business CEOs, professional athletes, or self-help gurus. It is fashioned after Jesus Christ, who perfectly modeled how to live life in complete submission and obedience to God.

The Christian life is not modeled after business CEOs, professional athletes, or self-help gurus. It is fashioned after Jesus Christ, who perfectly modeled how to live life in complete submission and obedience to God.

Christians who assume God would never ask them to make a sacrifice or endure suffering have never seriously considered the nature of Christ's call. Dietrich Bonhoeffer claimed, "Discipleship means allegiance to the suffering of Christ."[32] Over the years I have met many well-intentioned Christians who believed God wanted, above all, for them to be comfortable and happy. But the cross looms before every Christian, loudly declaring that the Christian life is not intended to be safe! The same Jesus who died an excruciating death on a cross bids us *follow him*. Early Christians often faced martyrdom. To this day thousands of Christians lay their life down for Christ each year.

To Western Christians this can be troubling. Christianity in America is "comfortable." Many Christians, therefore, are bewildered when Christ asks them to make a sacrifice or leads them on a path of suffering. I grew up on the mission field in Canada. Many people from the United States felt led by God to come and minister with us. Some heartily embraced the call and were used mightily by God. Others faced discomfort and lost heart.

For some the bitterly long, cold winters demoralized them and compelled them to return to the warmer South. Many were dismayed by the unexpected cultural differences. They missed the way ministry was done "back home," or college football, or favorite stores or foods unavailable in Canada. Still others felt God calling them to serve in Canada, but they could not fathom God's requiring them to leave their home state or their parents or grandchildren. Issues such as these proved unbearable to some who professed to follow Jesus but lacked the fortitude for costly service. Yet the same person who left the throne room of heaven to be born in a cattle stall would certainly not hesitate to ask us to leave our hometown or overcome our shyness or move away from our parents.

Those who have taken discipleship seriously have discovered this: though Christ may bid them to follow him into a season of sacrifice, he will also grant the requisite grace and peace so they experience his heavenly joy. Bonhoeffer noted: "In the hour of the cruelest torture they bear for his sake, they are made partakers in the perfect joy and bliss of fellowship with him. To bear the cross proves to be the only way of triumphing over suffering."[33]

John G. Paton was a Scottish Presbyterian missionary who set out in 1858, along with his wife Mary, to be missionaries in the New Hebrides islands east of Australia. Paton had a successful ministry in Scotland, but he and his wife felt God calling them to leave the comforts of their native land to take the gospel to cannibals who had never heard the good news. Upon learning he was leaving his current ministry, an older gentleman accosted Paton and attempted to shame him for leaving his present assignment and taking his family to a dangerous, unknown world. The man exclaimed: "The Cannibals! You will be eaten by Cannibals!" Paton retorted, "Mr. Dickson you are advanced in years now, and your own prospect is soon to be laid in the grave, there to be eaten by worms; I confess to you, that if I can but live and die serving and honouring the Lord Jesus, it will make no difference to me whether I am eaten by Cannibals or by worms; and in the Great Day my resurrection body will arise as fair as yours in the likeness of our risen Redeemer."[34]

Paton and his wife arrived on the island of Tanna on November 5, 1858, healthy, vigorous, and eager to minister to the locals. Paton had urged his wife to wait to come until after delivering their first child, but she insisted on accompanying him, since she felt equally called to minister to the people. Not knowing any better, they built their home at a low spot, near water which was rife with disease that was particularly hazardous to Europeans. Mary became sick while pregnant with their first child. In February she gave birth to their son. She was overcome with illness and died on March 3. Seventeen days later the baby followed her to the grave.

To read the account of Paton over the ensuing years is heart-wrenching. On numerous occasions the cannibals he was trying to minister to attempted to kill and eat him. He would be lied about and threatened. European sailors who occasionally passed through the area were evil and corrupt and turned the local people against him. Eventually, every other missionary who came to work with him died from disease or murder. Paton was ultimately forced to barricade himself in his house to escape certain death. Yet perhaps the most unsettling attacks Paton faced were the criticisms from his brethren back in Scotland who second-guessed his decisions and belittled his efforts. Paton was ultimately used to evangelize Aniwa, a neighboring island, until the entire population was converted. Paton stirred up much support for his mission work so his pioneering work on the island of Tanna ultimately bore much fruit as well.

Reading accounts of the early missionaries and the extreme price they paid in their service for God is humbling in an age when having a church service run five minutes late is considered a trial. The pioneering missionary C. T. Studd, served in India, China, and Africa over his long career. He declared: "If Jesus Christ be God and died for me, then no sacrifice can be too great for me to make for him."[35] He also boldly declared: "Some want to live within the sound of a church or chapel bell; I want to run a rescue shop, within a yard of hell."[36] Through the ages there have been those who understood that the same Savior who embraced his own cross would most assuredly have a cross for them as well. Many who vainly attempted to save their life ultimately squandered it. But others have resolutely taken up their cross and humbly followed their Lord. The kingdom of God has been greatly blessed and expanded as a result.

Conclusion

Every aspect of the Christian life finds its center at the cross. God will never send you on an undertaking that does not commence at Calvary. There is no such thing as Christianity without a cross. Likewise, there is no power without the cross. There is no victory over sin without the cross. Fools run from the cross, but the wise hurriedly make their way to the foot of it, for there they find forgiveness, power, and life.

Questions for Reflection/Discussion

1. What sacrifice is God presently asking you to make for him? How are you responding?

2. Is your life characterized more by a pursuit of comfort or a determination to obey God at any price?

3. How is God currently calling you to "lose" your life? How are you responding?

4. What sins have you resisted placing on the cross so they would be crucified?

5. Have you discovered the joy that comes from suffering for Christ? If not, do you need to ask God to grant it to you?

CHAPTER 11

GOD'S WAYS ARE RELATIONAL

"I am the vine; you are the branches. The one who remains in me and I in him produces much fruit, because you can do nothing without me."
(John 15:5)

For just as the body is one and has many parts, and all the parts of that body, though many, are one body—so also is Christ. For we were all baptized by one Spirit into one body—whether Jews or Greeks, whether slaves or free—and we were all given one Spirit to drink. Indeed, the body is not one part but many.
(1 Cor. 12:12–14)

One of the most tragic moments in Scripture occurs after Adam and Eve have eaten from the forbidden fruit. "Then the man and his wife heard the sound of the LORD God walking in the garden at the time of the evening breeze, and they hid from the LORD God among the trees of the garden. So the LORD God called out to the man and said to him, 'Where are you?'" (Gen. 3:8–9).

This poignant moment raises many questions. Perhaps most importantly is: What does this reveal about God? God is omniscient. He knew his only two creatures had sinned. Surely he also knew exactly where they were. So, why did he come looking for them? Many have conjectured that it was God's regular habit to commune with the first couple in the cool of the evening. Imagine! God himself taking walks with his children. This, of course, was God's original plan. To regularly spend time walking closely with his creatures. He may have come on that occasion for their customary time of fellowship, but this time Adam and Eve were missing. Sin had separated them from their Creator.

This raises other questions. Why did God take time to fellowship with his creatures in the first place? He made them out of dust. They could seemingly contribute nothing to him that he needed. Within the context of administering an entire universe, why would God seek out the company of frail mortals each evening? God had myriads of angels at his disposal. The glimpses Scripture provides of heaven indicate it is filled with adoring spiritual beings who worship and serve God continually. Why should almighty God remain committed to this wayward couple when he could create millions more? For that matter, why not acknowledge the divine experiment had failed and eradicate the sin-prone human race? What is it about God that refuses to give up on people? And why did he care so much about rebellious humanity that he was willing to send his only Son to a despicable cross to redeem them?

One of the profound realities of God's ways is that he is relational. Even though God is entirely self-reliant, all-powerful, and needs nothing, something fundamental about God's nature values relationships.

God's Nature: Relational

God Is Trinity

The trinitarian doctrine, that God is Father, Son, and Holy Spirit (one God in three persons) confuses and perplexes many people. No other major religion views their god this way. The Trinity encompasses three persons in eternal, loving community within the Godhead (John 17:20–26). Had God never created another creature in heaven or on the earth, he would have enjoyed perfect fellowship with himself. Nevertheless, Scripture reveals that God created legions of powerful, angelic beings who worship and serve him. There was a time when they did not exist. Throughout Scripture we get glimpses of seraphim, cherubim, angels, and archangels. Presumably, God could create many more if he desired. And indeed, heaven may be populated with magnificent creatures we know nothing about. And still God chose to create mortals.

What motivated God to establish a race of beings that would ultimately cost his Son's life? How does he view people differently than he values angels? Why was Christ's death on a cross not also applied to the redemption of fallen angels? How is God's fellowship with people different from, or possibly more satisfying than, his communion with heavenly beings? We know God is, by nature, love. Perhaps God created humanity so he had beings on whom he could pour out his vast love. God may have created people with the capacity to express affection to him in ways heavenly creatures cannot. Scripture doesn't answer these questions.

Unlike Greek and Pagan Gods

In the ancient world, the Greek and Roman gods were largely disinterested in people's well-being. The mythical beings supposedly desired sacrifices so they could be nourished by them, but they generally had no desire to experience an ongoing personal relationship with mortals. It would have been inconceivable for people to walk in fellowship with Zeus, Poseidon, or Hades. These were selfish and temperamental gods. Although, at times, the gods were purported to disguise themselves to mingle among people, this was not so they could enjoy fellowship with them. Typically, people felt it more prudent to avoid the gods than to interact with them.

Of the other world religions, adherents do not generally believe they can enjoy close fellowship with God. Some religions view their god as distant and wrathful. Such a god inspires fear, not a desire for close communion. Other religions promote many gods who are everywhere. It is impossible to know them personally. Still other religions view god merely as an impersonal power force. You may tap into your god, but you do not fellowship with him. Then there are religions in which we, ourselves, are viewed as divine. There is no being for us to get to know or to spend time with except ourselves.

That is why the Judaic-Christian God is so distinct and attractive. He is awesome in his power and holiness, yet he desires people to love him and to enjoy being with him.

God in the Old Testament

The Old Testament reveals numerous personal ways God related to people. God spoke to Cain to warn him of the sin that sought to entrap him (Gen. 4:6–7). God related to Abraham as a friend (2 Chron. 20:7; Isa. 41:8; James 2:23). At one point God came in human form to share a meal with Abraham (Gen. 18:1–15). When Isaac was struggling, God appeared to him and encouraged him not to be afraid. God assured Isaac of his loving presence (Gen. 26:23–25). At a critical moment in Jacob's life, God, in the form of a man, wrestled with him all night (Gen. 32:24–32). God spoke to Moses face-to-face just as someone speaks with a friend (Exod. 33:11). At the outset of Joshua's leadership, God bolstered him (Josh. 1:1–9). King David likened his relationship with God to a sheep and a shepherd (Ps. 23). When Elijah grew discouraged, God met him on Mount Sinai and spoke to him in a soft whisper (1 Kings 19:12–13). At the height of King Nebuchadnezzar's power, he had three young Jewish men thrown into a fiery furnace because they refused to worship an idol. Yet, when the king peered into the furnace, he saw the three men walking around freely along with a fourth man who "looks like a son of the gods" (Dan. 3:25).

Before the coming of Christ, God's relationship with his people was loving, but a chasm existed between holy God and sin-addicted humanity. Thus, God seemed distant and unattainable. Yet God desired more for his people. Some, like Abraham and Moses, had close walks with God. But when Jesus came, the barriers between God and people were finally overcome, and intimate communion with the divine is now accessible to all.

God in the New Testament

The New Testament describes God's interaction with people as much more pronounced than in the time before Christ. The incarnation was the greatest miracle and most profound act of grace in human history. God had always loved his people and sought to guide and save them. Yet God was a perfect spirit who dwelt in heaven. The gap between holy God and sinful people was insurmountable.

Though we are familiar with the Christmas story, our limited understanding cannot fully grasp the magnitude of what it meant for God to take on the form of a frail human baby and live among his creatures. Scripture tells us, "The Word became flesh and dwelt among us. We observed his glory, the glory as the one and only Son from the Father, full of grace and truth"

(John 1:14). We cannot begin to comprehend the enormous act of grace that took place when the Son of God, Lord of the universe, humbled himself and came as an infant, wholly vulnerable and dependent on earthly parents. Why would almighty God care so much for his creatures that he would condescend to abandon heaven and live as a mere mortal among a sinful, imperfect people?

Jesus said, "The one who has seen me has seen the Father" (John 14:9). When we watch the way Jesus related to people, we see the ways of God the Father. Early in Jesus's ministry, he invited twelve disciples to be with him (Mark 1:16–20). At times he focused primarily on three of these disciples (Mark 5:37; Matt. 17:1; 26:37). At other times Jesus concentrated on larger groups, such as when he commissioned the seventy-two (Luke 10:1) or when he taught the five thousand (Mark 6:30–44).

It is instructive how Jesus enjoyed the company of others. He is often pictured eating meals with friends, sinners, and even Pharisees (Matt. 26:6; Mark 2:15; 14:3; Luke 10:38–42; 19:5; 24:30; John 2:1–12; 12:1–3; 21:12). In the Middle Eastern culture of Jesus's day, sharing a meal with someone was an act of fellowship. One of the early criticisms leveled at Jesus was that he attended parties thrown by "sinners" (Luke 5:27–31). Jesus had special friends, including Mary, Martha, and Lazarus (Luke 10:38–41; John 12:1–3). There was also a group of women who followed Jesus and supported his ministry (Luke 8:1–3). Jesus was no ordinary rabbi. Jewish rabbis traditionally kept themselves aloof from common people. Jesus, however, seemed to genuinely enjoy the company of others, and clearly many felt comfortable spending time with him.

Even on the night Jesus was betrayed into the hands of his enemies, he determined to share a meal with his disciples. He certainly had much on his mind as his appointment with Golgotha drew near. Yet Jesus chose to spend his last evening of earthly freedom fellowshipping with his closest friends. Even as he prayed in the garden of Gethsemane, he invited his disciples to share the moment with him. Jesus, the Son of God and Savior of humanity, was not a solitary figure. He surrounded himself with people throughout his ministry. Even as he hung upon the lethal cross, he had loyal friends with him. And, while enduring the most painful death imaginable, Jesus still took time to minister to others (Luke 23:39–43; John 19:25–27).

The Gospels show that Jesus typically had people around him. He was not a lone superhero. He did not remain "professionally aloof" from his followers or the crowds who sought him out. He spent time with people of all ages, from all walks of life, and regardless of their gender or social status. As the Scripture says, "God loved the world" (John 3:16). God could easily have washed his hands of his fallen creatures and created something better, but he did not. He did not give up on people, even when they rebelled against him. Though God disciplined and judged those who opposed him, he steadfastly worked out his eternal purposes to redeem his fallen creatures. From Genesis to Revelation, the evidence clearly demonstrates that God highly values relationships.

Our Response to God's Ways

Divine Fellowship

Knowing how much the Father loves us and desires time with us, how should we respond? We ought to be emboldened to draw as near to God as possible to enjoy this sublime communion (Heb. 4:16). It may have been shocking to someone like John, who was so close to Jesus, to observe, "He was in the world, and the world was created through him, and yet the world did not recognize him. He came to his own, and his own people did not receive him. But to all who did receive him, he gave them the right to be children of God" (John 1:10–12). God does not command us merely to submit to him as a vassal in his kingdom. Rather, the Father welcomes us into his family as adopted sons and daughters. Speaking from experience, Paul told Christians in Rome, "You received the Spirit of adoption, by whom we cry out, '*Abba*, Father!' The Spirit himself testifies together with our spirit that we are God's children, and if children, also heirs—heirs of God and coheirs with Christ" (Rom. 8:15–17).

Even more amazing, Jesus declared: "You are my friends if you do what I command you. I do not call you servants anymore, because a servant doesn't know what his master is doing. I have called you friends, because I have made known to you everything I have heard from my Father" (John 15:14–15). It is incredible that Christ should look to any mere mortal to be his friend. Such generosity is infinitely more than we deserve. The only thing more baffling than the fact God makes such a generous offer is that many, even Christians, choose not to fully avail themselves of the privilege.

Many believers assume they will eventually enjoy fellowship with their Savior once they die and enter heaven. The key from their perspective is ensuring their name is safely written in the Lamb's Book of Life so they gain admission into heaven one day. However, eternal life includes much more than everlasting life. It also encompasses a quality of life. It is life lived in close fellowship with God the Son and God the Father, through the Holy Spirit (John 17:3). This commences the moment we are born again. Jesus desires intimate fellowship with people now, not just in the afterlife. He likened the relationship he seeks to that of a branch and a vine (John 15:1–8). There cannot be any separation between a branch and a vine, or else the branch will die. Jesus urged believers to relate to him just as intimately.

Jesus told his disciples that, though he was going to return to his Father, he would not leave them as orphans, for he would send the Holy Spirit to reside within them (John 14:15–18). Jesus's disciples would have an even more intimate relationship with the Holy Spirit than they had with Jesus (John 16:7). What an amazing opportunity is available to everyone who believes!

In 1990, my father, Henry Blackaby, wrote his seminal book, *Experiencing God*. It proved revolutionary to many people's walk with God. People constantly told him how they had attended church all their lives without being taught that God wanted them to enjoy an experiential relationship with him that was personal and interactive. Sadly, some of the opposition to this teaching came not from unbelievers but from Christian leaders. Many recoiled at the thought that God "speaks" to people today. They argued that God did not need to communicate with people today because the Bible was available to answer people's questions. Others feared people would misunderstand what God was saying and be led into heretical teachings. Some decried this as "mysticism" and warned of dire consequences.

Still, the Scriptures clearly teach that God desires a close, personal relationship with people (Rom. 8:14–17). He enjoys fellowshipping with us. Our Father delights in communing with his children. He wants us to know him (John 17:3; Phil. 3:8–10). To simply be a church attender who worships God from afar or who merely performs a daily Bible reading is to drastically underestimate the quality and vibrancy of the relationship God desires to have with us.

The Church

It is not surprising that a God who values relationships so highly would expect his followers to prioritize them as well. It was said of the early believers: "They devoted themselves to the apostles' teaching, to the fellowship, to the breaking of bread, and to prayer" (Acts 2:42). Early Christians served and worshipped God together. The writer of Hebrews urged believers not to neglect meeting together (Heb. 10:25). The Bible does not promote solitary Christianity. Rarely do you find Jesus or Paul ministering apart from the companionship of others.

Paul described the church as the body of Christ (1 Cor. 12). He taught that the body consists of many parts and each member is crucial for the body's overall health. Today's culture celebrates independence. People exult in their freedom to do whatever they choose, accountable to no one. Yet Scripture promotes not independence but interdependence. Paul made clear that each part of the body is to be vitally connected to the other parts of the body. If one member suffers, then every member feels the pain (1 Cor. 12:26). Every member is responsible to their fellow believers.

I experienced this truth powerfully when I was a university student. One evening I attended a service at my church. I entered the auditorium looking about for friends to sit with, and an elderly widow named Mrs. Clark caught my eye. Her husband, Arthur, had died several months earlier. The thought entered my mind that with the passing of Mr. Clark the previous fall, Mrs. Clark would be solely responsible for the upkeep of her lawn that spring. I could not imagine this dainty and diminutive Englishwoman knowing how to start a lawn mower!

I sat down next to her and asked what her plans were to care for her yard. I will never forget the look that came over her face. She had been worried sick about the grounds around her humble home. She was a woman of modest means and had no experience dealing with service people. She feared her property would be so neglected that she would be forced to leave her house and move into a nursing home. I told her I would stop by on Saturday.

When I arrived at her house, the lawn was overrun with tall grass, weeds, and fallen tree limbs. It took several hours to tend her yard. As I was finishing, Mrs. Clark approached with a handful of money. She did not want to be a burden to anyone and insisted on paying me. I told Mrs. Clark that God had clearly told me to help so I could not take her money. However, I hinted that I was aware she was a marvelous baker. The next day as I entered the church building, I was struck by the powerful aroma of fresh baking. Mrs. Clark had been watching for me and eagerly pointed to a box of baked goods she had brought me. It was glorious! Henceforth, I went by her house every weekend to mow her lawn. She insisted I first sit down and have tea and home-baked treats (to keep up my strength!). She asked about my classes and how she could pray for me. We became dear friends. I cherished those conversations and prayer times. I learned that when you live your life like Christ, you become involved in the lives of others. College students will fellowship with widows, businesspeople will spend time with the poor, and men will take the fatherless under their wing. God has a marvelous way of bringing the most unlikely friends together!

I am a member of the church to which Truett Cathy, founder of Chick-fil-A, belonged. Though he was a billionaire who led a highly successful food chain, he took being a church member seriously. For over four decades he faithfully taught a fifth-grade boys' Sunday school class. Not only did he teach my son-in-law, Sam, as a boy, but he also taught Sam's father when he was young. Truett had all manner of boys in his class. Some were raised by single mothers. Some were from poor families. Nevertheless, Truett would invite the children to his home where they could ride all-terrain vehicles and enjoy themselves. He would often load several boys in his truck and take them to drop off meals for widows and poor families. At Truett's funeral, his pallbearers were all men who had once been his students. When people take God's ways seriously, they find that God connects them in creative and unexpected ways with people of all ages and backgrounds.

God has provided much help and instruction so we might enjoy robust relationships. Some of that wisdom includes:

1. Don't judge others, so you, yourself, are not judged (Matt. 7:1).
2. Do to others what you want them to do to you (Luke 6:31).
3. Don't withhold good from those you have the power to bless (Prov. 3:27).
4. Relate to others in humility (Prov. 16:18).
5. Be faithful and reliable to others at all times (Prov. 17:17).
6. Refrain from boasting (Prov. 27:2).
7. Keep your anger in check (Prov. 29:11).
8. Recognize when it is wise to speak and when it is wise to remain silent (Eccles. 3:7).
9. Always be quick to forgive (Matt. 6:12–15).
10. Carry one another's burdens (Gal. 6:2).

God has provided every resource necessary so we can cultivate God-honoring relationships. Christians ought to be gifted at building healthy relationships because we have Christ's example, the wisdom of Scripture, and the Holy Spirit to guide us. Christian marriages ought to be fulfilling and long-lasting because the Holy Spirit enables couples to love and forgive as Christ did. Christian families ought to be wholesome and joyful because God is at work in each member. Christian friends and colleagues ought to be a source of joy and encouragement because they have the Holy Spirit within them, guiding them to be a blessing.

I recently had a Christian explain to me that she did not need to attend church because she listened to three preachers on television each week who provided excellent teaching. She did not feel she was missing out by skipping church. This attitude, unfortunately, has become widely prevalent but is unbiblical and self-centered. Not only was this woman missing out on what a church family could offer her, but she was also withholding the blessing she could have been to others. Christians are not intended to relate to God solely in isolation. Individual worship and corporate worship are both essential to a Christian. We do not meet corporately merely to have our needs met; we also gather to encourage and meet the needs of others. The apostle Paul urged Christians to "carry one another's burdens; in this way you fulfill the law of Christ" (Gal. 6:2).

Many people have determined to give up on the church due to its many and obvious flaws. Yet Christ has not abandoned the church, so we have no right to do so. Christ loved the church enough to die for it (Eph. 5:25–27). How could we, then, feel justified in forsaking it? When we withdraw from the church, we withhold what God intended to supply the body through us (1 Cor. 12:17–22). Though lounging in your pajamas on the weekend while flipping through television channels looking for an interesting religious program might seem appealing, it fails to fulfill your divine calling to live in close relationship with your brothers and sisters in Christ.

Conclusion

Even God, who is supremely self-sufficient, cherishes fellowship. God's plan is to place us in a church body so we can live in fellowship with other believers (1 Cor. 12:18). Jesus said the way we treat those God places in our life is how we treat him (John 13:20). Western culture increasingly leans toward isolationism and self-reliance. Yet God's design is to place people in our life who can encourage us, help carry our load, speak truth to us, and hold us accountable. Christian fellowship should transcend all barriers and flow freely among believers of every background, financial status, educational level, and political perspective. Christians should be the most effective of all people at developing healthy relationships, for we have the Holy Spirit guiding and enabling us. Those who heed the Spirit's voice will inevitably be a blessing to others.

Questions for Reflection/Discussion

1. How would you evaluate the present condition of your relationships? Are they healthy? God honoring? Where do they need to be improved?

2. How would you evaluate your current relationship with God? Is it vibrant? Joyful? Growing? What might you do to enrich it?

3. What is one way you might become a greater blessing to someone in need?

4. Are you actively involved in a church family? If not, what is your justification for this?

5. Where do you struggle in your relationships? What next step can you take to improve the way you relate to others?

CHAPTER 12

GOD'S WAYS ARE JOYFUL, RESTFUL, PEACEFUL

But the angel said to them, "Don't be afraid,
for look, I proclaim to you good news of
great joy that will be for all the people."
(Luke 2:10)

Therefore, since the promise to enter his
rest remains, let us beware that none of
you be found to have fallen short.
(Heb. 4:1)

"If you knew this day what would bring peace—
but now it is hidden from your eyes."
(Luke 19:42)

How can you have joy, rest, and peace when your life is difficult and you are being treated unfairly? You can't. Unless you have Jesus. When Christ dwells within you, everything he is, and does, becomes a part of your life as well. As we have seen, God's character and ways are multidimensional. Yet there are three ways God acts that are closely interrelated and that can dramatically affect the Christian's life. These are joy, rest, and peace. These are fully experienced in heaven, but they can be ours today as well, even under the most trying circumstances.

God's Ways Are Joyful

The first time I ministered in the Middle East, I took my eighteen-year-old son Mike with me. I was somewhat nervous about how people would respond to us. We were being housed in a gated community, and upon our arrival, we drove up to the security checkpoint. An armed, uniformed officer approached our vehicle and asked who we were. When I told him my name, he broke into an enormous smile. "Richard!" he exclaimed, "Welcome!" "Where is Michael?" he asked, peering into the back of the SUV. Our host had registered us with the security service, and this officer wanted to personally greet us upon our arrival. I learned that his name was Charles. Every time we came or went, he would wave enthusiastically and smile as we passed by.

I eventually learned his story. He was a Christian from a Muslim country in Africa. People opposed to his faith had burned down his family store and left him impoverished. He was forced to move without his family to this Middle Eastern country to earn money as a security guard. He worked sixteen-hour shifts, six days a week. He could not go home to visit his family for two years. The other three men who worked with him were Muslim and often ridiculed his faith. One day an imam called on him. He pulled out a fistful of money and told Charles it was his if he would convert to Islam. As Charles told me this story, he looked at me and, with a huge smile said, "How could I forsake Jesus after all he has done for me?" Charles was one of the most joyful people I have ever met, yet he had also suffered far more hardships than most people I know.

God does not merely possess character traits. He embodies the fullness of those attributes. For example, God is not merely loving; he *is* love (1 John 4:8). Likewise, God not only tells the truth; he *is* truth (John 14:6). So it is with joy. God embodies joy. Nothing in the universe can diminish his joy to the slightest degree. Because he is joyful, everything God does is accomplished with joy.

God is not merely loving; he *is* love (1 John 4:8). Likewise, God not only tells the truth; he *is* truth (John 14:6)

God Acts Joyfully

The psalmist David described what it was like to be in the presence of almighty God. We might assume that in God's hallowed company we would be overwhelmed by his mighty power, or his august holiness, or his unrelenting love. Yet David wrote, "In your presence is abundant joy; at your right hand are eternal pleasures" (Ps. 16:11). As we consciously draw near to God, we will be overwhelmed by a profound sense of pure, unquenchable joy. It can wash over us during our morning devotions and captivate us in a worship service. Joy pervades God's presence and overflows to his children. That is, in part, what makes heaven so wonderful. We will experience an unlimited supply of joy in its richest, undiluted form for eternity.

Why is God's presence characterized by perfect joy? Is he oblivious to the evil and suffering people experience on the earth? Does he not see the cruelty being perpetrated upon the vulnerable? Is he unconcerned by the gross injustice suffered around the globe?

God is fully aware of sin's effects on the earth. The Scriptures, particularly the prophetic books, are filled with God's condemnations of oppressors and evildoers. The Lord is not indifferent to sin or suffering. But God has access to far more information than merely what is reported on the daily news. He sees the future. He understands how every problem on the earth will ultimately be resolved. He intends for every wicked person to receive the full justice due them. He has already written the final chapter of Earth's history. God also experiences the exquisite bliss of heaven. He knows that a day is coming when "he will wipe away every tear from their eyes. Death will be no more; grief, crying, and pain will be no more, because the previous things have passed away" (Rev. 21:4). God understands that righteous people who suffer in this life will be more than recompensed in the age to come (Luke 16:19–24; Rev. 7:17; 21:4).

In our day God's causes can appear to be thwarted at every turn while evil gains momentum daily. However, while all can appear gloomy from our earthly perspective, we do not see what God sees. We only have glimpses of the masses of people coming to faith in Christ in countries officially closed to the gospel. We never hear of the many miracles taking place around the globe. We cannot know where revival and spiritual awakening are pending. But God does.

God's joy is also sustained by his eternal vantage point. When we lose a loved one to a terminal illness or a tragic accident, we suffer a profound sense of loss. We understandably grieve over not seeing them again in this life. But God resides on both sides of eternity. He knows that believers who depart from this life are gloriously welcomed into heavenly bliss. God sees how infinitesimally brief this life is compared to what awaits us in the next. He recognizes that the tribulations of this life will be quickly swallowed up and forgotten as we enter his all-consuming presence in heaven. God maintains his joy, regardless of what we face, because he sees our circumstances in their proper light.

We tend to live with happiness, not joy. Happiness is based on circumstances. If the weather is miserable, traffic is worse than usual, or the news is filled with troubling stories, our happiness evaporates. Joy, on the other hand, emanates from God's mighty, loving, victorious presence. When we abide in God's presence, joy is found in abundance (John 15:11). We can be certain that the angelic hosts don't lose even an ounce of their joy because of what people, or weather, or economies are doing on Earth. There are no cherubim in heaven's courts wringing their hands because a dictator has come to power or a pandemic has spread. They see God upon his throne, and they know his will is always perfectly accomplished. Angelic beings have watched him rule the universe throughout the ages, and they have never known him to be anything less than resoundingly victorious in every circumstance. They glory in his enormous power and profound wisdom. Knowing you serve a God who is always victorious causes exuberant joy.

The apostle John could have been vulnerable to losing his joy. He was an old man sent to prison on an unjust charge. His life was difficult. He was concerned for the church's survival. Powerful enemies opposed the church. The unpopular emperor Diocletian was enforcing his cruel rule across the empire. Churches that had once been bastions of God's kingdom had grown lukewarm or had forsaken their first love. The risen Christ drew near to John and invited him into a special viewing of heaven so he could see how its residents perceived the world's problems:

> Immediately I was in the Spirit, and there was a throne in heaven and someone was seated on it. The one seated there had the appearance of

> jasper and carnelian stone. A rainbow that had the appearance of an emerald surrounded the throne.
>
> Around the throne were twenty-four thrones, and on the thrones sat twenty-four elders dressed in white clothes, with golden crowns on their heads.
>
> Flashes of lightning and rumblings and peals of thunder came from the throne. . . .
>
> Day and night they never stop saying, Holy, holy, holy, Lord God, the Almighty, who was, who is, and who is to come.
>
> Whenever the living creatures give glory, honor, and thanks to the one seated on the throne, the one who lives forever and ever, the twenty-four elders fall down before the one seated on the throne and worship the one who lives forever and ever. They cast their crowns before the throne and say, Our Lord and God, you are worthy to receive glory and honor and power, because you have created all things, and by your will they exist and were created. (Rev. 4:2–5, 8–11)

John did not witness happiness. Heaven was not conducting a typical office party. Heavenly creatures were basking in the Lord's presence. They could clearly see him seated on his throne so they knew there was no reason to forfeit their joy. When you experience the joy that emanates from God's presence, your natural response is worship. Heaven can worship God freely because there is no problem, no enemy, and no crisis that can separate them from almighty God. When John gazed into heaven's court, it did not eliminate his problems. It put them in their proper perspective.

You can be certain of this. If you were carried to heaven and, from there, you considered your life on Earth and its problems, you could not help but experience joy. For now you would see Christ upon his throne and be amazed by his power, love, and wisdom. You would observe angelic beings shuttling about the universe, carrying out the Creator's every intention. You would see invincible heavenly legions prepared to vanquish any foe. You would learn of God's plan for humanity that he has been steadily implementing day by day, undeterred throughout the ages. You would be transfixed by the joy that exudes from Christ himself at the center of heaven. Such is the joy that awaits you.

Responding to God's Joyful Ways

How should you worship, pray to, and serve a God who radiates joy? What should your communion with God be like if, every time you draw near to him, you encounter fullness of joy? Jesus commanded his disciples to abide in him; that is, to continuously remain intimately connected to and in fellowship with him. Jesus explained: "I have told you these things so that my joy may be in you and your joy may be complete" (John 15:11). You cannot live in the epicenter of joy and not feel its effect (Ps. 16:11). The closer you walk with Jesus, the more joy you experience.

You cannot live in the epicenter of joy and not feel its effect (Ps. 16:11).

The world assumes that joy results from an abundance of pleasure and an absence of problems. If we could just regain our health, or find a new job, or purchase that house, *then* we could be joyful. But joy comes from basking in God's presence. It is available regardless of the burdens or trials that assail us. After an arduous challenge of rebuilding the wall around Jerusalem, Nehemiah encouraged the people by saying: "Do not grieve, because the joy of the LORD is your strength" (Neh. 8:10).

Likewise, when the kingdom of Judah was assaulted by a massive enemy army during King Jehoshaphat's reign, God sent word that he would deliver them. The next day the choir preceded the army into battle, singing praises and shouting for joy (2 Chron. 20:13–29). The battle was won while the people praised God! Joy came before the victory, not after.

If we could just regain our health, or find a new job, or purchase that house, *then* we could be joyful. But joy comes from basking in God's presence.

A joyless Christian is a contradiction in terms. Since Christ is risen and rules the universe, everything a believer does, regardless of outward circumstances, can be permeated with joy. That was Paul and Silas's experience. Evil men who had been exploiting a vulnerable woman lied about them to the leaders of the city of Philippi. The civic authorities had them humiliatingly stripped in public and then brutally beaten. Then they were placed in stocks in the inner prison reserved for the worst offenders. The two men had every reason to be miserable. Yet, at the darkest apex of the night, they were joyfully singing hymns (Acts 16:16–34). They had been unjustly robbed of their dignity; they were battered, bruised, bleeding, naked, and mocked, but none of that could separate them from God's presence. And that is where joy can always be found.

Even the smallest inconvenience can rob us of our joy if we allow it to distract us from abiding in Christ's presence. Sadly, you do not have to look far to encounter joyless Christians. It might be Christian businesspeople who allow the demands of work to stress them out or parents who are so immersed in the daily grind of child-rearing that their home is a somber place. Some allow political tension to hijack their joy. A cranky boss, a loss in sports, a less than competent store clerk, a traffic jam—a never-ending list of factors make people's joy vaporize daily. Even "career Christians" can lose their joy. Pastors have grown bitter because of the way a few grumpy souls in their congregation treat them. Missionaries become so frustrated with the management of their organization that they descend into joylessness, even as they share the good news of the gospel. There are Christian families that dutifully but joylessly attend church each week.

Jesus assured his disciples that no one could steal their joy (John 16:22). Yet too often God's people surrender it.[37] Paul and Silas experienced, in the depths of the Philippian jail, that no circumstance could remove God's presence, so their joy remained intact. However, when we base our joy on our feelings or present situation, we are always one rude comment or insensitive act away from misery.

Christ has called us to be his ambassadors (2 Cor. 5:20). The role of ambassadors is to embody the government ruler or nation they represent. It is a gross dereliction of duty for Christ's ambassadors to represent him joylessly. Christianity is, by its nature, a joyful religion (Luke 1:14, 44; 2:10). Our faith is based on the gospel, which literally means "good news." How could we not serve such a God joyfully?

God's Ways Are Restful

God Gives Rest

One of the mysteries concerning almighty God is why he chose to rest after six days of creation (Gen. 2:1–3). While creating a universe is no small matter, it seems that a divine being who could speak galaxies into existence would not need to recuperate after six days' labor. Theologians have speculated for centuries as to why God rested. It may have been to set an example for his creatures, as they did not have divine powers for their labor as he did. It could be he took time to enjoy the work he had accomplished. He may have ceased working so all creation could bring him glory. Perhaps it was because everything he had created was good and nothing more needed to be done. What is certain is that God affirmed and modeled the value of finding respite from work.

If anyone should have been utterly exhausted and on the verge of burnout, it was Jesus. Yet there was an unmistakable serenity to his life and actions. It is important to note that, even though Jesus was the Son of God and capable of performing jaw-dropping miracles, he did not have superhuman strength or endurance. In taking on flesh, Jesus experienced all the physical limitations we do. He grew tired from physical and emotional exertion. He needed sleep and food like every mortal. He enjoyed peace and quiet. He needed rest. On one occasion Jesus was so tired he fell asleep in a boat, and even a fierce storm did not wake him (Mark 4:38). Clearly, there were occasions when Jesus was completely exhausted.

Moreover, everywhere Jesus went, people clamored to see him, talk with him, and be healed by him. He was constantly being scrutinized and criticized by self-righteous Pharisees and a wide array of enemies. He generally had twelve men with him, so he rarely had privacy. What's more, those disciples, though enjoying constant access to him, seemed never to master the teaching he regularly gave them (Matt. 16:22–23; John 14:9). Jesus ministered to large crowds, yet he did so without the assistance of modern technology. He walked most places in sandals in the heat of the day. He did not have the benefit of air-conditioning, sound systems, or green rooms before he spoke.

Jesus would have endured many emotional pressures as well. He dealt with oppressed, exploited, and demoralized people. He was regularly called upon to minister to demon-possessed, sick, and even dead people. He dealt with racism and sexism. He performed his ministry knowing he had a close associate who would one day betray him. Moreover, Jesus performed his ministry with the specter of a cross looming before him at Calvary. How did Jesus manage to do so much, under such challenging conditions, and not suffer an emotional or physical breakdown? He regularly did four things. The first two are commonly recognized. The second two are often neglected by his followers.

Jesus Withdrew

Jesus regularly took his disciples to a deserted place away from the crowds to rest and recuperate (Mark 6:1–2; 9:2; Luke 9:10). Because Jesus ministered from the confines of a limited, human body, he could not work all the time. He had to withdraw from the crowds for restoration. Of course, Jesus knew that every time he taught, preached, healed, or cast out demons, he made people's lives better. It may have seemed cruel or selfish to retreat from the crowds when he had the power to set people free from their afflictions, but Jesus never displayed any sense of guilt for withdrawing from people and resting. Perhaps because Jesus knew how demanding his schedule was, he was more intentional about taking time to restore his strength.

Jesus Found Strength by Communing with God

Modern pundits and self-help gurus might posit that Jesus "lacked balance." He did not keep regular office hours or schedule annual vacations. Though he sought to withdraw from the crowds, the crowds often found him, nonetheless. Jesus's primary source of renewal came not from his holidays but from his communion.

Jesus made a regular practice to spend extended time in fellowship with his heavenly Father. Prayer was not merely a spiritual discipline or a religious obligation for Jesus. He found strength and renewal in prayer. At times this meant praying at the end of a long day of ministry or praying through the night (Mark 1:35; 6:46; Luke 5:16; 6:12). Though it meant less physical rest, prayer restored Jesus spiritually. Regardless of how busy he was, he always made time to spend with his Father. Not surprisingly, when Judas considered how to betray Jesus to his enemies, he knew the most predictable place to find him was at his place of prayer.

After a demanding day of work, we might feel as if we are too tired to pray. But Jesus found strength in prayer. Imagine how physically and emotionally exhausting it was to teach more than five thousand men and their families all day, without the means of a loudspeaker. Then feeding the multitude. Surely breaking that much bread and fish, even miraculously, must have been wearisome. Yet at the end of that long day, Jesus told his disciples to take the remainder of the evening off while he personally dismissed the crowd (Mark 6:45). After sending the last person home, Jesus climbed a mountain to pray through the night. Surely Jesus's prayer life was of a different quality than ours, for he came away from his prayer times refreshed and invigorated rather than depleted. Prayer times restored him in ways that no amount of sleep could.

Jesus Found Strength and Comfort from Friends

One cannot read far into the Gospels without soon detecting that Jesus enjoyed people. He relished fellowship with his friends Mary, Martha, and Lazarus at their home in Bethany, outside of Jerusalem (Luke 10:38–42; John 12:1–8). Jesus attended parties

(Luke 5:29–30; John 2:1–12), even inviting himself to some (Luke 19:5). Jesus carried the greatest responsibility of anyone who ever lived, yet he still took time to cease from his work and enjoy time with friends.

Because the Gospel writers placed a priority on Jesus's crucifixion and resurrection accounts, as well as his teaching, we can sometimes miss other aspects of Jesus's life that were important. One of these is how much he enjoyed the fellowship of friends. Jesus was not a robot. He had deep feelings. And, though he was the Messiah with history's greatest task awaiting him, he still took time to enjoy the company of others. I, for one, would love to hear Jesus's laugh. I suspect he laughed often. It may have been of the kind that fills a room when it erupts at a humorous moment. No one would have savored the simple pleasures of life or seen the humor in ordinary situations any more than he did. This may well be why he was on so many people's party guest list. Elton Trueblood wrote a book entitled, *The Humor of Christ*.[38] Perhaps one of the ways Jesus was able to endure the constant criticism of his opponents or to restore his emotions after casting out a demon from someone in horrific bondage was to keep his sense of humor. Jesus always had friends around him. Clearly this was, in part, to teach them. But it may well be that he also genuinely enjoyed being around people because he found refreshment from their company.

Jesus Lived at a Divinely Ordered Pace

No one had more demands upon their time than Jesus. Yet he never seemed in a hurry. He was never rushing down the street, late for an appointment. Nevertheless, Jesus completed every assignment his Father gave him (John 17:4; 19:30). People did not set Jesus's agenda; the Father did. People were constantly telling him what they thought he should do (Matt. 4:1–11; 12:38–39; 16:22; Mark 1:37; 3:21; Luke 8:19–21; John 7:1–5).

Yet Jesus lived his life at the divinely set pace his Father assigned him.

There are many ministers today suffering from burnout. They are emotionally and physically depleted because of their multitudinous responsibilities. Yet Jesus understood that God would empower him to accomplish everything he assigned him. Burnout typically results from micromanaging and taking on responsibilities God has not assigned. Ministers often take on extra work out of a sense of guilt, to please people, or because they do not trust others to do the work properly. Jesus always remained supremely in control of his schedule. Though others constantly suggested additional tasks for him to do, he knew he had one master: God the Father. I work regularly with CEOs of large companies. At times they feel stressed and overwhelmed by their enormous responsibilities. I often remind them that they are the boss. They are responsible for their own schedules. They can say no. Much of their overwork comes from choices they make and not from work that is imposed on them. Saying no to unnecessary tasks frees them to say yes to God. Jesus refused to let anyone but his loving heavenly Father set his agenda.

John Mark Comer says, "After all, this is the man who waited three decades to preach his first sermon, and after one day on the job as Messiah, he went off to the wilderness for forty days to pray. Nothing could hurry this man."[39] Jesus never hurried, yet he always had space in his life for people. Even though his daily schedule appeared to be a continuous interruption, he never acted like a type A, task-driven executive walking briskly down a hallway with his head down so as not to be diverted from his destination. Jesus was never too busy or distracted to recognize a divine appointment.

When Jesus entered a Galilean city, the crowds were so thick that he and his disciples could barely make their way down the street. Jairus, a synagogue official, rushed up and fell at Jesus's feet, begging him to come to his house and heal his gravely ill daughter (Mark 5:21–24). Time was critical. Jesus began to follow him, but suddenly he stopped and asked who had touched him. His disciples were incredulous. Half the town seemed to be brushing against him! But Jesus realized someone had just been healed by touching him, and he wanted to identify who it was. It was a woman who had been bleeding for twelve years. Jesus took time to bless her. Before he could continue his journey, word came that Jairus's daughter had died. To people like Jairus, it may have seemed that Jesus should have been in a greater hurry. The delay may have cost his daughter her life. Though Jesus didn't arrive on Jairus's schedule, he would perform an even greater miracle than had been called for and raise the girl from the dead (Mark 5:35–43). Jesus never rushed through life. He always moved at a divinely set pace. Though some might have wished Jesus would move more quickly, he accomplished everything his Father assigned to him each day.

Jesus never rushed through life. He always moved at a divinely set pace.

As Jesus and his disciples passed through Jericho on their way to Jerusalem, mobs of people, desperate to see the famous Teacher and Healer, pressed in upon them. Jesus and his companions had almost made it to the city's outskirts when Jesus stopped, having just spotted the most notorious tax collector and sinner in the region (Luke 19:2). Jesus insisted on going to his house for lunch. The disciples were aware they still had seventeen miles to go to their destination, much of it uphill. Time was critical. Yet Jesus refused to be hurried. He always had time to join his Father's activity.

Jesus set aside periods of quiet and refreshment. He took time to fellowship with people. He was always open to a divine "interruptions." Nevertheless, because of the way Jesus conducted his life and ministry, he left nothing undone. After only three and a half years of public ministry, Jesus exclaimed, "It is finished!" (John 19:30). Because of Jesus's divinely orchestrated pace of life and work, he accomplished more than anyone in history, and he launched a worldwide movement that continues to this day.

Responding to God's Way of Rest

How do you follow someone who takes rest seriously? How do you model yourself after a person who never felt overwhelmed by his workload or discouraged by his responsibilities? The rest Jesus offers is not merely a physical respite. It includes spiritual and emotional restoration. Jesus said: "Come to me, all of you who are weary and burdened, and I will give you rest. Take up my yoke and learn from me, because I am lowly and humble in heart, and you will find rest for your souls. For my yoke is easy and my burden is light" (Matt. 11:28–30). When you follow Jesus, he will certainly lead you to build a Sabbath rest into your life. He will teach you to regularly cease from your labor. He will guide you into the divinely orchestrated cycles of work and rest.

There is a rest that goes much deeper than physical rest. This is a spiritual rest that comes from intimate fellowship, or abiding in Christ. David wrote: "I am at rest in God alone. . . . Rest in God alone, my soul. For my hope comes from him" (Ps. 62:1, 5). While Jesus did not always enjoy as much physical rest as he might have wished, he never failed to regularly seek spiritual restoration. For believers, "rest" can include ceasing from striving to obtain our own salvation and understanding that our righteousness and acceptability to God come not from our efforts but Christ's. True spiritual rest involves taking our life's burdens and casting them upon our Savior (1 Pet. 5:7). Godly rest means refusing to worry about tomorrow and, instead, trusting the problems of each day into God's hands (Matt. 6:25–34). It is possible to be the busiest person on the earth and yet to daily experience God's rest. It is also possible to live a life of extravagant luxury and idleness and yet be weighed down by anxiety and stress.

The Sabbath was not widely practiced in the ancient world. For societies living on the brink of hunger and poverty, work was a daily necessity. For God to command his people to labor only six out of the seven days in a week was asking them to trust him to make up the difference so they did not become destitute. Farmers who observed the Sabbath would have noticed tasks left unfinished. Fields still needed to be plowed, sown, or harvested. Animals required care, and repairs demanded attention. Farmers would have been tempted to forgo rest to catch up on their work. Forcing oneself to refrain from labor and to focus instead on physical, spiritual, and emotional rest was an act of faith for people with so much work to do.

The same problem plagues many Christians today. Is it surprising that pastors struggle to rest? Many who "serve God for a living" are physically and spiritually drained. They constantly pour out, but they neglect taking time to fill up. They are weary from the load they carry, but they feel guilty if they rest from their labor. Burnout is a widespread problem among Christian leaders. This is ironic, for many ministers are wearing themselves out serving someone who knew how to rest. Needing rest is God's way of reminding us that we are mortal and have limited strength. Apart from abiding in Christ, we can do nothing (John 15:5). Every time you feel the need for rest, you are being reminded of your need for God.

What does this mean for Jesus's followers? We must learn to live in a divine rhythm of work and rest. We must trust our work, finances, and cares into God's hands and allow him to carry the burden for us. This will happen as we let God determine our priorities so we focus on the most important work each day. We must tap into the deep wells of emotional and spiritual rest that restore us, even as we pass through troubled and stressful times. We can ask Christ to replenish us when we have spent all we have in his service fulfilling our responsibilities. When we live our life God's way, we regularly draw on God's rest so we have the strength to complete everything he puts before us.

Every time you feel the need for rest, you are being reminded of your need for God.

God's Ways Bring Peace

God's Nature

You will not find a place in the Bible where God is presented as frantic, distressed, or anxious. God is always at peace, for nothing can surprise, alarm, or harm him. He exists in perfect tranquility. God is omniscient and eternal. He has no need to receive daily angelic briefings about the latest developments in the universe. He has always known what will happen today, and he has had an eternity to prepare for it. Your doctor's office may have called and asked you to come in to discuss the most recent lab results. This might alarm you and cause you to worry. But long before you were born, or your grandparents were born, God knew you and was aware of what those lab tests would reveal. He has been preparing you all your life for the upcoming appointment. You are better equipped for it than you know. God knows your body better than your doctor does. He sees your future. He knows what he intends to do as he works in your health. Ultimately, he understands what awaits you on the day you finally meet him face-to-face. You may be troubled by the unknown, but with God there is no unknown.

Jesus is the Prince of peace (Isa. 9:6). He is supreme at experiencing and dispensing peace. There is no greater reservoir of peace than God's storehouse. There are many ways to describe God's peace. It is a state of absolute calm, regardless of what is occurring. It includes tranquility, confidence, trust, and faith that all is well, regardless of the circumstances. A powerful king may feel at peace as he sits securely upon his throne. A baby may feel at peace as her mother holds her tightly. God can bring peace while you undergo painful trials. People have experienced God's unshakable peace even as they endured cancer or the loss of a spouse. God's peace is so pure and strong it can guard your mind and heart even while you endure life's worst circumstances.

**You may be troubled by the unknown,
but with God there is no unknown.**

Scripture describes God as a fortress, a stronghold, and a rock (Ps. 59; 62:1–8). The psalmist David knew full well the value of a strong fortress. Much of his life was plagued by enemies. He endured numerous troubles and threats. But he learned that God, himself, was his safe place. God would not merely grant David peace; he would *be* his peace (Micah 5:5; John 14:27). The key, as David came to understand, was remaining in the stronghold of God. David said:

> "Lord, I seek refuge in you. . . . Be a rock of refuge for me, a mountain fortress to save me. For you are my rock and my fortress. . . . For you are my refuge. Into your hand I entrust my spirit. . . .

> You know the troubles of my soul and have not handed me over to the enemy. You have set my feet in a spacious place. . . .
>
> But I trust in you, LORD; I say, "You are my God." The course of my life is in your power. . . . Make your face shine on your servant; save me by your faithful love. . . .
>
> How great is your goodness, which you have stored up for those who fear you. . . . You hide them in the protection of your presence; you conceal them in a shelter from human schemes, from quarrelsome tongues. . . .
>
> Be strong, and let your heart be courageous, all you who put your hope in the LORD." (Ps. 31:1–5, 7–8, 14–16, 19–20, 24)

During the Middle Ages, whenever an enemy invaded the land, peasants farming in the countryside would hurriedly race to the castle for protection. The farmers were no match for the rapacious hordes descending upon their farms. Their only hope for survival was to enter the castle. Once inside, with the drawbridge closed, they were safe from their enemies. The king and his forces would defend the castle and sally forth to combat the enemy. The key for the peasants was not to fight the enemy but to remain safely within the fortress.

God is our tower of strength. He is not intimidated by any enemy that comes against us. He laughs at them (Ps. 2:4). Even human castles and strongholds can be overcome but not the refuge of God. Whatever is entrusted to him is entirely secure. This should bring us deep, abiding peace.

The book of Revelation demonstrates God's unequaled power in language that is deeply reassuring: "Then I saw an angel coming down from heaven holding the key to the abyss and a great chain in his hand. He seized the dragon, that ancient serpent who is the devil and Satan, and bound him for the thousand years. He threw him into the abyss, closed it, and put a seal on it so that he would no longer deceive the nations until the thousand years were completed" (Rev. 20:1–3).

Countless evil people throughout history have brought great suffering to millions, but none compares to the diabolical evil embodied in Satan. No one has brought more grief, pain, and destruction upon humanity than he has. He has deceived the smartest people on the earth. He has instigated devastating wars that led to the deaths of millions. He has destroyed a multitude of marriages, misled untold numbers of prodigals, enslaved countless addicts, and brought dishonor to God's name throughout the ages. How does one arrest and imprison the world's most fiendish villain? We would assume that for such a Herculean task, God would dispatch an archangel like Michael or Gabriel, accompanied by battalions of angels. They would storm Satan's battlements and overwhelm his sinister forces. But this is unnecessary. Instead, according to John's vision, God commissions one lone angel. He is not even named. He has no legion in reserve. No resistance is mentioned. No battle is fought. If there is, it is so inconsequential it does not merit mention in Scripture's hallowed pages.

This is humanity's greatest foe. And when God's patience reaches its end, he is summarily dispatched to the abyss. Understand this: you have no enemy, no critic, no naysayer who compares to Satan's destructive capacity. If God can so easily overcome your most powerful threat, you certainly have nothing to fear from a lesser foe.

Why are God's ways always peaceful? Because there is nothing in the universe powerful or evil enough to disturb his serenity. He is all-powerful. In every conflict there is never any doubt as to who will be victorious. Just as God once cast Satan out of heaven, so he will most assuredly have him hurled into a lake of fire (Rev. 20:10). Though your troubles and enemies may seem invincible to you, they are as nothing in God's sight (Rev. 19:19–21; 20:1–3). If you take refuge in almighty God as your stronghold, you can remain in perfect peace.

Why are God's ways always peaceful? Because there is nothing in the universe powerful or evil enough to disturb his serenity.

Our Response to God's Ways of Peace

Peace does not result from an absence of problems. It comes from abiding in Christ. Peace in our heart and mind stems from having peace with God (Rom. 5:1). When we are at peace with God, he makes us his heir rather than his enemy (Rom. 5:10; 8:14–17). Peace with God frees us from shame and guilt. It alleviates our fear of death. It fills our life with the love and joy of God. When we become children of God, he gives us his Holy Spirit to apply his peace to every corner of our life. Peace with God makes us God centered rather than self-centered. When we focus on God, our mind and heart are enveloped in divine well-being. Isaiah declared: "You will keep the mind that is dependent on you in perfect peace, for it is trusting in you" (Isa. 26:3). Jesus said, "Peace I leave with you. My peace I give to you. . . . Don't let your heart be troubled or fearful" (John 14:27).

Though our peace comes from God, we must respond to him in faith if we are to experience it. Like every divine promise, God will not force his provision upon us. We must trust him for it. The Bible says to "cast your burden on the LORD, and he will sustain you; he will never allow the righteous to be shaken" (Ps. 55:22). Yet many Christians refuse to do so. It is tempting to cling to our fear. We often fail to trust God to manage our concerns. We regularly rehearse our anxious thoughts. When we refuse to surrender our worries, they eat away at us, even though peace that surpasses understanding is available to us in abundance.

Paul urged believers to walk in the Spirit (Gal. 5:16). This involves living our life with a daily conscious awareness of and surrender to the Spirit's leading. When we walk in the Spirit, a natural by-product will be God's peace reigning in our hearts and minds (Gal. 5:22). If we are not experiencing God's peace in ever-increasing measure, then we are not walking in the Spirit. We may be attending church services or doing Bible readings, but if we are not seeing the fruit of peace in our life, that is a sure sign we are not abiding in Christ. When we embrace the Spirit's work in us, he will saturate our hearts and minds with peace.

If we are not experiencing God's peace in ever-increasing measure, then we are not walking in the Spirit.

To experience God's peace, we must be people of prayer. Paul declared, "Don't worry about anything, but in everything, through prayer and petition with thanksgiving, present your requests to God. And the peace of God, which surpasses all understanding, will guard your hearts and minds in Christ Jesus" (Phil. 4:6–7). There will inevitably be disconcerting circumstances in our lives. The enemy roams the earth like a lion, looking for those he can destroy (1 Pet. 5:8). We are daily engaged in spiritual warfare (Eph. 6:10–17). Yet, regardless of what we face, we can immediately go to God in prayer and lay the entire matter before him.

John Paton, nineteenth-century missionary to cannibals, whose life was in constant peril, observed: "Did ever a mother run more quickly to protect her crying child in danger's hour, than the Lord Jesus hastens to answer believing prayer . . . ?"[40] He adds, "Truly all are safe who are in God's keeping."[41] As we lift our concerns to him, God infuses our hearts and minds so thoroughly with his heavenly peace that there is no room left for worry or fear. God's peace is undaunted by our worst problem or fiercest enemy. It is counterintuitive to remain calm when our health is suffering, the nation is in political turmoil, or the economy is undergoing a massive downturn. Yet such is the peace of God.

God's Peace and the News

I once was speaking at a conference on the difference Christ makes in a believer's life, and after one session a couple approached me. They appeared deeply troubled. They shared with me their many concerns for the nation, as well as for the world at large. They were clearly devoid of peace and joy. I was curious and asked how much news they consumed each day. They estimated they watched or listened to an average of eight hours per day, since the news was on whenever they were home. Then I asked how many hours a day they read their Bible and prayed. Somewhat sheepishly, they confessed to doing so roughly fifteen minutes per day. They had no peace because they regularly filled their minds with the world's perspective and concerns, while taking only a hurried glance at what God had to say. It is impossible to enjoy close fellowship with the Prince of peace and remain troubled and anxious.

It is impossible to enjoy close fellowship with the Prince of peace and remain troubled and anxious.

Conclusion

It is easy to believe that residents of heaven experience joy, rest, and peace. God, however, makes these experiences available to us as well, even during our frenetic, demanding, and troubled moments. The world offers shallow substitutes for joy, rest, and peace, but these cannot satisfy our deepest longings. It is possible not only to experience these ways of God but to make them a pattern in our life. There is a way for us to live and work joyfully, restfully, and peacefully. It is God's way.

Questions for Reflection/Discussion

1. Would those who know you best consider you to be a joyful person? What is the evidence?

2. How easy do you find it to rest? Do you feel guilty for regularly seeking physical, emotional, and spiritual restoration? How might Jesus's example help?

3. How do you use prayer for spiritual and emotional restoration?

4. How serious of a crisis must you encounter before you lose your sense of peace?

5. How does the amount of time you spend consuming the news compare with how much time you spend in prayer?

CHAPTER 13

GOD'S WAYS ARE BEAUTIFUL

God saw all that he had made, and
it was very good indeed.
(Gen. 1:31)

I have asked one thing from the LORD*; it is*
what I desire: to dwell in the house of the LORD
all the days of my life, gazing on the beauty of
the LORD *and seeking him in his temple.*
(Ps. 27:4)

On April 3, 1860, Charles Darwin confessed to Asa Gray, "The sight of a feather in a peacock's tail, whenever I gaze at it, makes me sick."[42] Darwin acknowledged that nature's beauty was problematic for an evolutionist seeking a utilitarian, pragmatic reason for its existence. Vibrant colors can certainly make birds or animals attractive to mates. But they also make them highly visible to predators, and this seems to run contrary to the natural selection of the species. One would think that over time the animals and birds that survive would be those that were least noticeable and most bland. Evolution is hard-pressed to explain creatures with dazzling beauty.

A larger consideration is, Why do humans take delight in or experience a sense of wonder about that which is beautiful? No other members of the animal kingdom (that we know of) experience awe when looking at a sunset or gazing upon a majestic mountain. There is something innate within human beings that recognizes when a sight, sound, or smell is pleasing to the senses. Likewise, people find deep pleasure in exalted music, artistic masterpieces, and classic literature. Darwin struggled to explain the function of a Shakespearian sonnet in terms of the survival of the fittest. In fact, Darwin came to despise the works of Shakespeare. People have no need of poetry to preserve their genes for the following generation. There is, however, an inborn quality within human beings that delights in beauty.[43]

God's Ways are Good and Beautiful

When we first read about God in the Bible, he is creating good things (Gen. 1:4, 10, 12, 18, 21, 25, 31). The psalmist proclaimed: "The heavens declare the glory of God, and the expanse proclaims the work of his hands. Day after day they pour out speech; night after night they communicate knowledge" (Ps. 19:1–2). Paul described the heavens in a similar fashion: "For his invisible attributes, that is, his eternal power and divine nature, have been clearly seen since the creation of the world, being understood through what he has made. As a result, people are without excuse" (Rom. 1:20). The Greek word used here to mean "that which is made" is translated "workmanship" in Ephesians 2:10. We derive the English word *poetry* from it. As people gaze into the heavens or consider the intricate craftsmanship of the human body, they see God's artwork—his masterpieces. David, Paul, and other biblical writers believed that God, as Creator, left his personal imprint on creation. Therefore, to see the vastness, intricate complexity, and breathtaking beauty of creation is to glimpse into the mind and heart of its Creator.

The universe presents us with numerous impressions concerning God. Its immensity certainly reflects on God's power. Even the most powerful telescopes yet made cannot detect the edge of the cosmos. Why create a universe so enormous? The people occupying Earth use only a miniscule fraction of a universe consisting of trillions of stars and planets. God made the universe far larger than was necessary for humanity to appreciate or enjoy. Could it be that he made it not only for us but for his own pleasure? When considering the bleak nature of other planets in the solar system, Earth is a magnificent and beautiful place. Why did God design Earth the way he did? Why create beautiful mountain ranges, waterfalls, forests, plains, lakes, and rivers? Why make sunrises and sunsets so spectacular? Why include such a wide array of flora and fauna? As countless landscape artists have demonstrated through the ages, Earth abounds with beauty. God must have known that by creating beauty in nature, such as the forbidden fruit in the garden, people would be tempted to worship nature rather than him. Yet God valued beauty so much that he filled the earth with it, even though he knew it would compete for our affections.

The deeper issue is: What makes one thing attractive and another banal or even repulsive? What makes people appreciate one sunset or mountain range over another? What makes one painting a masterpiece and another one fit only for a garage sale? Are certain objects innately lovely, or is it that God identifies certain things to be lovely? Are objects, vistas, sounds, or smells delightful in themselves or because people delight in them? We know what we like. But do we understand why?

Throughout Scripture, God directed people to construct objects that were beautiful. God clearly understood what made something attractive. God exhibited high standards when he instructed people to build a tabernacle for worship purposes, yet he also valued what was appropriate for each situation. He did not command farmers to gild their barns with gold, yet the tabernacle was to be so furnished. The ark of the covenant, representing God's presence with his people as well as the altars and utensils were intricately designed by God. Daniel Blackaby notes: "With the tabernacle, the temple, and the ark of the covenant—the three physical Old Testament structures symbolic of God's physical dwelling amongst men—the biblical text reveals that the blueprints and design patterns are given to man directly from God himself" (Exod. 25:8; 1 Chron. 28:19).[44] The ark of the covenant was to be overlaid with gold (Exod. 25:11), though it would only be seen by a high priest once a year. There were two golden cherubim that towered over the ark (Exod. 25:18–20; 37:7–9). These, too, were only visible annually to a single high priest. Even the inside of the ark was to be gold although only God ever saw it. God is an invisible spirit. Perhaps that is why he cared about the furnishings representing his presence.

God also gave detailed directives for the garments, breastplate, diadem, and turban of the high priest (Exod. 28). The breastplate for the high priest was to be made of blue, purple, and scarlet yarn and inlaid with precious stones (Exod. 15–30). Instructions for the priest's robe and turban were explicit (Exod. 25:31–38). Even the tabernacle curtains were precisely designed using costly blue, purple, and scarlet yarn. Moreover, figures of cherubim were to be woven into them (Exod. 36:8–14). Construction of the tabernacle and items for worship were not left up to Israelite volunteers. God appointed Bazalel, from the tribe of Judah, to be the chief artisan. Of him, Moses declared: "He has filled him with God's Spirit, with wisdom, understanding, and ability in every kind of craft to design artistic works in gold, silver, and bronze, to cut gemstones for mounting, and to carve wood for work in every kind of artistic craft" (Exod. 35:31–33). Daniel Blackaby notes: "Interestingly, the first biblical record of a person being filled with the Spirit of God is an artist and a craftsman, not a king or prophet."[45]

God provided a detailed and unique recipe for the anointing oil as well as the incense used in the tabernacle (Exod. 30:22–38). He specified how burnt offerings were to be sacrificed so they produced a "pleasing aroma" to the Lord (Lev. 1:9, 13, 17). Lest anyone presume that any type of ornamentation or worship was acceptable, God made an example of Nadab and Abihu, the sons of Aaron. These two offered up "unauthorized fire" before the Lord (Lev. 10:1–3). Clearly they did not follow the precise formula God had given. Consequently, God struck them both dead. From the outset of the Israelite's worship, God made it exceedingly clear that he has high standards for how people worship and relate to him.

God is spirit, yet he cares deeply about how things look, smell, and sound. As music with voice and instruments was developed for worship, especially under David, all five senses were incorporated. God, who is spirit, does not have a physical nose, ears, or eyes. Yet he cared about such details as how incense offered to him smelled. What kind of aroma is pleasing to a spirit?

Blackaby observes that throughout Scripture, God directs the most amazing story ever told as he redeems his fallen creatures. The drama and high-quality storytelling included in the Bible's pages have inspired much of the West's great literature down through the ages. Novels, poetry, and plays about human failings and a savior coming to make things right are universal in scope. Parables Jesus told, such as the prodigal son and the good Samaritan have been viewed through the centuries as masterful storytelling. There is something profoundly compelling about a well-told story, a striking painting, a spectacular sunset, a symphonic masterpiece, or the fragrance of a rose garden that appeals to an innate aesthetic, spiritual, human dimension.

Perhaps we know why we find certain things attractive and others repulsive, but why does God delight in things that are beautiful? Why does it matter to God how something looks, smells, or sounds? How does God evaluate whether something is good, beautiful, or pleasing to experience? What is it about the way God designed us that makes us consider one painting a masterpiece and another worthless? Why are Beethoven's symphonies cherished around the world, but a middle school band's clarinet performance is painful even for parents to hear? While there is certainly a wide range in tastes among people, God clearly designed humanity to delight in certain forms of beauty.

Our Response

Out of everything God brought into existence, only humans were created in his image (Gen. 1:26–27). Theologians have debated for millennia what exactly this means. Is it that he gave us eternal souls, unlike any other creature? Is it that we are rational beings, able to use reason? Clearly, God made us to be moral beings who can be held accountable for our actions. While the extent and exact nature of how God's image is reflected in humans is uncertain, it is obvious that God created humankind with qualities and characteristics that set us apart from every other inhabitant on Earth. A key distinctive about humans is not just our ability to *appreciate* beauty but also our ability to create things that are aesthetically attractive.

Creating and appreciating beauty must certainly encompass a part of what it means to reflect God's image. Here are four ways we can embrace our God-given capacity to appreciate and create beauty.

Delight in What God Does

As we have seen, God, as Creator, takes pleasure in things that are excellent and lovely. God values aesthetics. If it mattered to him if certain objects were made of gold or tin, or whether a color was purple rather than beige, or if music is harmonious rather than off-key, how should this affect how we live?

Surely our Creator wants us to find pleasure in what brings him delight. We can be intentional in seeking out and paying attention to beauty in its wide variety of forms. There are countless ways to do this: spending time outdoors, tending a flower garden, visiting an art gallery, attending a symphony, reading a classic book or good poetry. We are surrounded by beauty, but we must take time to appreciate it.

Parents and grandparents can teach their children to appreciate beauty that is found in the world whether in nature or in the arts. When I took my family to visit the Grand Canyon, I was taken back by its enormity and beauty. I stood in awe of this masterpiece of nature. Suddenly I heard my children squealing with joy. They had just seen a squirrel. They were not even looking in the direction of the canyon. But, perhaps, my children were on to something. Though there are far more squirrels than wonder-of-the-world canyons, even the smallest of animals is an awe-inspiring exhibit of the Creator's handiwork.

Over the years I have taken my children to places like the Louvre and the British Museum. Love of beauty is often more caught than taught. Two of my children developed a list of the top one hundred works of literature throughout history and have made a point of reading them. We have a family book club wherein we read a challenging book together and then meet over lunch to discuss it. They have all learned to savor the delightful aroma one experiences when opening a brand-new book. Perhaps your family is drawn to art or enjoys seeing plays together. We have friends who love to gather and play instruments and sing together. Many families go on hikes together or camp in the beautiful outdoors. This is living according to God's ways.

Create Beautiful Things as You Are Able

Not everyone is gifted artistically or musically. We certainly are not all poets. Yet there are numerous ways to create beauty around us. We can decorate our homes, grow a flower garden, play pleasant music, burn a scented candle, or keep a well-manicured yard. We might set out a birdbath and feeder and enjoy watching the birds they attract. A fountain can provide soothing sights and sounds.

Jordan Peterson, in his book *Beyond Order: 12 More Rules for Life,* provides an interesting rule for people to live by. Rule 8, "Try to make one room in your home as beautiful as possible."[46] Peterson is a psychologist, not a theologian. He suggests: "We live by beauty. We live by literature. We live by art. We cannot live without some connection to the divine—and beauty is divine—because in its absence life is too short, too dismal, and too tragic."[47] Peterson suggests that people find one room or space in their home and make it lovely. He argues that everyone needs something of beauty in their life for both spiritual and psychological reasons. He says: "Making something beautiful is difficult, but it is amazingly worthwhile. If you learn to make something in your life truly beautiful—even one thing—then you have established a relationship with beauty. From there you can begin to expand that relationship out into other elements of your life and the world. That is an invitation to the divine."[48]

Peterson's thoughts may reflect God's command to Adam and Eve to exercise dominion over the earth (Gen. 1:28; 2:15). By naming the animals, Adam joined God in the creative process (Gen. 2:19–20). The descendants of Adam and Eve continue to share the responsibility of taking what God entrusted to them and, with the resources God gives them, making their world more attractive. Daniel Blackaby has pointed out that the four rivers listed in Genesis 2 found their origin in the garden of Eden and flowed out into the rest of the world (Gen. 2:10–14). It seems that the beauty and treasures of Eden were ultimately to be shared with the surrounding world.

When I was a child, my parents bought my brother Tom and me a new bunk bed. Attached to the end was a small desk, and as the older brother, I claimed that tiny space as my own. I carefully lined up my books on it and gathered the most attractive keepsakes and bookends I could muster. The first time I ever dusted anything was when I rubbed my little desk until it gleamed in the light. Our family included five children compressed into a three-bedroom bungalow that also housed church guests, including summer missionaries. That small space at the edge of my bed became an oasis for me. There I placed everything attractive I owned. As I sat at my desk, my eyes feasted on the array of my favorite earthly objects. There I would read my leather-bound Bible and enjoy the rich texture of its pages and the intoxicating aroma of bonded leather. I learned, even as a child, that when you live in a crowded, noisy, humble home, even a small, beautiful space will minister to your soul.

There are numerous ways we can make a small corner of our world beautiful. We might start with our own body. Clearly we have not all been given the same physical qualities. However, our divine mandate is to take what we are given and manage it into its best condition possible. Scripture instructs us that our bodies are temples of God (1 Cor. 3:16). As Paul notes: "For God's temple is holy, and that is what you are" (1 Cor. 3:17). When we allow our bodies to become out of shape, or we do not properly bathe or groom ourselves, we reflect on our Maker. The way we dress can also reflect how we view ourselves as God made us. When we dress slovenly or allow our home or office space to be overrun with clutter, there can be spiritual consequences. I have found that when I lose excess weight, exercise, and tidy up my world, my walk with God improves. Surely, if we would make the world a beautiful place, we should start with ourselves.

We can do as Peterson suggests and make our bedroom or office or living room or backyard or deck a place of beauty that nurtures our spirit. I know men who have done that with their garage, and to them it is not a place filled with oily tools and scattered car accessories but an oasis in their frenetic world. Doing something as simple as turning off the loud, intrusive television programming and commercials blasting into our home and replacing these with peaceful, exalted music can constitute reclaiming the airwaves of our home. My wife Lisa is gifted at doing this. She decorates our home simply and tastefully without spending a lot of money. She keeps tranquil music playing softly. She burns scented candles. As a result, we don't merely live in a comfortable home; we reside in our own retreat center, one that ministers to the souls of those who enter.

A popular current trend is decluttering. Daniel Levitin notes that, until 1600, the average family lived in a one-room house.[49] Today, people typically reside in multi-roomed homes filled with items they rarely use. One study found a typical home with 2,260 visible objects just in the kitchen and two bedrooms! Three out of four Americans report their garages are too full to park a vehicle in them.[50] Levitin notes that living in a cluttered world can be exhausting. He explains that when our mind is having to cancel out extraneous sights and sounds, it becomes too distracted to properly focus on what matters most. For some people, fulfilling God's commission to "have dominion" over the earth begins by taking control of their own life and surroundings. An uncluttered, thoughtfully decorated home can truly be an act of worship.

My wife wages a constant battle against clutter. We keep a goodwill box by the door to the garage at all times. Anything that is no longer needed or useful is carted off to a charity store where someone else can benefit from it and we can keep our shelves and spaces free for items we will use. Hoarders hold on to everything they have for fear they might need it someday. I know people who cannot sleep in their bedroom anymore because it is filled with items they never use. It can be an act of faith to reduce your possessions to the point where you have space for everything you own. Not only will this minister to your soul, but you will be able to park your car in your garage! There are some excellent Christian podcasts full of great ideas on how to simplify and declutter your life.

Imagine what would happen if every Christian made a practice of trying to make their surroundings a little more beautiful. When we go to work, we seek to improve the appearance and functionality of the workplace. I have a friend who noticed a well-known, wealthy, Christian businessman walking from his car to a store. On his way from the parking lot, he stooped down to pick up a piece of litter and took it to the nearest garbage can. Why would a billionaire do such a thing? Why would it matter if one piece of trash was removed from a massive parking lot of a retail outlet he did not own? Yet he chose to make a parking lot just a little more attractive. As a general lifestyle, Christians should make the world lovelier as they pass through it. Doing so can be an act of worship.

Worship in Beauty

God is beautiful. The psalmist David wrote: "I have asked one thing from the Lord; it is what I desire: to dwell in the house of the Lord all the days of my life, gazing on the beauty of the Lord and seeking him in his temple" (Ps. 27:4). Worship is intended to be an aesthetically pleasing experience. Music is to be pleasing to the ear. Sermons ought to be clear and compelling. Prayers should speak to people's hearts and point them heavenward.

Views on worship have changed radically through the generations. Traditionally, people dressed in their finest attire to worship almighty God. Church buildings were built as an act of worship. The architecture of cathedrals was intentionally designed to lead people into an act of worship merely by entering the building. The vertical lines drew people's gazes upward. The shadows as people entered were displaced by light as they approached the altar. The stained glass beautifully proclaimed the gospel. Anyone who has entered a cathedral understands the unique experience it engenders.

During the Reformation, and particularly under the Puritans, there was a reaction against the gaudy ostentatiousness of many churches of that time. In response, places of worship were stripped of their beauty and made to fulfill a solely pragmatic function. Stained-glass windows were out. Emphasis was placed on the preached Word rather than on the furnishings or music. While there is no question that the preached Word is far more important than a flying buttress, it could be argued that something was lost when much of the wonder, majesty, and beauty of the worship experience was discarded. Protestant worship tended to focus on the auditory aspect of the Word preached. More traditional worship, or "high church," incorporated sound but also sight, smell, touch, and taste through such vehicles as incense, candles, and receiving Communion. Could it be that we miss important aspects of worship because we engage so few senses? Could it be that by downplaying beauty in our services we forgo aspects of worship that could speak deeply to our souls? It is certainly possible to worship God in a plain, unadorned room or even a prison cell. But beauty resonates in our souls. If God delighted in golden cherubim and embroidered curtains, along with customized incense in a place of worship, perhaps we could deepen our worship if we enhanced its beauty.

Beauty and a Potted Plant

When I graduated from seminary, I was called to be the pastor of a small church. It had experienced numerical decline for seven years and was suffering the consequences of pastoral neglect. I, of course, developed the best sermons and Bible teaching I could muster. I met everyone at the door with a smile. I zealously reached out to members who had stopped attending. But something bothered me. The auditorium was tired and drab. The carpet and curtains were out-of-date. The platform and furniture were shabby. I came to believe that if we could "liven up" the auditorium, it would affect our worship. We didn't have much money so we couldn't afford to do anything drastic. I removed some outdated, dusty, artificial plants, and I strategically positioned some live potted plants on the platform.

I had a well-intentioned church member who was extremely pragmatic. He wondered why we would waste money on plants when we needed to address drainage issues on the side of the building. Bringing live plants into the auditorium simply meant someone had to water them, an unnecessary frivolity as far as he was concerned. We had an ongoing debate for most of my tenure as pastor. It can be hazardous to remove dated, tired-looking decorations from churches! Congregations have split over less. I still believe that when it comes to the place where you worship God, you should make it as pleasing to the senses as is reasonably possible.

Do Everything to the Glory of God

The way we live reflects our Creator. Our work is an expression of worship to the one who commanded us to exercise dominion over the earth. I minister to many businesspeople. They are just as called to their work as pastors and missionaries are to theirs. The apostle Paul urged believers, "And whatever you do, in word or in deed, do everything in the name of the Lord Jesus" (Col. 3:17). He also exhorted: "Whatever you do, do it from the heart, as something done for the Lord and not for people" (Col. 3:23). This is the way God's people should approach our tasks. Our labors become an act of worship. Work done well brings glory and honor to God. The writer of Proverbs advised: "Do you see a person skilled in his work? He will stand in the presence of kings. He will not stand in the presence of the unknown" (Prov. 22:29).

Our work is an expression of worship to the one who commanded us to exercise dominion over the earth.

Western culture has largely dismissed the importance of "work as worship" as an archaic and even explosive notion. The goal for many is to do the least possible for the greatest remuneration. A sense of entitlement pervades many workplaces. Yet, for a Christian, work is not merely a means to earn a living; it is a calling. God may have gifted you with certain skills and abilities you use each week at your workplace. To only use a small percentage of your capacity is to dishonor your Creator. Likewise, if you believe God is the one who gave you your job, you dishonor him by not giving your best in the role he provided.

This attitude can, of course, be distorted into justifying workaholism. However, the greatest beauty is that which shines through our character and a life well-lived. Mother Teresa, who devoted her life to caring for the world's poorest people, died within a week of Princess Diana. Diana was a beautiful, glamorous, jet-setting princess who captured the world's hearts and imaginations. Both women did many good works for the benefit of others. Mother Teresa may not have had the same outward beauty as Diana, but she lived a beautiful life and truly was a lovely person. Perhaps hers was the greatest beauty of all.

Whether you are serving as a Sunday school teacher at your church, as a volunteer at your child's school, or at a local homeless shelter, you should be known as someone who not only *gives* their best but *is* their best as they serve. Others might merely put in their eight-hour shift at work, but you take time to straighten up the workroom. Others drive the company truck, but you take a minute to haul in the garbage others left behind. Others neglect the house they are renting because it is not theirs. You take time to weed the flower beds and to maintain the property out of courtesy for the owners. More importantly, you do so with grace and humility. Many would mock such an attitude and claim it is wasted and unnecessary. But Christians are different. We bear God's image. We delight in beauty and order and in doing good. This not only honors God and brings him delight; it also blesses others.

As a parent, one of my chief goals was to teach my children that they should always give their best. The world today does not encourage young people to do that. It often advises them to do the least. I have one child who, before handing over his midterm exam for my inspection, would always inform me of what the class average was. If he were just one percentage point above average, he would explain to me that he was "above average"! I would routinely ask him, "But was this your best?" The point was not to be at the top of the class. It was to reach the full potential God had created in him. I regularly reminded my son that God had certainly not made him "average"!

One of Satan's most insidious lies is to convince people to accept less than God's best. That is what he attempted to do with Jesus. The Father had prepared a spectacular story of redemption that was in the process of being played out ever since the garden of Eden. But Satan suggested Jesus take shortcuts that could attract a crowd quickly and bypass a painful cross. It would be "good enough." God intended to give a centenarian man a son so everyone knew his descendants were a miracle from God. But Abraham succumbed to using an acceptable worldly method and slept with his wife's maid.

The way we care for ourselves, our work, our marriage, our children, and our possessions reflects on God.

Just as in Old Testament times when God refused to accept blemished and second-rate sacrifices, so God expects us to live to the best of our ability in this generation. The way we care for ourselves, our work, our marriage, our children, and our possessions reflects on God. Life is a gift and a privilege. It must be handled with care. As Christians, we should live our lives with God-honoring intentionality as we seek to create a beautiful life that reflects the majestic qualities of God himself.

As Christians, we should live our lives with God-honoring intentionality as we seek to create a beautiful life that reflects the majestic qualities of God himself.

Conclusion

When God created the earth and all that is in it, he made it good and lovely. God delights in beautiful things. As salt and light (Matt. 5:13–16), Christians push back darkness and transform ugliness into reflections of divine beauty. It is a high calling. Master painters, musicians, and architects have at times accomplished this on a grand scale, but it is also possible in the humblest cottage and within the poorest family. You might not be able to afford to gild your palace with gold overlay, but you could expend some effort to beautify your living space. When you create beauty, even on a small scale, you bring glory to God.

Questions for Reflection/Discussion

1. What in your environment is the most beautiful?

2. How could you enhance your surroundings to make them more pleasant?

3. How are you cultivating the habit of appreciating the loveliness God has placed around you?

4. How could a cluttered area or room, if tidied up, make the most positive difference in your home?

5. How do your work habits reflect on your Creator?

CHAPTER 14

GOD'S WAYS ARE COUNTERCULTURAL

Where were you when I established the earth?
Tell me, if you have understanding.
(Job 38:4)

But the person without the Spirit does not
receive what comes from God's Spirit, because
it is foolishness to him; he is not able to
understand it since it is evaluated spiritually.
(1 Cor. 2:14)

Some friends of mine love learning about other cultures. One Thanksgiving they invited some international university students to their home for dinner. They thought these young people would enjoy experiencing one of their host nation's holiday traditions.

After their guests arrived, my friends explained the history of Thanksgiving and showed them around their home. Small talk ensued, and all seemed to be going well. But when dinner was announced, the students suddenly did a peculiar thing. They each took a dinner plate and went outside into the backyard. The hosts were puzzled. They were even more perplexed when they found the students pouring dirt from the flower beds onto their plates in a ritual cleansing ceremony! The students sheepishly explained that, due to their religion, they could not eat food on plates that were not cleansed. This dear couple can tell many such stories from over the years as they have courageously sought to develop relationships with people whose ways are entirely different from their own.

While learning about other country's cultures can be challenging, relating to an all-powerful, perfect, eternal Spirit can be far more daunting. Fortunately, God has revealed much about himself and his ways so we may properly relate to him. Nevertheless, though God has revealed his ways to us, that does not mean they have automatically become *our* ways. Throughout this book, we have examined some of the major areas of life in which God's ways are different from our own. But there are many, many more.

One of the most common mistakes among Christians is to assume that our ways are just like God's. In fact, they typically are not. God's ways are often countercultural. The reason we can struggle to do things God's way is because we may well have been raised all our life to act in the opposite manner. Society may praise the opposite response to God's preferred action. Others may criticize you or be offended when you behave in the manner God prescribes. The following is a quick overview of additional examples wherein God expects us to function *his* way rather than the *world's* way.

God's Ways Often Contradict Popular Opinion

Humanity does not have the final say on what is true and what is false. God contends that what he says is always true, even when it contravenes popular opinion. Jesus regularly challenged commonly accepted beliefs and practices. He declared, "You have heard that it was said, . . . But I tell you . . ." (Matt. 5:21–22, 27–28, 31–32, 33–34, 38–39, 43–44). During the Sermon on the Mount, Jesus presented the prevailing norms of that day and the views of "experts"; then he taught what God said about these matters. Modern society recoils at the notion of absolute truth, of right and wrong. The belief that the Bible's viewpoint trumps popular opinion is offensive to many. That is why the Bible has often been accused of being intolerant.

The Bible claims that God made people to be either male or female (Gen. 1:27). But today's culture provides a plethora of options. The Bible declares that all of life is sacred, including life in a mother's womb (Ps. 139:13–16; Jer. 1:5). Yet many argue that life has no value until it is outside the mother's body. Jesus said he is the only way to God (John 14:6; 2 Tim. 2:5). Yet the world claims that many religions, beliefs, and practices can safely navigate us into the afterlife.

If we live by God's absolute truth, we will inevitably offend others with what the world calls narrow mindedness and bigotry. It is hazardous to build our life upon fickle, frequently shifting societal opinions. Far better to base our life and eternity on the bedrock of God's unchanging truth.

God's Way Prioritizes Loyalty to Christ

A common misconception is to assume Christ will not call us to act contrary to our preferences and desires. He would never ask me to: live far from my parents, reject ungodly attitudes held by my family and friends, leave a lucrative and secure job and enter the ministry, go on an international mission trip when I am afraid of flying, or generally ask me to do anything I don't want to do. Prioritizing self, or family, over Jesus can prevent us from following him. Many people told Jesus they wished they could follow him, but it would upset their parents (Matt. 8:18–22). Jesus declared that our commitment to him ought to far exceed our loyalty to our parents and extended family (Luke 14:26). He wants no voice to carry greater weight with us than his. Furthermore, he claimed we ought to love him even more than we love ourselves. This is counterintuitive and certainly opposes modern culture, which deifies self. How often do we wish we could follow Christ, but we are uncomfortable with the sacrifice involved? In a world that perpetually urges us to affirm ourselves, we can treat Jesus as if his role is to support our goals and desires rather than to act as our Lord. Jesus commanded us to surrender our goals, desires, preferences, fears, and insecurities to him and then follow him wherever he leads.

God's Way Is to Submit

One of the most abominable words in the English language today is *submit.* The term connotes weakness and being controlled by someone more powerful. It is considered humiliating to submit ourselves to anyone. Yet God values submission. We are charged with submitting to him (James 4:7). Believers are told to submit to one another (Eph. 5:21). Perhaps most culturally offensive to Western culture, wives are instructed to submit to their husbands (Eph. 5:22; 1 Pet. 3:1). Almost as troubling in our modern day, believers are advised to submit to governing authorities (Rom. 13:1; 1 Pet. 2:13). Nowhere does Christ tell us to subjugate others. Rather, our calling is to voluntarily surrender ourselves out of our love for Christ and for others. In an age valuing independence and freedom, God's kingdom is characterized by submission. Many today, even in the church, despise this message.

God's Way Is Obedience

The apostles declared: "We must obey God rather than people" (Acts 5:29). Today this word *obey* is as offensive as *submit*, but it is the natural outcome of submission. You won't obey God if you do not first surrender control to him. There are Christians who would sing worship songs to God all day long but cringe at obeying him. Yet God declares that obedience pleases him more than worship (1 Sam. 15:22). Jesus did not describe his friends as those who liked to worship him or pray to him or study about him; he identified his friends as those who obeyed everything he commanded (John 15:14). I often work with Christian CEOs of large companies. These people are used to being in charge. It has been fascinating to watch them learn how they, too, must be God's bond servants. God isn't looking for upper and middle managers for his kingdom. He is looking for servants. The word *obedience* has become almost as anachronistic as *thee* and *thou* in modern parlance, even when discussing parenting. It seems Christians are among the few who still value it today.

God's Way Is to Discipline

There is much heated debate today regarding whether parents should discipline their children. It is considered brutish for parents to reprimand their offspring. Yet God is clear that he disciplines every one of his children. He loves us too much to ignore our sinful or harmful behavior. In fact, God's discipline is evidence that we are his children (Heb. 12:8). God's discipline, however, is perfectly designed to accomplish his purposes in our life. Rather than being discouraged by God's chastening, we should be encouraged that he continues to work in us as he steers us into his perfect will.

God's Way Is to Serve

One of Jesus's most controversial statements was: "The Son of Man did not come to be served, but to serve" (Matt. 20:28). Jesus was the long-awaited Messiah. Everyone anticipated he would lead the Jewish people to overthrow their Roman oppressors and establish his earthly kingdom in Jerusalem. Even as the Jewish people watched the Roman legions marching along their highways, they comforted themselves in knowing that one day their Messiah would destroy Rome and its minions and establish a new, glorious, and powerful kingdom on Earth. Yet Jesus declared that his mission was to lay down his life on behalf of others. These were not the words expected from a great conqueror!

Moreover, Jesus also said, "Whoever wants to become great among you must be your servant, and whoever wants to be first among you must be your slave" (Matt. 20:26–27). Voluntarily serving others can be humbling. Servants are not the most powerful people; they are the weakest. The world celebrates those who have a host of people at their beck and call, meeting their every need. Yet Jesus told his followers that greatness was expressed not by how people served you but by how you served others (Luke 22:24–27).

This is without a doubt one of the most difficult ways of Jesus for people to emulate. If we suffer insecurity about our identity or self-worth, we may find it impossible to willingly serve others. Yet our worth is not dependent on our earthly relationships. It is based on our relationship with God. In fact, since we are beloved children of the King, we can take delight in serving in the lowest rank because we know this in no way diminishes our value to our heavenly Father. Only those who don't find their value in their relationship with God need to augment their status by seeking importance the world's way.

God's Way Is to Take Responsibility

Today's society enables irresponsibility by loudly proclaiming, "It's not your fault!" "You are not to blame!" Society loathes taking responsibility for its actions. Many believe criminals need counseling rather than jail time. Businesses that fail declare bankruptcy and receive bailouts. It seems unkind to make people bear the consequences for their actions. But that is what God calls us to do. Because ultimately, "we must all appear before the judgment seat of Christ, so that each may be repaid for what he has done in the body, whether good or evil" (2 Cor. 5:10). Those who embrace God's ways understand they will give an account to him for every word and deed. Knowing this should profoundly affect how we live.

There are two important dimensions to God's call for assuming responsibility. First, God does not commission us to make others take responsibility. Today's culture often delights in policing others' behavior and calling them out on social media if they break the rules. But God calls us to focus on taking responsibility for our *own* actions. Jesus encouraged us to quit worrying about correcting someone with a splinter in their eye when we had a beam in our own (Matt. 7:3–5). Ironically, it is often the people who cannot see well themselves who take it upon themselves to judge how others behave! God's way is for us to make a priority of addressing our own issues and to leave others to the convicting work of the Holy Spirit.

Second, we can resolutely accept the blame for our sins because when we do, God will respond to us with mercy and grace (Eph. 2:4–6). God's focus is not on our humiliation and suffering but on our redemption and freedom. He knows that when we confess our sins and turn from them, we will be set free (Acts 2:37–40; 1 John 1:9). The sooner we take responsibility for our life, the sooner we can experience the abundant life he intends for us (John 10:10).

This also includes apologizing for our wrongdoing, which is certainly countercultural! Many who are caught red-handed still justify, or excuse, their behavior rather than taking ownership of it. Christians, however, ought to be quick to seek forgiveness when we are in the wrong. This can include inadvertent or thoughtless actions wherein we meant no harm. We are called to live in peace with others and to avoid causing anyone to stumble because of our actions (Ps. 34:14; Luke 17:2). Paul went so far as to claim that if eating meat caused a fellow believer to stumble, he would never eat meat again (1 Cor. 8:13). The world may flee from taking responsibility, but God's way is to quickly embrace it.

God's Way Is to Forgive (Often)

Jesus lived in the Middle East where vengeance was common. Yet, when he was asked how often people should forgive those who offended them, he replied, "I tell you, not as many as seven . . . but seventy times seven" (Matt. 18:22). In other words, there is no limit to how often you should forgive. This, like most everything else Jesus said, goes diametrically against worldly thinking. Society argues that some offenses are unforgivable. No amount of penance is adequate. To forgive appears to condone the sin or invite further offense. Yet Jesus claimed his kingdom citizens were to repeatedly forgive. He did not grant exemptions to forgiveness based on the gravity of certain offenses. In fact, Jesus claimed that God would forgive us in the same manner we forgive others (Matt. 6:12–15). We are to forgive because God has shown us grace and forgiven us. We are to treat others in the same manner God has treated us (Matt. 18:21–35).

God's Way Is to Go the Second Mile

In Jesus's day, the occupying Roman army claimed the right for a soldier to force a bystander to carry his pack for a mile as he traveled down the road. This pressured local subjects to submit to Roman authority in the most humiliating manner. Yet Jesus said, rather than becoming angry and resentful at such demeaning treatment, they should graciously offer to carry the soldier's pack an additional mile (Matt. 5:41). We can't imagine in our day how radical and horrifying this sounded to Jesus's listeners. Yet Jesus was never motivated to say things that were popular. Today's society is hypervigilant to protect ourselves from exploitation or oppression. Jesus commanded his followers to respond to unfair behavior not with anger but with grace. He said if someone slaps us on our right cheek, rather than retaliating in kind, we should turn our left cheek for them to slap as well (Matt. 5:38–39). Or, if someone sues us for our coat, we should throw in our shirt for good measure (Matt. 5:40). This would have been an unpopular and astounding teaching in its day, as it is in ours. These ways of God clearly cut across what the world, or most Christians, are willing to practice. Only by the Holy Spirit's enabling can we possibly live God's way.

God's Way Is to Love Our Enemies

One of the most radical commandments Jesus ever issued was for people to love the ones they would naturally hate the most (Matt. 5:44). To this day this command is largely ignored. When encouraged to do so, Christians immediately, and often angrily, spew all manner of excuses why they do not have to comply. Their enemies are evil people, out to destroy them. Their enemies ought to be judged, not loved. Their enemies aren't acting lovingly toward them. People will cite Jesus's recriminations of the Pharisees or money changers in the temple as proof they do not have to behave lovingly toward *everyone.* As Jesus acknowledged, it is not difficult to love those who love you. The real test is whether you will love those who are the most humanly impossible to love.

Of course, God's way is also holy. He never condones sin. It is possible to love someone without condoning their behavior. However, modern culture tends to condemn wrong behavior *and* the person committing the act. It is not surprising that shortly after Jesus gave this command, he concluded this section by saying, "Be perfect, therefore, as your heavenly Father is perfect" (Matt. 5:48).

God's Way Is for Us Not to Judge

Jesus commanded his disciples; "Do not judge, so that you won't be judged" (Matt. 7:1). This is easier said than done. It's tempting to take sinful delight in the downfall of others, especially those we don't like. We might also find pleasure in virtue, signaling as we loudly call out the shortcomings of others. It is a congenital human weakness to enjoy feeling holier than others. Jesus warned, however, that as surely as we have condemned someone, we will find ourselves in a similar situation yet be disqualified to receive mercy (Luke 18:9–14). How often have we heard preachers or politicians vociferously highlight someone's moral or ethical failure, only for them to later be exposed for committing the same sin?

Of course, Jesus was not saying we should condone sin or turn a blind eye to evil. Christians are not called to be naïve. Like most of what Jesus said, he focused on our heart. He was forbidding self-righteousness. We are not to eagerly criticize people while assuming we are free from any transgression ourselves. James cautions us from trying to usurp God's role as the only legitimate judge of humanity. He advises: "There is one lawgiver and judge who is able to save and to destroy. But who are you to judge your neighbor?" (James 4:12). It is far better to leave judgment to God and to prepare ourselves for the day we will give an account to Christ ourselves (2 Cor. 5:10). Knowing we are sinners ourselves should cause us to deal with our sinful brethren with humility and grace.

It is far better to leave judgment to God and to prepare ourselves for the day we will give an account to Christ ourselves.

God's Way Is to Take Sin Seriously

The world makes excuses for sin and even widely celebrates it. But God's way is never to make light of our transgressions. Jesus cautioned, "And if your right hand causes you to sin, cut it off and throw it away. For it is better to lose one of the parts of your body than for your whole body to go into hell" (Matt. 5:30). The world argues, "No one's perfect." "Everyone sins." "If it feels right, how can it be wrong?" But Jesus clearly taught about the gravity of sin. With God no sin is insignificant. A single, innocuous sin can bring spiritual death and dramatically affect eternity. Christians ought never to flirt or toy with sin or temptation, for they know the horrific consequences and the enormous pain it has caused through the ages. While others minimize and excuse their wrongdoing, our way should be to immediately and thoroughly address each sin so it no longer exercises a hold on us.

God's Way Is to Prioritize His Kingdom

Responsible people have bills to pay, retirement income to build, and mortgages to pay off. Putting food on the table and clothing our family are legitimate concerns. Yet Jesus said, "But seek first the kingdom of God and his righteousness, and all these things will be provided for you" (Matt. 6:33). Before you turn your attention to the mundane issues of life, invest yourself in building God's kingdom. It is tragic for us to pad our investments while God's work is left wanting. Have we truly been successful if our business is thriving while our church is withering? The advancement of God's kingdom should bring us more satisfaction than the success of our career. To give our best effort to God's business instead of our own might appear irresponsible. Yet God did not command us to neglect paying our bills or to be careless with our affairs. He told us to make his kingdom our foremost concern. In response he would provide for our secondary matters. Unbelievers may wonder why we give so much money to missional causes or turn down a promotion that would involve more travel from home or volunteer at a homeless shelter. But we do so because our life's priorities have a God-oriented rather than a self-centered focus.

God's Way Is to Seek Perfection

The most difficult and daunting command Jesus ever gave may well have been this one, when he said, "Be perfect, therefore, as your heavenly Father is perfect" (Matt. 5:48). There could be no greater challenge than this. It is difficult enough to strive for excellence. But seeking to attain the perfection of God is an entirely different matter. The Greek word for *perfection* can also mean "complete" or "mature." Nevertheless, adding "as God is complete/mature" still places the command well beyond our reach.

Anyone who has attempted to keep a New Year's resolution knows how challenging it can be to better oneself. Many people simply accept themselves as they are, flaws and all, and make no serious effort to improve. Christians should constantly seek to grow toward the perfect example set by God himself. We know this is a process that requires God's assistance. But we also realize God never commands something without also providing the requisite power and resources for success (Phil. 4:19). Therefore, the way of the Christian is continuous improvement. None of us fully achieve perfection in this life, but we draw closer each day (2 Tim. 3:17; James 1:4). While some may be content to repeatedly succumb to the same sins and flaws, Christians are called to grow in greater Christlikeness every day. One day in heaven we will be perfect! But until that day we keep striving.

Conclusion

If you live your life according to God's ways, as exemplified through the life of Christ, you will inevitably live in stark contrast to society at large. Be prepared to be misunderstood, criticized, and persecuted. The temptation will be to reduce God's commands to a way of life that is more palatable to modern culture. Jesus's ways will seem harsh, or stringent, or impractical, or impossible to practice in the modern age. A. W. Tozer warns, "It is a grave responsibility that a man takes upon himself when he seeks to edit out of God's self-revelation such features as he in his ignorance deems objectionable."[51] Better than trying to downsize or explain away God's ways you find off-putting, allow God to transform your heart and mind until his ways become second nature to you, as they were to Christ.

Questions for Reflection/Discussion

1. Of all God's commands, which one do you find the most difficult to obey?

2. What are some immediate actions you could take that would help you better live your life God's way?

3. As you seek to live according to God's ways, where have you encountered the most misunderstanding and resistance?

4. What has God particularly impressed upon you as you have read this book?

5. How have you inadvertently sought to soften or alter your Christian lifestyle to make it less strenuous or offensive to others?

CHAPTER 15

LEARNING TO LIVE BY GOD'S WAYS

Teach me your way, L*ORD, and I*
will live by your truth.
(Ps. 86:11)

Now if any of you lacks wisdom, he should
ask God—who gives to all generously and
ungrudgingly—and it will be given to him.
(James 1:5)

With America's sixteenth presidency as the ultimate prize, the battle over who would win the 1860 Republican presidential nomination proved to be a watershed in American history. The Civil War loomed. The nation hung in the balance. Several powerful politicians aggressively campaigned for the nomination. New York senator William Seward, Ohio governor Salmon Chase, and Edward Bates from Missouri were strong candidates. Yet they would be caught by surprise when they were bested by a self-educated, relatively unknown political upstart by the name of Abraham Lincoln. Upon winning the presidency, Lincoln surprisingly asked his rivals to take prominent positions in his cabinet. Lincoln also invited three former Democrats—Gideon Welles, Montgomery Blair, and Edwin Stanton—to join his team. Stanton had been disdainful of Lincoln in the past. Doris Kearns Goodwin noted, "Every member of this administration was better known, better educated, and more experienced in public life than Lincoln."[52] What's more, each of them believed he would make a far better president.

Initially, the other men experienced everything from shock to bewilderment at Lincoln's methods. He clearly did not approach governing in the same way they did. Each one vainly attempted to adjust the way Lincoln led, so it better aligned with his own methodology. But each one, to varying degrees and often grudgingly, eventually conceded that Lincoln's ways were superior to his own. To this day, Lincoln is routinely rated as the greatest president in American history. Yet at the time, his ways seemed a mystery to some and ludicrous to others. In time, however, some of Lincoln's associates, such as Seward and Stanton, grew to love him. Stanton was inconsolable after Lincoln's death. These men realized it had been their supreme privilege to serve with someone of such greatness.

Perhaps the most important challenge of our life will be learning to relate closely to God, whose ways are far higher, wiser, and nobler than ours. We will be tempted to reinterpret God's ways so they are more like our own. But that is an unfortunate and oftentimes tragic exchange. Instead, it ought to be our life's ultimate quest to live our lives God's way.

Learning to Walk in God's Ways

God's ways don't come naturally to us. In fact, they may be the opposite of what we have practiced all our lives. How can we learn them? The following steps may prove helpful.

Consider Your Current Behavior

We often behave instinctively. "That's how I have always done it!" we exclaim. Perhaps we mimic what our parents modeled for us. Or we may have developed habits out of self-preservation as a child or in response to hurts we suffered, but just because we have always acted a certain way does not mean we should continue in like manner. Some people find themselves continually embroiled in conflict. They assume this is natural, as it's all they've ever known. They don't stop to consider that perhaps it is due to the way they treat others. I know a young woman who was fired from three jobs in a row. She assumed it was because she suffered the misfortune of having three terrible bosses. She failed to make the connection that her employment woes might be related to her work ethic.

God urged his people, "Think carefully about your ways" (Hag. 1:5, 7). The psalmist confessed, "I thought about my ways and turned my steps back to your decrees" (Ps. 119:59). The world is continually pulling us away from God's standards and commands. We are often unaware of the battle that rages around us as the media bombards us with worldly messages. Jesus claimed we would be blessed when we lived our lives according to his instructions (Matt. 5:3–10). Yet many Christians are miserable and assume their lack of joy is due to life's difficulties. They may fail to realize that their woes are the result of the way they have chosen to live their lives.

As King Solomon was dedicating the temple in Jerusalem, he offered an insightful and prophetic prayer:

> When there is famine in the land, when there is pestilence, when there is blight or mildew, locust or grasshopper, when their enemy besieges them in the land and its cities, when there is any plague or illness, every prayer or petition that

> any person or that all your people Israel may have—they each know their own affliction—as they spread out their hands toward this temple, may you hear in heaven, your dwelling place, and may you forgive, act, and give to everyone according to all their ways, since you know each heart, for you alone know every human heart. (1 Kings 8:37–39)

Solomon warned, ironically, that a time would come when people would no longer follow God's guidance. When that happened, God would allow people to reap what they had sown. He would permit them to experience hardships and trials designed to humble them and drive them back to God. Solomon prayed that God would give to everyone "according to all their ways." Why is it crucial to think and act God's way? Because God will bless or discipline you based on your behavior. He does not bless efforts that use the world's ways (Prov. 14:12). If your life continually undergoes defeat, loss, and disappointment, you may be experiencing the results of your own choices. God urged people to examine the fruit of their lives. Your current life may provide a strong indication of the way you have been living.

Ask God to Teach You His Ways

Moses requested of God: "Now if I have indeed found favor with you, please teach me your ways, and I will know you, so that I may find favor with you" (Exod. 33:13). The psalmist David prayed, "Make your ways known to me, Lord; teach me your paths. . . . Teach me your way, Lord, and I will live by your truth" (Ps. 25:4; 86:11). Moses and David knew God better than most people in human history. Yet they understood they could not discover God's ways on their own. God would have to teach them. They both spent their lives learning God's ways, and as a result, few people enjoyed the influence with God and people they did.

Study and Apply God's Word

God has revealed his ways in his Word. Whenever you read the Bible, ask yourself some key questions: "What does this teach me about God and his ways? What does this say about me and the way I am living? What adjustments must I make so I am living according to God's ways?" These questions will help you better understand God's ways and how they impact the way you live. For example, suppose you read Galatians 6:2, "Carry one another's burdens; in this way you will fulfill the law of Christ." As you consider what this reflects about God, you realize that God is constantly coming alongside people in need and helping them ease their load. Galatians even calls this a "law" of Christ.

Then you consider your own practice. You can't think of anyone whose burden you are currently helping to carry. Yet you know many people at your church, workplace, and among your neighbors who are carrying heavy loads. You realize you have been excusing your lack of concern for others by your busy schedule. The Holy Spirit convicts you that you have not been open to reaching out to help others. In response, you ask God to help you overcome your natural self-centeredness and to make you more thoughtful and helpful. The next day you receive an invitation to a baby shower for a young, impoverished couple. Your first thought is that you don't know them well and the shower is on your day off when you typically relax at home. You don't enjoy attending showers. Your instinctive response is to decline the invitation, but you sense the Holy Spirit leading you to make time to attend and to be generous. In a small way God has reoriented you to be the kind of person who does things his way. Never be satisfied until your life matches what you find in Scripture.

Heed the Holy Spirit

David wrote: "LORD, you have searched me and known me. You know when I sit down and when I stand up; you understand my thoughts from far away. You observe my travels and my rest; you are aware of all my ways" (Ps. 139:1–3). The Holy Spirit is fully aware of every area of our life where our ways do not match his. He has numerous means with which to guide us into his ways. It might be that we have treated someone rudely. They might respond to us angrily. As we depart from the confrontation, the Spirit immediately begins to convict us of how we just behaved. He helps us see how our actions have caused offense and alienation. Or perhaps we are tempted to be dishonest while filling out a tax form. Even as we enter incorrect numbers, the Spirit convicts us of our deceitfulness. The next moments are crucial. What we do next reveals what we believe about God. We have just received an opportunity for a course correction. We can sink deeper into sin or adjust our behavior to be more Christlike.

Be alert to the Holy Spirit's voice when you encounter a Scripture. The Spirit may grip your attention and cause you to realize that the verse you are facing applies to you. When possible, have a journal nearby to record whatever impressions the Spirit places upon your heart. Or perhaps you are listening to a sermon at church, or a Christian song, or you are speaking with a Christian friend, and suddenly your heart begins to race. You become aware that the Spirit of God is speaking to you. The Holy Spirit will use a variety of means to correct you when your ways do not align with those of the Father.

I remember an incident in my life when the Holy Spirit corrected me concerning how I was behaving. Some friends invited my wife and me to go to dinner with them. They were a wonderful couple. The husband was in between jobs at that time. Over the meal they graciously asked me where I had recently traveled in my speaking ministry and what books I was writing. I told them about recent conferences where I had spoken. I mentioned my current writing assignments. It was a delightful time. On our drive home I noticed my wife was unusually quiet. I asked if anything was wrong. Lisa is gracious and was trying to think of a kind way to tell me what she had noticed. She pointed out that I had done the lion's share of the talking during the meal, yet I had not asked our friends any questions about their lives or work. Initially, I grew defensive and explained that I was just answering their questions and besides, our friend was currently unemployed, and I did not want to ask him any awkward questions that might make him feel self-conscious. Lisa, however, was not buying it. "You could have asked them about their children. They are active in their church. They have lives too." I, of course, did not like this line of thinking. However, when we arrived home, I went to my office and began to reflect on what had happened. The Holy Spirit led me to audit the way I was treating my friends.

I sat at my desk and opened my Bible. Soon I was in Proverbs. I had not liked the way I had acted, and I was not happy being out of unity with my wife. Something was wrong. As I turned the pages, I asked the Holy Spirit to speak to me. I read Proverbs 10:11, "The mouth of the righteous is a fountain of life." Proverbs 10:19, "When there are many words, sin is unavoidable." Proverbs 10:21, "The lips of the righteous feed many." The Holy Spirit showed me what my words could have done for our friends. I could have blessed and encouraged them. Instead, I had bragged about myself. Then I turned to Proverbs 27:2, "Let another praise you, and not your own mouth." The Holy Spirit was making sure I didn't miss his point! And, lest I become angry at my wife for confronting me, I noticed three verses further, "Better an open reprimand than concealed love" (Prov. 27:5).

I have found that the Holy Spirit is usually gentle with those who accept his rebuke humbly and with an open mind. I sensed he wanted to grow me in that moment so my ways became more like his. I knew the Lord was telling me to make specific adjustments. First, even when people asked me to talk about myself, I would stop, before long, and intentionally ask questions about them. In fact, I would try in every conversation to do the least talking. Further, I would guard my mouth from the temptation to brag about what the Lord was doing in my life and ministry. Instead, I would seek satisfaction in talking with God about those things. God also challenged me to intentionally strive to bless people in every conversation. Often, this could be done simply by showing genuine interest in their life.

I cannot say I have always followed through with everything God showed me that day. But I changed. I also learned there are many other areas in my life the Holy Spirit will also improve if I will pay attention.

The world's ways are so deeply ingrained in us it takes time to weed them out so God's ways become our own. But the effort is worth it! Can you imagine what the world would think if God's people stopped acting like everyone else and began behaving the way Jesus did? The world was always attracted to Jesus. He was invited to parties. Sinners wanted to talk with him. If our lives are like Christ's, people will be drawn to us too, for the right reasons. It is religious hypocrites that no one has time for.

If our lives are like Christ's, people will be drawn to us too, for the right reasons.

Conclusion

The world desperately needs to see and experience genuine Christianity. Many have been turned off or offended by the church. That is a shame. The church was designed to be the body of Christ on Earth that demonstrated to a watching world what Jesus is like. But too often, we Christians have been seduced by the world's ways, and we have not noticed how deeply imbedded worldly practices have become in our lives. The church keeps trying to do God's work the world's way, and the world is having none of it.

It should be a wake-up call when our ways are indistinguishable from the world's. When we realize how far we have departed from God's ways, we should call fellow believers into an emergency prayer meeting and plead with God to forgive us. Christ commissioned the church to be in the world, but too often the world is in the church. Oh, that God would grant us the humility to confess that we have been dazzled by secular ways. We prefer being first over being last. We want to be served rather than to serve. We want to strike back rather than to forgive. We want to serve God but not be holy. Yet we have been too proud to admit that the world's ways have not worked. God has not blessed, and we are barren of his power.

Fortunately, God is exceedingly gracious and patient. He will welcome us home and teach us his ways once more. I believe that nationwide and worldwide revival is not necessarily far off. But we must hunger and thirst for God's ways in our lives and churches. We must discard worldly thinking and practices that dishonor Christ and be humble enough to let the Holy Spirit refashion us into instruments through whom he is pleased to work powerfully. Then perhaps we will be prepared for the prophecy of Micah to be fulfilled at last: "In the last days the mountain of the LORD's house will be established at the top of the mountains and will be raised above the hills. Peoples will stream to it, and many nations will come and say, 'Come, let's go up to the mountain of the Lord, to the house of the God of Jacob. He will teach us about his ways so we may walk in his paths" (Mic. 4:1–2).

We must hunger and thirst for God's ways in our lives and churches.

Questions for Reflection/Discussion

1. How are you intentionally seeking to learn God's ways? What are some additional practices you could begin?

2. What do you sense the Holy Spirit is convicting you to change right now as you have read this chapter?

3. How open are you to godly feedback from other people? How do you respond to it?

4. How might you study God's Word differently, so you learn the ways of God? After reading this book, what are some of God's ways that you feel led to focus on in your life in the coming days?

NOTES

1. Henry T. Blackaby and Roy T. Edgemon, *The Ways of God: How God Reveals Himself Before a Watching World* (Nashville: B&H Publishing Group, 2000).

2. Blackaby and Edgemon, *The Ways of God.*

3. A. W. Tozer, *The Knowledge of the Holy* (New York: Harper One, 1961), 3.

4. Tozer, *The Knowledge of the Holy*, 2.

5. Jonathan Haidt, *The Happiness Hypothesis: Finding Modern Truth in Ancient Wisdom* (New York: Basic Books, 2006), 1–22.

6. Jonathan Haidt, *The Righteous Mind: Why Good People Are Divided by Politics and Religion* (New York: Pantheon Books, 2012).

7. Tozer, *The Knowledge of the Holy*, 110–11.

8. Dallas Willard, *Hearing God: Developing a Conversational Relationship with God* (Downers Grove, IL: IVP Books, 1984; reprint ed. 2012), 232.

9. J. C. Pollock, *Moody* (Grand Rapids: Baker Books, 1963; reprint ed., 1995), 77.

10. Daniel Kahneman, *Thinking, Fast and Slow* (New York: Farrar, Straus and Giroux, 2011), 53.

11. Kahneman, *Thinking, Fast and Slow*, 62.

12. Tozer, *The Knowledge of the Holy*, 104.

13. Tom Holland, *Dominion: The Making of the Western Mind* (London: Abacus, 2019), 15.

14. Tozer, *The Knowledge of the Holy*, 98.

15. Brother Lawrence, *The Practice of the Presence of God* (Springdale, PA: Whitaker House, 1982), 81.

16. I develop this thought much further in Richard Blackaby, *Putting a Face on Grace: Living a Life Worth Passing On* (Colorado Springs: Multnomah Books, 2006).

17. John Milton, *Paradise Lost* (New York: Penguin Books, 2000), ed. John Leonard, 32–33.

18. See George M. Marsden, *Jonathan Edwards: A Life* (New Haven: Yale University Press, 2003), 357–74; Iain H. Murray, *Jonathan Edwards: A New Biography* (Carlisle, PA: Banner of Truth Trust, 1987; reprint ed., 1992), 311–70.

19. Corrie ten Boom, with John and Elizabeth Sherrill, *The Hiding Place* (Washington Depot, CT: 1971), 106.

20. Ron Chernow, *Titan: The Life of John D. Rockefeller* (New York: Vintage Books, 1998), 181–82.

21. Henry T. Blackaby, Richard Blackaby, Mike Blackaby, and Claude King, *Experiencing God: Knowing and Doing the Will of God* (Nashville: Lifeway Press, 2022).

22. Tozer, *The Knowledge of the Holy*, 41.

23. C. S. Lewis, *Mere Christianity* (New York: Macmillan, 1943; 1960 ed.), 120.

24. J. C. Pollock, *Moody* (Grand Rapids: Baker Books, 1963; reprint ed., 1995), 26.

25. Arthur Wallis, *In the Day of Thy Power* (London: Christian Literature Crusade, 1956; Reprint ed. Columbia, Missouri: Cityhill Publishing, 1990), 204–05.

26. I discuss life's seasons in Richard Blackaby, *The Seasons of God: How the Shifting Patterns of Your Life Reveal His Purposes for You* (Colorado Springs: Multnomah Books, 2012).

27. Ron Owens, *Ron Dunn: His Life and Mission* (Nashville: B&H Publishing Group, 2013), 216.

28. Courtney Anderson, *To the Golden Shore: The Life of Adoniram Judson* (Grand Rapids: Zondervan, 1956), 36–45.

29. You can read more of Carrie's story in Henry Blackaby, Richard Blackaby, Mike Blackaby, and Claude King, *Experiencing God: Knowing and Doing the Will of God* (Nashville: Lifeway Press; 1990; 2022 ed.), 51.

30. Dietrich Bonhoeffer, *The Cost of Discipleship* (New York: Macmillan, 1963; original ed., 1937), 99.

31. An inspirational book that discusses this is V. Ray Edman, *They Found the Secret: 20 Transformed Lives That Reveal a Touch of Eternity* (Grand Rapids: Zondervan, 1960; reprint ed., 1984).

32. Bonhoeffer, *The Cost of Discipleship*, 101.

33. Bonhoeffer, *The Cost of Discipleship*, 101.

34. John G. Paton, *John G. Paton: Missionary to the New Hebrides* (New York: Robert Carter and Brothers, 1889; reprint ed., (London: Forgotten Books, 2015), 91.

35. Norman P. Grubb, *C. T. Studd: Athlete and Pioneer* (Wheaton, IL: Sword of the Lord Publishers, 1946), 129.

36. Grubb, *C. T. Studd*, 152.

37. For a more in-depth discussion, see Richard Blackaby, *Unlimiting God: Increasing Your Capacity to Experience the Divine* (Colorado Springs: Multnomah Books, 2008).

38. Elton Trueblood, *The Humor of Christ* (New York: Harper and Row, 1964).

39. John Mark Comer, *The Ruthless Elimination of Hurry* (Colorado Springs: Waterbrook, 2019), 91.

40. Paton, *Missionary to the New Hebrides*, 267.

41. Paton, *Missionary to the New Hebrides*, 309.

42. Charles Darwin, "Letters from Charles Darwin to Asa Gray, 3 April 1860," In *The Life and Letters of Charles Darwin,* vol. 2, ed. Francis Darwin (London: John Murray, 1887), 296.

43. My son wrote his PhD dissertation arguing that sublime literature was an apologetic for the existence of God. Daniel R. Blackaby, *An Argument from Sublime Literature: How Language, Beauty, and Literature Point toward the Existence of God* (PhD dissertation, Southern Baptist Theological Seminary, December 2018).

44. Blackaby, *An Argument from Sublime Literature*, 196.

45. Blackaby, *An Argument from Sublime Literature,* 197; see Exodus 35:31.

46. Jordan Peterson, *Beyond Order: 12 More Rules for Life* (New York: Penguin/Portfolio, 2021), 201–27.

47. Peterson, *Beyond Order*, 203.

48. Peterson, *Beyond Order*, 202.

49. Daniel J. Levitin, *The Organized Mind: Thinking Straight in the Age of Information Overload* (New York: Dutton, 2014), 78.

50. Levitin, *The Organized Mind.*

51. A. W. Tozer, *The Knowledge of the Holy*, 80.

52. Doris Kearns Goodwin, *Team of Rivals: The Political Genius of Abraham Lincoln* (New York: Simon and Schuster, 2005), xvi.

ABOUT THE AUTHOR

Richard Blackaby is the oldest child of Henry and Marilyn, and the president of Blackaby Ministries International (www.blackaby.org). Richard has a PhD in church history from Southwestern Baptist Theological Seminary. He has served as a senior pastor and as a seminary president. Richard travels extensively and speaks internationally on spiritual leadership, experiencing God, revival, and God in the marketplace. Richard regularly works with Christian CEOs of Fortune 500 companies. You can follow Richard on Twitter at @richardblackaby, Facebook at Dr. Richard Blackaby, or his podcast at *The Richard Blackaby Leadership Podcast.* Richard and his wife Lisa live in Atlanta, Georgia. Their three children all serve in ministry.

Richard has coauthored numerous books with his father, including: *Experiencing God*, *Experiencing God: Day by Day*, *Experiencing God Study Bible*, *Fresh Encounter*, *Spiritual Leadership*, *Hearing God's Voice*, *Called to Be God's Leader: Lessons from the Life of Joshua*, *God in the Marketplace*, *Being Still with God*, *When God Speaks*, and *Flickering Lamps: Christ and His Church.* Richard has also written: *The Seasons of God*, *The Inspired Leader*, *Unlimiting God*, *Putting a Face on Grace*, *Living Out of the Overflow*, *Rebellious Parenting*, *Experiencing God at Home*, *Spiritual Leadership Coaching*, and *Developing a Powerful Praying Church.*